Customer
Visits

Second
Edition

Edward F. McQuarrie

Customer Visits

Building a
Better
Market
Focus

Second
Edition

SAGE Publications
International Educational and Professional Publisher
Thousand Oaks   London   New Delhi

For information:

SAGE Publications, Inc.
2455 Teller Road
Thousand Oaks, California 91320
E-mail: order@sagepub.com

SAGE Publications Ltd.
6 Bonhill Street
London EC2A 4PU
United Kingdom

SAGE Publications India Pvt. Ltd.
M-32 Market
Greater Kailash I
New Delhi 110 048 India

Printed in the United States of America

Library of Congress Cataloging-in-Publication Data

McQuarrie, Edward F.
    Customer visits: Building a better market focus/
Edward F. McQuarrie.—2nd ed.
        p. cm.
    Includes bibliographical references and index.
    ISBN 0-7619-0883-8 (Cloth: acid-free paper).
    ISBN 0-7619-0884-6 (pbk.: acid-free paper)
        1, Industrial marketing—Research. 2. Communication in marketing.
    3. Consumers—Attitudes. 4. Customer relations. I. Title.
    HF5415.1263.M37   1998
    658.8′34—dc21

98 99 00 01 02 03 04 10 9 8 7 6 5 4 3 2 1

Acquiring Editor:	Harry Briggs
Editorial Assistant:	Anna Howland
Production Editor:	Astrid Virding
Production Assistant:	Karen Wiley
Typesetter:	Marion Warren
Indexer:	Teri Greenberg
Cover Designer:	Ravi Balasuriya
Print Buyer:	Anna Chin

Contents

Introduction

At some point during the 1980s, the word *customer* began to appear more and more often in business conversations. CEOs used it in speeches, magazines used it in cover stories, and business people everywhere began to pronounce the word with extra emphasis. I will leave to some future historian the task of tracing the evolution of this growing preoccupation with the customer. Certainly, the book *In Search of Excellence,* by Tom Peters and Robert Waterman, played a role, as did the soul-searching by American managers whose firms lost ground to global competition.[1] Suffice to say that by 1990 there was no escape from talk about the customer and the importance of being market driven, and that throughout the 1990s, more and more organizations began to emphasize the importance of the customer. The underlying premise appeared to be that a focus on customer needs had become *the* critical success factor in business. An effective orientation to market needs, not cost control, not participative management, not technological prowess, was now the key.

So today, everyone is talking about the customer; but it is far from clear that much of anything has changed in how business is actually conducted. The problem is not so much bad faith as lack of knowledge. How *do* you move an organization so as to make it market driven? How do you organize product development so that real user needs are addressed? How do you change hearts and minds so that employees take responsibility for customer satisfaction? These are the difficult questions that have to be addressed by firms that seek to be customer focused.

The businessperson will find few books and articles that address these questions of implementation. Whereas exhortations to focus on the customer abound, practical advice is scarce. Good conceptual work *has* been done in the areas of defining market orientation and demonstrating its profitability, and Chapter 1 will introduce the reader to this research. However, the focus of this book is the implementation gap that continues to handicap contemporary businesses in their attempts to be customer focused. I believe the pressing need today is for action plans, not definitions. What can you do, tomorrow, to move yourself, your people, and your organization closer to customers?

Here it is helpful to consider another term that began to pepper business conversations during the 1980s and that continues to be an important concept today: *quality.* It is my impression that the people championing the cause of quality have always been action oriented and focused on implementation. Early in the 1980s, the tool of choice was quality circles; by the middle of the decade, quality function deployment (QFD); by the beginning of the 1990s, total quality management (TQM). Our future historian will be curious about both the hidden connections and the mutual blind spots among those concerned with quality on the one hand and the customer on the other. This book will provide a framework for thinking about ways in which the customer can be made an integral part of efforts to enhance quality. In fact, I will argue that a focus on quality that is not simultaneously a focus on customers is doomed to failure. Ideally, the two approaches are complementary, with knowledge of how to be customer focused providing strategic direction, and TQM procedures showing the way to mobilize the organization in response to knowledge of the customer.

Customer focus, market driven, total quality: all new terms, all promising a new way of conducting business. Most observers would agree that for any organization desiring to change, the essential first step is to obtain the commitment of top management to the values underlying these philosophies.[2] On the assumption that this commitment is in hand, the purpose of this book is to help you with the second step: devising action plans that are affordable, accessible, and able to generate momentum for change. The target audience is businesses that market to other businesses, with a special emphasis on product categories that are technically complex.

FOCUS OF THIS BOOK

In a *customer visit,* managers and engineers leave their office and travel to the customer's place of business. They interview buyers and users and they tour the work site. In a *program* of customer visits, a dozen or more visits are planned and conducted systematically. You can expect four major benefits:

- Better information on what your customers really need.
- Closer relationships with customers.
- A common vision, shared across your organization, of what customers expect.
- A change of heart within your organization, in the direction of greater commitment on the part of all functional areas to satisfying customer needs.

You will not find the customer visit technique featured in any market research textbook. In fact, academics did not invent the practice of programmatic visits to customers. It emerged spontaneously at companies like Hewlett-Packard. The practice of customer visits was developed by such firms as a response to the unique marketing challenges faced by technology firms selling complex products to business users.[3] Firms that market to other businesses face a different set of problems than firms that market to a mass audience of individuals or families.[4] In business-to-business (BTB) markets, products are often more complex, the selling process is much more prolonged and complicated, buyer and seller are more interdependent, and the marketing function is more dependent on other functions. These challenges are even more pronounced for technology firms. Important characteristics of technology firms would include a high dependence on new products, as measured by the percentage of revenue attributed to products introduced within the past 3 years; substantial investment in technological innovation;

and a very high degree of product complexity. In the case of technology firms, the speed and complexity of change demands that marketing intelligence be nimble, future oriented, and optimized for discovery. For BTB firms overall, interdependence among the functions within the vendor organization combined with interdependence between vendor and buyer demands that intelligence gathering be "owned" by intelligence users, and not delegated to specialists. These are among the most important factors that have driven BTB marketers in general, and high technology firms in particular, to develop the idea of a program of customer visits.

In the United States, BTB firms came late to the marketing concept.[5] In recent decades, these same firms have been under-served by academic research in marketing. The combination of ignorance of marketing principles, together with a failure of textbooks to customize basic marketing principles so as to address the uniquely demanding aspects associated with business users and technical products, has produced a pervasive sense of uncertainty and discomfort. There is an understandable reluctance on the part of industrial marketers to simply mimic the time-honored approaches that have worked so well in the marketing of soap, snack foods, and soft drinks. Although basic marketing principles might be acknowledged as universal, most managers of technology businesses nonetheless retain an uneasy sense that in their own case, the execution of marketing and marketing research will have to be modified to a greater or lesser degree. In summary, although the idea of competing on technical innovation and excellence alone grows increasingly suspect, the precise adaptation of basic marketing principles to the BTB and technology context remains unclear.

This book is written for managers caught in this dilemma. It provides an orientation to, and specific advice regarding, market research in a BTB context. Every aspect of the book is focused on the manager who wants to act, now. Arguments are supplied to convince the skeptical, and explanations produced to motivate the reluctant. But the heart of the book takes the form of recipe knowledge. It describes specific steps to be taken in order to produce the desired result: an organization that is attuned to customers and motivated to satisfy their needs. More and more leading firms are conducting organized programs of visits for this purpose. I share with you their insights into the benefits (and risks) of visiting customers.

BACKGROUND

My involvement with customer visits began in 1985, when I participated as a professional interviewer in a series of visits conducted by the Computers Systems Division at Hewlett-Packard (HP). At that time, I was completing a PhD in social psychology and had been working for several years as an interviewer for Burke Marketing Research, an independent supplier of market research services. What HP requested for this project seemed very unusual at the time. They wanted Burke to supply professional interviewers, but they also wanted to send a team of their managers to accompany the interviewer. Normal practice in market research, as described in textbooks, is quite different. The standard procedure is for the manager to develop a set of research objectives, and then find an outside research firm to execute them. The research firm goes off, conducts interviews on its own, and delivers a report. The manager stays home and waits for that report.

At Burke we approached that initial HP project with trepidation. We envisioned all kinds of difficulties: that the HP managers would start to argue with the customers as we tried to interview them, or ask biased questions, or otherwise ruin the validity of the data. Instead, I came to view this project as one of the more successful in my experience. Two impressions stood out: First, because the HP managers received the information firsthand, directly from customers, the findings had more impact than was normally the case. Second, the interviews themselves were unusually productive. These managers knew a lot more about computer technology, and they were able to ask follow-up questions that would have escaped me. These interviews opened my eyes to the importance of putting technically knowledgeable managers face-to-face with their customers.

Several years later I was approached by Corporate Marketing Education at HP about designing a course on customer visits. They indicated that the practice of customer visits was widespread at HP (although typically, professional interviewers were *not* involved). Like many technology companies in the 1980s, top management at HP had decided that the firm needed to become more market driven and less technology driven. The establishment of Corporate Marketing Education and the strengthening of the market research function were but two examples of initiatives in this direction. One motivation for the course on customer visits was the perception on the part of

HP's market research function that many customer visit projects were misconceived or poorly executed. Hence, the rationale that guided course design was to build on the basic value of face-to-face contact with customers by improving planning and execution. Since 1988, I have presented the material in this book to more than 2,000 people at HP and other firms in seminars held all over the United States and in Europe as well. I am familiar with the application of customer visits within dozens of product categories and across a wide range of research questions. The dialogue with course participants has refined my understanding of critical success factors and pointed out the aspects of visit programs most likely to cause difficulty. You, reading this book, get the benefit. Besides HP, I am familiar with the efforts of a range of other leading firms that also conduct programs of customer visits. These include Sun Microsystems, IBM, Compaq, Apple, Digital Equipment, Unisys, and Amdahl in the computer industry; Microsoft, Symantec, Lotus, and Cadence in software; Motorola, Fluke, Tektronix, and Varian in electronics; and Sealed Air, Pitney-Bowes, Trane, and CIGNA in the BTB category. Discussions with managers at such firms allow me to supplement the conceptual arguments in the book with the testimony of experience. It soon became apparent that HP was not the only firm engaged in systematic attempts to visit customers, and that nothing about the methods described in this book is unique either to HP or the computer industry.

Because my understanding was forged through give-and-take with seminar participants, I chose to write this book using a relatively informal style. Whenever possible I directly address you, as if we were face to face and you had just asked for my advice. My fondest hope is that some day I will be sitting on a plane and the person next to me will open a briefcase and pull out a dog-eared, well-thumbed copy.

Developments Since the First Edition

The text of the first edition was more or less complete by late 1992. In the intervening 5 years, several factors emerged that influenced this revision. First, as the number of firms for whom I consulted increased, I gained the benefit of a wider range of questions and comments from seminar participants. I am more confident that the techniques described in this book are generally applicable across a variety of BTB and technology markets. In response to these gains in experience, the seminar materials also evolved, and this second edition reflects that evolution, catching the book up with what I have been presenting orally. All of the chapters describing specific procedures contain new material, generally in the form of expanded coverage.

The most important addition is Chapter 3, "A Typology for Customer Visits." Prior to the first edition, most of my efforts were focused on organized programs of a dozen or more customer visits where market research was the primary agenda. I gradually became sensitized to the fact that the bulk of face-to-face customer visits did not fit this model. In fact, most customer contacts occur one at a time, in the service of agendas other than research, and this will probably always be the case. Although there certainly are many organizations that would benefit from conducting more customer visit programs, this is not to say that the ad hoc customer visits that currently occur are wrong or useless. All that needs to change is that systems be put in place to harvest the wealth of information potentially available from these ad hoc visits. Chapter 3 suggests how this may be accomplished. It also describes a variety of alternatives to programmatic visits.

Another influential factor was a change in the nature of the seminars. What began life as a 2-day course organized according to conventional training principles (i.e., a series of presentation-learning exercise-discussion sequences) became, under the pressure of business in the 1990s, a 1-day seminar, which in turn, when combined with other topics, sometimes became a half-day seminar. Condensing the lecture material into half a day created the opportunity to spend the afternoon in hands-on consultation with a team planning a specific upcoming visit program. The repeated opportunity to apply general principles to specific cases proved both fascinating and educational—I learned more than when I simply presented a course. What became apparent during these consultation sessions was that deciding on objectives, selecting a sample, and designing a discussion guide were challenging endeavors for most teams. Hence, those topics are among the most heavily expanded in this second edition.

A third factor was writing *The Market Research Toolbox: A Concise Guide for Beginners.*[6] The chance to work out the relationships between customer visits and other market research techniques was helpful in reinforcing my understanding of the unique strengths and limitations of the customer visit technique, and that is reflected in this revision. The position of customer visits within the market research toolbox is always a lively focus of discussion in seminars. The present volume can be combined with *The Market Research Toolbox* for a more complete understanding of when to use customer visits and when to do some other kind of market research instead.

In one respect, little has changed since the first edition: Conventional accounts of market research continue to pay scant attention to the idea of in-person visits to customers by cross-functional teams. Furthermore, most engineering degree programs continue to ignore tools and techniques for obtaining customer input and including it in product design. Hence, this book continues to fill a need by making up for a gap in the education of engineers and managers. The basic rationale for customer visits has not changed since the first edition. The power of the technique has worn well over the past 5 years, and I believe that most marketing and engineering personnel in technology firms can benefit from the advice herein.

WHO SHOULD READ THIS BOOK

Product Manager in a Technology Firm. You are expected to be the expert on all aspects of your product: who uses it, for what purpose, and why; who the competitors are and the strengths and weaknesses of your product relative to each; key trends in the marketplace, along with emerging threats and opportunities; and so forth. You crave knowledge in all these areas and are already immersed in market research data.

This book can help you in two ways. First, it tells you how to use customer visits to gather the knowledge you need to execute your responsibilities as product manager. Second, it provides a resource that you can use to educate your counterparts in other areas of the organization. Many of your decisions require buy-in from these counterparts. One of the best ways to get that buy-in is to visit customers jointly.

R&D Project Manager. You are inclined to believe that "market research is too important to be left to marketers." Because you have overall responsibility for product design, and because product design must have input from customers, you recognize that you must get directly involved with some market research. Customer visits are among the techniques you will use most frequently. This book tells how to do it right.

Engineer-Scientist With a Technology Firm. You have visited customers from time to time as part of product development efforts. You have the nagging feeling that this visit activity has often been less efficient or effective than it could have been. This book will be food for thought and a source of practical tips for improving your customer visits.

Marketing Manager-Strategic Planner. You understand the importance of customer feedback, you are familiar with various market research tools, and you probably have an MBA. You will find this book a handy reference. You will also appreciate the emphasis on BTB marketing, as opposed to the consumer packaged goods emphasis that may have dominated your graduate training.

Market Research Manager. You are looking for a better way to do exploratory market research. You have grown dissatisfied with focus groups (the conventional solution) because the available moderators often do not have the necessary technical background.

Quality-Customer Service Manager. You are charged with monitoring and improving customer satisfaction. You are familiar with customer satisfaction surveys, but have been troubled by the limitations of such data. This book offers you an alternative means of making the customer visible and important within your organization.

Executive in a BTB or Technology Firm. You know that your firm must become more market driven if it is to survive and prosper. You've made the speeches; now you are on the lookout for a practical tool that will help you implement the new focus. This book offers you a wealth of suggestions.

Instructor. You are seeking supplementary reading material for a course on Market Orientation, BTB Marketing, or Marketing Research. This book can be used to cover the topic of personal interviews and qualitative research. It can also support assignments that require students to gather information from customers. You will find it particularly well received by part-time MBA students who work full time for BTB or technology firms.

This book is organized to meet the needs of the people just described. It makes copious use of checklists, procedural models, a problem-solution format, and the like. If you have not visited customers in the past, I tell you how to get started. If you already do this, I suggest how you might improve your practice.

NOTES

1. See Peters and Waterman (1982).

2. See Webster (1988, 1992) for an overview of these issues.

3. The true origins of the practice of visiting customers apart from any immediate sales agenda probably lie far back in time. Some speculations on the history and future of customer visits are offered in the final chapter.

4. See Webster (1978) for an overview of industrial marketing.

5. See Feldman and Page (1984) and Kelly and Hise (1979) for evidence on this point.

6. Published by Sage in 1996.

Acknowledgments

Since publication of the first edition, I have had the opportunity to present this material to many firms and business units new to me. I would particularly like to acknowledge invitations from Bob Fulon at Microsoft, Kris Jones at Fluke, George Bertram at Sealed Air, Staci Hartman at Tektronix, Calvin J. Huntzinger at Varian, Carolyn Casey at Hewlett-Packard, Margie Spyers and Katie Dunnington at CIGNA, and Gordon Eubanks at Symantec. A very special thanks goes to Bob Aron at Motorola University, whose early interest did so much to make the first edition a success.

I also had the chance to meet and learn from some of the many other authors and consultants working in the general area of market focus, voice of the customer, user-centered product design, and the like, including Chris Allen, Bill Barnhart, Jose Campos, John Carter, Dan Dimancescu, Michael Eckhardt, Christian Homburg, Sheila Mello, and Hermann Simon. I owe a special debt of gratitude to my editor at Sage, Harry Briggs, who brought both the first and second editions of this book into being.

Many people contributed to making the first edition of this book possible. In rough chronological order, I would like to thank Nick Calo, formerly of Burke Marketing Research, for introducing me to qualitative market research; Katherine Tobin and Mike Ward, now or formerly of Hewlett-Packard, for organizing the first customer visit program that I ever encountered; Shelby McIntyre of Santa Clara University, for inviting me to come to Santa Clara, for encouraging me to believe that customer visits were a worthy research topic, and for all his helpful advice as a colleague on this manuscript and earlier papers; Valerie Taglio, formerly of Corporate Marketing Education at Hewlett-Packard, for asking me to design a course on customer visits; Connie Cavanaugh, Nancy Gordon, Linda Rough, Anne Morton, and Ben Spencer-Cooke, also of Corporate Marketing Education, for their efforts to improve the course; Eng Tan and Klaus Hoffmann of Hewlett-Packard, for inviting me to teach this material in Europe; Fred Webster, formerly executive director of the Marketing Science Institute, for encouragement and financial support when it counted the most; George Day, Rick Staelin, Paul Root, Kathy Jocz, Nicolene Hengen, and Marni Clippinger, also of the Marketing Science Institute, for support both financial and moral; the 33 individuals whom I interviewed at Metropolitan Life, IBM, Polaroid, Du Pont, Milliken, Cigna, Fluke, and Raychem, for showing me that customer visits were not an isolated practice; Tom Kendrick, John Birk, and the Project Management Council in Corporate Engineering at Hewlett-Packard, for their willingness to support data collection; Bill BonDurant and Edith Wilson of Hewlett-Packard, and Chuck Powers and Tyzoon Tyebjee of Santa Clara, for stimulating exchanges; Dave Stewart of the University of Southern California, for his careful reading of the first edition manuscript; Richard Paynting of Bose Corporation, Fredric Laurentine, Lew Jamison, and Karen Thomas of Sun Microsystems, and others, too numerous to name, for invitations to teach; Mike Kuhn of Burke, for support through the years; and Karen Graul of Santa Clara, for typing so many drafts so cheerfully and so well.

Most of all, I would like to thank the participants in my customer visit seminars. Their eagerness to learn and searching questions laid the foundation for this book.

CHAPTER ONE

The Contribution of Customer Visits to a Market Focus

Most businesses are guided by one of the following fundamental orientations. See which one best characterizes your firm:

1. Financially oriented: The business is primarily viewed as a capital asset that produces income for shareholders.
2. Technology oriented: The core function of the business is to invent new things or come up with better ideas.
3. Quality oriented: The business is focused on processes—the goal is to do the right thing the first time and every time.
4. Market oriented: The business exists to create and keep customers. Discovering needs and satisfying these needs is the core function.

None of these orientations is wrong and every one contributes a piece of the puzzle so far as business success is concerned. Who would invest in a firm that didn't strive to provide shareholder value? Who would want to compete without the aid of new technology? Who would want to hire a manufacturing manager who didn't care about process quality?

1

What has changed in recent years is the recognition that customers must be placed at the center. When resources are limited and competition is keen, customers provide the guidepost. Only by finding and keeping customers can we provide value for shareholders.[1] Only by focusing on customers can we choose among technologies and invest appropriately in processes. A market orientation is not the only thing a business needs, but it is the central thing, the core that anchors the rest.

In turn, the primary justification for customer visits is the impetus they provide toward achieving a market focus. If all you need is a piece of information, then there will often be alternative kinds of market research that can provide that piece of information more quickly, more comprehensively, and more inexpensively. However, if what you need is an integrated understanding, and even more, an acceptance of customers and the legitimacy of their needs, then customer visits will often be the best kind of market research to conduct.

The idea of a market orientation dates back at least to the 1950s.[2] Here are two formal definitions that reflect current thinking:[3]

Definition 1: "Market orientation is a business culture committed to the continuous creation of superior value for customers."

Definition 2: "Market orientation is the organization wide *generation* of market intelligence pertaining to current and future customer needs, *dissemination* of the intelligence across departments, and organization-wide *responsiveness* to it."

The two definitions point to some important considerations that have to be taken into account by anyone seeking to move an organization closer to its customers. The first definition emphasizes that a market focus represents a business *culture*: something reflected in the shared values held by employees, the statements made by managers, and the totality of actions taken by the firm.[4] If, today, your firm is not customer focused, or not sufficiently customer focused, then you require a change of culture—no small thing. Because cultural change may be required, you cannot rely on directives or edicts from top management. In fact, it has been shown empirically that the top-down approach to achieving a customer focus is not effective.[5] Such edicts provide a beginning, and are probably an essential prerequisite for success insofar as they communicate a commitment on the part of top management, but they only lay the foundation. To complete the task you have to change hearts and minds at all levels of the organization. Understanding that customer focus is a matter of business culture thus identifies the magnitude of the task facing you and your firm as you attempt to change.

The first definition also reminds you of the central task of all customer visits—to understand what customers value. You cannot prosper as a firm unless you offer something for which customers are willing to pay. Unfortunately, what customers actually value may not be the same as what they say they want. If customer visits were a simple matter of asking customers what they want and then going back and building that answer, there would be no need for a book on the topic. However, discovering what customers really value, and matching that to some competence of your firm that allows you to deliver *superior* value, is not easy. That will require understanding your competitors as well as your customers. Here customer visits may play a role but are unlikely to be sufficient, which serves as a reminder that successfully implementing a market focus will require more than just excellence in customer visits.

The second definition is useful because it begins to specify some of the activities that characterize a market-focused business. Such a business will be mightily concerned with intelligence: not just facts, not just data, but meaningful information organized into patterns and themes. Most important, as emphasized by *organization wide,* the gathering of intelligence in such a business will not be delegated to the marketing research department. A key challenge that must be addressed in building a market focused culture is how to bring about a shared vision of the customer, at all levels, and across all departments. More strongly, a customer focused business must neither expect nor allow the marketing function to monopolize the activity of gathering market intelligence. In particular, engineers must not rely solely on customer information communicated to them second-hand.

This is a radical notion: that you cannot rely exclusively or largely on marketing personnel, much less marketing research personnel, to generate market intelligence. If you do, you fail the test: Your business is *not* going to be customer focused. Your employees, in particular your technical people, are *not* going to develop a shared commitment to customer satisfaction. Later in this chapter, I will explain why marketing cannot carry the burden of intelligence gathering; here it is sufficient to highlight the fact that a market orientation is neither a common nor an obvious way of managing a business and demands real changes in conventional modes of organization. Do not confuse *market orientation* with *marketing orientation*—it is customers that have to be placed at the center, *not* the marketing function. Market focus is not about giving dominance to those employees who hold marketing jobs; it is a matter of bringing everyone to focus on customers. Organizations where marketing fences off the customer, and insists on controlling all access, are among those least likely to succeed in implementing a market orientation as defined earlier.

MARKET ORIENTATION
AND FINANCIAL PERFORMANCE

The definitions quoted previously were produced in the course of work sponsored by the Marketing Science Institute (MSI) beginning in the late 1980s. Around that time, MSI declared customer and market focus to be a core research topic based on expressions of interest received from industry sponsors. In addition to conceptual work aimed at clarifying the meaning and measurement of market orientation, a stream of empirical research investigated the financial implications of succeeding or failing in the effort to become market focused.[6] After all, if market orientation cannot be connected to business profit, and ultimately shareholder value, how important is it, really?

A typical study in this vein might investigate several dozen business units (SBUs). The investigators would measure the degree of market orientation of each SBU, then take standard measures of the financial performance of each business unit (return on investment, operating margin, etc.), and then examine the correlation between the two. Over the last decade, a variety of such studies concluded that in fact, the more market oriented a business tends to be, the more profitable it is. This result has been obtained in comparisons of SBUs within a single firm, and in comparisons of business units across firms. It has been obtained in studies of U.S. firms and also in studies of international firms.

Of course, causal conclusions from such correlational studies are always open to challenge. Thus, perhaps more profitable firms are more able to indulge in the "luxury" of focusing on customers, so that market orientation is an expression rather than a cause of profitability. A more compelling research design, that to my knowledge has not been pursued, would be to recruit a sample of SBUs with a relatively low degree of market orientation, divide them into two groups, and apply to one group an intervention designed to increase market orientation. A demonstration that profitability increases when market orientation increases would nicely supplement the existing correlational studies.

Nonetheless, a substantial body of evidence already exists to indicate that market orientation and financial success go hand in hand. Given this positive association, the primary question reverts to this: How can a business successfully implement and sustain a customer focus? This is where customer visits come to the fore.

MARKET FOCUS AND QUALITY

Returning now to the second definition, it is in the area of organization wide responsiveness that practitioners of TQM have excelled. The procedures associated with TQM, derived in part from the application process for the Malcolm Baldrige award,[7] provide specific advice about how to mobilize an organization in response to an identified market need. But it is important to understand that a focus on quality that is not simultaneously a focus on the customer will be at best, blind and at worst, wrongheaded. Despite its prominent mention in the Baldrige Award application, this fact is often missed. Because some of the outputs of TQM are valued by most customers most of the time (e.g., reduced cost, fewer defects), practitioners of TQM have not always recognized or emphasized that quality cannot be defined by the vendor firm in isolation. Left to its own devices, the vendor firm cannot know what to measure or what should be continuously improved.

Here is a specific example of how a focus on continuous improvement in production processes can lead a firm astray. Recently, a major chemical firm analyzed its output of a particular product and found several contaminants that current production procedures failed to remove. Committed to a goal of eliminating defects, the firm vowed to drastically reduce the level of these trace contaminants. By means of a substantial redesign of the production processes, it was able to achieve this goal. Whereupon, the firm promptly lost two of its largest customers. It turned out that these customers expected to find those "contaminants" in the product and, in fact, relied on their presence to calibrate their own production processes![8]

The chemical example illustrates what might be called the "quality trap," which comes about when you emphasize perfecting processes rather than satisfying customers. Without practical steps to move the organization closer to the customer's perspective, the TQM process is vulnerable to becoming a new gloss on an old fallacy: an encouragement to focus on the *thing* you make rather than the *need* you fill. Under a market orientation, business success is not a function of making more and more perfect things, but of producing higher and higher levels of value for customers.

PROMISE OF CUSTOMER VISITS

It is the thesis of this book that a simple, practical step that should be considered by any organization that seeks to be market focused is to increase the number and range of employees who visit customers and improve the sophistication of these visits. I believe that a personal encounter with customers has unique potential to transform how an employee views his or her task. Only when the customer becomes visible as a person with legitimate needs, and there is the opportunity for employees to build a shared perspective with customers, can a firm make dramatic progress toward increasing its market orientation. Contact that is limited to executives, or remains the special province of the sales and support groups, will not do the job. In fact, the prime targets for participation in customer visit programs are first, engineers and scientists, and second, production and manufacturing personnel. It is individuals such as these, who are typically shielded or prevented from encountering customers firsthand, who most need to increase their level of face-to-face contact. The firm that does not allow or encourage its engineers to visit customers is a firm that will not succeed in building or holding a customer focus. Here is a quote to illustrate the point:

> My background is in production and I'll be quite frank with you, sometimes the customer has been more of an adversary rather than a friend. You know, he has complained about everything, he is not real-

istic, he just demands things. Back then we had an attitude that here is what we can do, here is when we can do it, take it or leave it. I was in the company for several years before I met a customer and honestly, sometimes when you are back in Production, you don't look on customer contact as necessary, you look at it as an evil. I know that's not right, but you tend to do it.[9]

Having made a strong pitch for the importance of firsthand experience of customers, it is now necessary to introduce some qualifications. Most important, face-to-face contact with customers is so valuable and important an activity that it has to be managed with the utmost care. The claim in this book is *not* that face-to-face contact is magically effective; on the contrary, it can be undertaken in such a way as to be misleading or even harmful. For example, suppose that the vice president of engineering were to issue a decree that all engineers in the unit will make at least one visit per year to a large customer. The vice president reasons that such contact will do wonders for improving engineers' understanding of customer needs. To see why this might be problematic, one has only to ask such questions as: Which customers will be visited by which engineers? What will they talk about? What will keep this visit from being a waste of time for the customer (and the engineer)? Questions such as these must be addressed if your firm is to get full value from its customer visits.

To reap the maximum value from customer visits, here are three rules to observe. These constitute the foundation for effective practice in customer visits:

1. The key decision makers must personally participate in the visits.
2. The visits should be conducted by cross-functional teams.
3. The visits ought to be organized as a program, complete with:

   a. Stated objectives
   b. A careful selection of customers
   c. A discussion guide
   d. A plan for reporting the results

These steps are required if you are to act on the proposition that personal encounters with customers are crucially important. The bulk of this book is addressed to the practical questions that arise once you commit to visiting customers in this way. The remainder of this chapter develops the underlying conceptual rationale for taking the specific step of conducting a program of customer visits as part of a commitment to market orientation. A later chapter will compare the benefits and risks of customer visit activity against other specific options for hearing the voice of the customer (e.g., focus groups).

WHY DO CUSTOMER RESEARCH OF ANY KIND?

This book develops the potential of customer visits as a kind of marketing research. Before a specific justification of customer visits can be offered, it is important to back up a step and ask, Why do *any* kind of customer research at all? Why not direct research solely at *markets*—the aggregate level where basic trends are set? This question can be addressed by examining the alternative of *not* doing research that directly involves customers. Clearly, there would be no need for such market research if managers and engineers already understood customers and their needs. However, evidence has accumulated that managers and professionals often delude themselves on this score. In one study, a sample of vendor-customer dyads was interviewed.[10] The vendors were asked a series of questions to assess their self-perceived degree of customer focus, and then the customer of each vendor was asked the same questions. There proved to be *no significant association* between vendors' self-perception of how customer focused they were, and their customers' perceptions!

Along similar lines, a large body of empirical research on success and failure in new product development supports the following points:

1. The less the investment in user needs research, the greater the odds of failure.
2. The more narrow and restricted the range of research activities, the greater the odds of failure.
3. The less proficient the research, the greater the odds of failure.
4. The later in product development that research was conducted, the greater the odds of failure.

In short, successful new products tend to be those backed by an early, substantial, diverse, and proficient customer research effort.[11]

Additional evidence comes from the study of technological inno-vation.[12] Here, two models of the invention process can be distin-guished: *technology push* and *demand pull*. In the technology push model, you would hire bright people, lock them in a lab, provide incentives such as stock options, stand back, and wait for insanely great products to emerge. In the demand pull model, you would first identify an unsolved customer problem, and then direct invention toward solving that problem. Research has shown that 70% of *successful* innovations fit a demand pull model. Technology push can and does succeed; but if you wish to play the percentages, you are better off researching needs and then inventing a response, rather than inventing something and then searching after the fact for cus-tomers who might need it. In short, a great deal of empirical evi-dence exists to show the importance of customer research broadly conceived.[13]

From a conceptual standpoint, in thinking about why customer research might constitute a critical success factor in business it may be helpful to use the metaphor of *entropy*. The idea of entropy derives from the second law of thermodynamics, and might be paraphrased as: "the amount of disorder and disorganization within a system can only increase over time." I propose to you that entropy is a funda-mental characteristic of the system that links producers and consum-ers. Entropy captures the notion that due to changes in the larger environment, a producer of a good or service is *always* in the process of losing touch with customer needs. Note, not "in danger of losing touch," but actually drifting apart, at a variable but unceasing rate. Whereas this process of drift and disengagement can be accelerated through failures of management, it can never be halted or abolished no matter how enlightened the leadership. It is a structural feature of markets; a matter of natural law. Only by continuously refreshing its understanding of customers can an organization succeed. Hence, the necessity of ongoing investment in efforts to gather marketing intel-ligence.[14] Your business must become a learning organization if you are to overcome marketing entropy.[15]

WHY PERSONAL VISITS?

Having provided a broad justification for customer research in general, we can now develop a more specific rationale for customer *visits.* Why is it necessary for decision makers to *personally* visit the customer site?[16] Several converging arguments, based on communication theory, social psychology, studies in organizational behavior, and the knowledge utilization literature, suggest that personal visits may be very important. In addition to existing theory, it is possible to develop the contribution of personal visits in logical and commonsense terms. Finally, the case can be made in experiential terms. That is, throughout this and the next section the conceptual arguments will be supported with verbatim quotes drawn from businesspeople who have experience in this activity (see Exhibit 1.1 for a description of the source of these quotes).[17]

Exhibit 1.1

Customer Visits at Leading Firms

Between 1989 and 1991, the Marketing Science Institute sponsored a project to determine whether or not customer visits represented an isolated activity or a more widespread practice among business-to-business marketers. For this project I visited eight firms—four in the electronics industry (IBM, Raychem, Fluke, and Polaroid), two material suppliers (Milliken and Du Pont), and two financial services firms (CIGNA and Metropolitan Life)—and interviewed 33 people.

These interviews provided valuable insight into the motives for visiting customers, the expected rewards, and possible problems (see Chapter 2 for additional discussion). Quotes drawn from these interviews are provided to supplement and make more vivid the conceptual rationale for customer visits. Each quote is labeled according to the job title of the speaker to provide the reader with some context while protecting the privacy of those quoted.

Value of Face-to-Face Communication

One approach to analyzing the strengths and weaknesses of personal visits lies in research on the properties of different communication media, including interactive face-to-face communication, video interaction, telephone conversations, and written documents. Here it has been found that interactive face-to-face communication is the richest of all media.[18] Richness is a function of the amount and variety of information that can be conveyed. Specifically, research has shown that interactive face-to-face communication grows superior in effectiveness to the extent the information to be exchanged between two parties is complex, novel, or ambiguous. By contrast, less rich media may be equally effective in those cases where relatively simple, routine, and definite information has to be exchanged.

This research suggests that there may be no need to visit the customer site if the information you need is simple, involves nothing very new, and primarily concerns matters of fact. To put the matter more strongly: you probably cannot justify the cost, in dollars or time, of a customer visit program if most of your questions could be answered with "yes," "no," "three times a week," "two people," "about $12,000," and the like. A series of telephone calls, or a survey of some sort, ought to be adequate when matters are this straightforward. On the other hand, consider the type of information you need during the early stages of new product development, or as you research opportunities for fundamental technological innovation. Consider also the kinds of subtle and intangible factors that may have a crucial impact on customer satisfaction. More generally, consider the complexity of the products sold by BTB marketers and technology firms. Under these circumstances, interactive face-to-face communication may be imperative if you are to succeed in learning about customers. Managers have begun to recognize this fact:

It's important to know how our products are being used and who is using them. Without that knowledge one is groping, and while there are many ways to get that knowledge, the most direct way, the most efficient way that I know of, is face-to-face with experienced, knowledgeable people talking directly to users in their place of work—not in an artificial environment, in their place of work. *(applications manager)*

Thought Worlds

In addition to the advantages of face-to-face communication, there is a more subtle but equally important argument for on-site visits that draws on research in sociology and social psychology. Here the key notion is referred to as the *thought world*.[19] Each of us lives in a thought world shaped by our background, membership in social groups, and current task demands. A thought world consists of tacit and taken-for-granted assumptions about what is important, relevant, or necessary.

Your perspective on the product you sell is shaped in countless ways by your thought world. Unfortunately, your customer probably inhabits a very different thought world. You are a software engineer, she is a financial analyst. You are a chemist, he is a lab technician. You are an instrument designer, he is a manufacturing supervisor. You do not have the same education, you are not subject to the same task demands, and you do not belong to the same social matrix. Even when backgrounds are similar, as when engineer visits engineer, thought worlds are often different. Vendor engineers tend to live in *Lab World*, whereas the customer's technical people tend to live in *Task World*. In Lab World, bits, bytes, and baud rate are a source of fascination and the focus of attention. The product itself is valuable and interesting. In Task World, the priority is to accomplish some job, and the product is merely a means to that end. The product and its underlying technology have value only insofar as they contribute to this task. Often there is a deep chasm between Lab World and Task World, as these remarks suggest:

It is difficult to get people out of the plants, but when we do, it is terribly beneficial. They gain a much better understanding of what the customer really needs. It gets them out of that mode where they're working on cost reductions and efficiencies at the plant, and it opens up a vision of what the company is really trying to do out in the marketplace. And they identify with that, and it sticks for a while. *(development manager)*

One of the benefits is for individuals in engineering and manufacturing who might have thought previously, "The stupid customer, how could they possibly use it this way. There is nothing we can do if they are going to abuse our products this way." But the awakening comes when they go out and see that it is not that far-fetched and people are human. *(quality manager)*

The argument from thought worlds is helpful because it drives home the point that the customer information that you lack is often not a matter of facts or details. Instead, what is missing is a key perspective, a basic principle or a bedrock assumption:

> We're going to try to do some surveys that will give us a measure of how we are doing. Chart the trends. But I think as much as we try to measure things, the most important thing we can do is learn how to listen to the customer and just hear what is going on. *(quality manager)*

If the key business problem is how to overcome a gap in thought worlds, then how likely is this to happen as the result of reading a document? Will a formal written communication—the report of a research study, say—allow you to bridge the gap that separates the customer's thought world from your own? I think not. Instead, you need to be there. To see the world through your customer's eyes, to put yourself in their shoes, it helps enormously to leave your own turf and to encounter the customer, in the flesh, on his or her home ground. A fundamental argument in favor of customer visits is precisely this need to escape from the blinders of one's own experience of the product category and marketplace, and grasp the very different experiences of customers. As one R&D manager put it,

> This just really blew my mind because I had never been in the field, and I was at this customer's shop and they were criticizing us because we had changed a parameter on something that appeared on the user's computer terminal. And they went through how they had to retrain 400 users, etc., and what a cost it was to them. Now I'm sure that the developer was completely unaware of the effect that that change had. What he was thinking about was how beautiful that change was. And he probably tried it out on his buddy at the user meetings and they thought it was beautiful, too. It had never been tried out on the management or the implications of what that kind of a change would do to the organization. So the guy was spending time on the wrong issue. *(R&D manager, electronics firm)*

Here is an example of a gap in thought worlds that will be familiar to anyone who frequently makes presentations using an overhead projector. When I arrive at a firm to make a presentation, of course I expect to find a room with overhead fluorescent lighting. Most of the time, this room will also have a built-in projection screen that

drops out of the ceiling—it is a training room or other space dedicated to meetings and presentations. And nine times out of ten, that
room will have a fluorescent light situated immediately in front of
the screen that acts to wash out the projected image—and no way to
turn off that light without turning out all the other lights!
Clearly the people who design electrical wiring arrangements for
buildings and the people who install ceiling light fixtures do not live
in the same thought world as people who make their living giving
presentations using overhead transparencies. Electrical-system designers live in a thought world that emphasizes providing enough
illumination evenly spread through the room, while minimizing the
number of switches and separate wiring grids. The idea of an audience who must be able to comfortably view a presentation while
having enough light to take notes and review written materials never
enters their thought world.

Knowledge Utilization

The communication channel and thought world arguments can be
supplemented with arguments from the knowledge utilization literature.[20] It is one thing to collect information on customers, and
another thing entirely to respond to that information. As an R&D
manager once remarked, "I submit that everybody trusts their own
judgment before they trust someone else's." Information that is
acquired firsthand is more credible and compelling. The requirement
that customer information be credible is particularly important in
situations where an organization is attempting to change its culture
in the direction of becoming more customer focused. Similarly,
technology firms are often dominated by technical and engineering
personnel, with marketing a weak or marginalized function. In that
situation, compare the rhetorical force of these two statements:
"Marketing says the customer wants X," versus "The customer told
me he wouldn't buy the product if it couldn't do X." If we want
technical and engineering personnel to act on customer information,
it helps enormously if they receive that information firsthand:

> Any time you talk directly with the end user, and you concentrate on
> what they are saying, a new insight emerges on what is important about
> the characteristics of the product. Let's say you are a manufacturing
> manager, and every day you're looking at quality control data and you

are seeing that the density, the degree of blackness in your film products, varies. Now you go into a medical installation, where density is extremely important, and suddenly you see that your product is going to fail in some percentage of the cases. Now when you go back, you're going to be thinking about how you are going to handle that. *(applications manager)*

The research on utilization of market information has shown that there are two types of research that are particularly likely to be ignored or rejected: studies that are exploratory in nature, and studies that produce surprising results.[21] The implications are chilling: It is precisely when the market is about to turn, or when the firm has lost touch with its market, or is examining a new market, that managers are most likely ignore or gloss over the customer information that professional researchers have obtained for them. The credibility of information gathered firsthand thus becomes an important practical advantage that favors the customer visit technique.

A related advantage of in-person visits is their flexibility. Because you are conducting the visits, rather than delegating this contact to someone else, you have the opportunity to capitalize on unexpected developments. Because the visit takes the form of a loosely structured interview, you can probe answers in depth, and customize your questions to accommodate the specifics of each customer you visit. Personal visits not only make surprising information more credible, they make it more likely that you will have the opportunity to be surprised in the first place.

Importance of Observation

The justification of in-person visits to the customer workplace is now halfway complete. Note that the arguments given thus far would largely apply even if you interviewed your customers in a white-walled room hidden away in a shopping mall. Why, then, must the personal encounter take place at the customer's place of work? The answer rests on the kinds of things that can be learned through observation. More strongly, observation goes beyond conversation to provide information not obtainable in any other way.

Here are two anecdotes that help to establish the importance of visiting the customer workplace. A manufacturer of test equipment used in factories told me that as part of each customer visit, they would examine where and how their test equipment was set up. They soon noticed that the testing area tended to be crowded with a wide variety of instruments, often more than the space could comfortably hold. In particular, customers for this vendor's test equipment resorted to a variety of jury-rigged attempts to locate the machine at eye level. After these visits, the vendor came up with a new model of the instrument that they dubbed "Skyhook." This was the same basic instrument, but with a hook welded to the top of the casing, making it an easy matter to suspend the instrument from the ceiling at any desired height anywhere in the testing area. The new modification was quite successful.

To return to the example, imagine yourself merely sitting in a conference room with the user of the test equipment and asking, "What could we do to improve this product?" How likely is it that a customer would respond, "Oh, you need to put a 2-inch metal hook on top of the instrument case"? It isn't going to happen—the customer himself doesn't realize that this is exactly what he needs. Whereas you, understanding your product intimately and given the chance to see it in use on site, may very quickly realize, "Hey, we can make this better." Again, what the customer says to you may only be a small part of what you learn as a result of making in-person visits to the customer site. What can be learned through conversation is limited by what you know to ask and by what is sufficiently top-of-mind for the customer to volunteer. The anecdote serves as a reminder that so many aspects of a user's experience with a product are tacit and will go unvoiced unless prompted.

The second anecdote comes from a manufacturer of tubing and closures. On a visit to a customer factory (the closures were one component of a product assembled by the customer), a member of the visit team from the logistics department in production stopped short and said, "My gosh, I just can't believe that." He had observed that a similar part shipped by a competitor was causing the customer a great deal of difficulty. The product had been stacked for shipping in such a way that it took longer to unload, was more difficult to unload, and was more prone to breakage than ought to have been the case. When the visit team returned home, that logistics person implemented new shipping policies that specified the kind of stacking and packaging that should be used for best results.

This anecdote emphasizes the need for the decision maker to be personally present. I doubt if I could tell whether parts were stacked properly, no matter how closely I peered at them. I doubt that I would even think to look! Only someone with the appropriate expertise would be likely to notice such a thing. A marketing manager is not an expert on logistics, nor is an R&D manager. Yet, problems with shipping can interfere with total customer satisfaction just as much as problems with product functionality. Again, the decision maker, whatever his or her job title, must be the one to visit.

WHY VISITS BY CROSS-FUNCTIONAL TEAMS?

The advantages of personal interviews under conditions of high uncertainty and complexity have long been recognized in market research textbooks. However, such textbooks typically assume that the personal interviews will be conducted by either a professional research consultant, a specialist from the vendor's marketing research staff, or someone in the marketing or sales function. The implicit or explicit rationale for this specialization and division of labor is the notion that conducting an interview, like constructing a survey, demands a high degree of skill and is best left to specialists. One of the most important messages in this book is that such an assumption can be dangerous and counterproductive in technical markets specifically, and BTB markets more generally. Although good interview skills are helpful, the overriding concern is to have the right people encounter customers firsthand. In BTB and technology markets, that means technical personnel must participate in visits.

Communication Line Loss

So why is it not sufficient to hire a market researcher to conduct in-person interviews with your customers? Engineering staff reading this book are likely to argue that surely a division of labor is both natural and necessary. Let engineers concentrate on design, production staff on process improvement, and let marketing travel around and talk to customers. Isn't that marketing's job? To report back on what the customer wants so we can design and build the product accordingly?

In a word, no. Not if you wish to be customer focused. If engineers delegate customer contact to the marketing function, and expect to

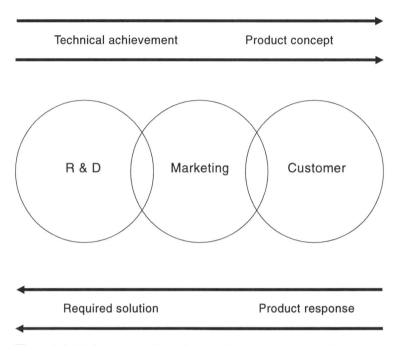

Technical achievement   Product concept

R & D   Marketing   Customer

Required solution   Product response

Figure 1.1. Linear model of interfunctional relations in new product development.

receive the necessary market intelligence secondhand, problems inevitably arise.[22] To see why, examine Figure 1.1. This presents a simplified model of the case where the new product development process is structured so as to place the marketing function in an interface or go-between role. I will refer to it as the conventional model. Any organizational arrangement in which marketing specialists are positioned as the go-between linking design engineers and customers will take the basic form shown in Figure 1.1. The process is assumed to work as follows: R&D engineers are the source of technical breakthroughs and emerging capabilities. In an effort to avoid being technology driven, these technological developments are conveyed to marketing, which in turn expresses them to the customer in the form of one or more product concepts that are the focus of market research. Customers offer feedback on how the product could be made more useful so as to better match their needs. This feedback is then analyzed by marketing, so they can inform R&D about how the technical advances need to be modified or supplemented in order to achieve new product success.

Two things are immediately apparent from an examination of Figure 1.1. First, it suggests a commanding role for the marketing function. This is essentially a hierarchical communications network in which engineers and customers can only communicate with one another through marketing. Second, in this model individuals in the marketing function have to perform a two-way translation task, both effectively transmitting to the customer an impression of what the new technical advances offer, and effectively conveying back to R&D the nature of the customer's response. This process can work well if and only if marketers can function as a kind of "superconductor," offering essentially no resistance to the passage of information in both directions. In fact, this model places an impossible burden on the marketing function. There is no reason to believe that marketers can function as a superconductor, and every reason to expect blockages, delays, distortions, and loss of information. The difficulty is twofold: marketing's inability to convey the totality of the customer's response to R&D, and marketing's inability to adequately convey R&D's emerging technical capabilities to the customer.

Strengthening the marketing function, or offering the marketing function a dominant role, is *not* what is meant by customer focus. In fact, a concentration on the marketing function is probably unhelpful in making the transition to a customer focus. In BTB and technology markets, R&D is too important to be kept isolated from the customer. Moreover, customers value direct contact with technical staff, and technical staff often desire direct contact with customers:

The customers are always very appreciative of having manufacturing people, or research people involved. They perceive it, I think, as an interest—that we are really interested in their business and went to the trouble to have various people come up and attend a session with them. *(development manager)*

There's a lot I get out of visiting customers. I get unfiltered information. In addition, I have a different set of eyes, I can hear things that are different from what my marketing and sales counterparts hear. The customer is the one who has the information I need to design products. *(R&D manager)*

Over time, I believe more and more marketers in technology firms will understand that their proper function is not to interpose themselves between technical staff and customers, but to facilitate the appropriate amount and kind of direct contact between engineers and customers. Anything less saddles the marketing function with the thankless task of trying to single-handedly *make* people be customer focused. By contrast, when given appropriate leadership and guidance, engineers can naturally develop a customer focus if they have an opportunity to encounter diverse customers and build and test mental models of how the customer interacts with the product. Absent such direct contact, I do not see how an engineer can visualize the customer in enough depth to shape product development decisions in the direction of total customer satisfaction. If scientists and engineers are not committed to this goal, it is surely not possible for total customer satisfaction to be added back in to the product at some later point.

Problems With Delegating Customer Contact

The problems with delegating customer research to specialists, together with the advantages of cross-functional visits, were clearly recognized by the managers I interviewed. In their view, the key handicap that made the use of outside professionals problematic was a lack of familiarity with the business:

> What my group brings to the party, that market research doesn't have, is the breadth and depth of their applications and product knowledge. A market researcher doesn't know that much about the application. They can ask all the right questions and they can statistically interpret them, but the applications specialist knows the products, knows the applications, and therefore has greater insight, in my judgment, in these interactions. *(applications manager)*

More generally, when the interviewer is intimately familiar with the business issues under examination, there is an opportunity to achieve in-depth understanding:

> Market research does a pretty good job of answering *what* is important, but in almost all cases it does not do a very good job around the *why*. It is not enough for customers to tell you what they want unless they can tell you why. *(R&D manager)*

All right; there are evidently some problems with delegating customer visits to market research specialists. But here the counterargument often raised is, "What about the sales force?" Because the sales force has regular, ongoing, on-site contact with customers, why can't they gather the necessary information? In reply, perhaps in theory the sales force might be able to get this information (although the typical incentive structure militates against this sort of "paperwork"); but according to the managers I interviewed, asking the sales force to obtain and report customer information simply was not the optimal approach:

> In the old way, the sales guy would have been the lead person who would have come back and told us this is what needs to be done, because I've just talked to the customer and he said this. So we would have gone off to our labs, done some stuff, and then sent him some samples. He would have gone in and talked to the customer and then come back and said: "We still have these issues . . ." Then we would have gone through that cycle, undoubtedly, a number of times. *(R&D manager)*

To summarize, the problem with delegating visits to the sales force is twofold. On the one hand, working through a salesperson produces a longer communication channel with the attendant inefficiency and loss of information. On the other hand, neither the incentive structure faced by salespeople nor their native talents are always appropriate to the kind of patient inquiry that good research demands. The field sales force does have a crucial role to play in an effective customer visit program, as will be developed later; here, I simply want to argue that visits cannot be off-loaded onto the sales force.

So far, the argument has been that in-person contact with customers cannot be delegated to people in the marketing area; but the same argument also holds in reverse: Problems will result if engineers attempt to shut out the marketing function. Although this gambit is not uncommon in technology firms, its pitfalls were ruefully acknowledged by one engineering manager:

> There is a tendency for the R&D folks to be a little myopic, to focus on technology-related issues and miss some of the other issues. I, as an engineer, tend to get so engrossed in talking with this engineer, who is having fun talking about what he is doing, and it's easy to get bogged down in trivia. We have done some products that are very good techni-

cally, but in some cases they miss the customers' real problem. I think in some respects the marketing person is a little bit better at keeping the focus on the agenda, and making sure we don't overlook things. *(R&D manager)*

Organizational Benefits of Team Visits

The argument for cross-functional visits goes beyond the quality of the information that technical personnel can gain through direct customer contact. Cross-functional visits also help to address the longstanding problem of how to integrate and harmonize the marketing and R&D functions.[23] Ultimately, what is required is that marketing, R&D, and the rest of the firm share a common vision of who the customer is and what he or she wants. Instead, turf battles, poor communication, and the failure to coordinate these two departments are all too common. In fact, one study of hundreds of new product development efforts found that moderate to severe disharmony between the marketing and R&D areas characterized nearly 60% of the projects examined. More pointedly, this study also found that the greater the disharmony between marketing and R&D, the more likely the product was to fail.[24]

Years ago, the solutions advanced to the problem of functional integration tended to take the form of formalized coordination procedures imposed from above. More recently, it has been recognized that informal interactions have much more power to build teamwork than formal procedures.[25] In this regard, consider what happens in cross-functional visits to customers. Marketers and engineers drive around in a rental car together, have breakfast together, and interact all day around a common focus on customers and their concerns. This suggests that team building may be a secondary gain from such customer visits. Customer visits early in the development cycle "cut down on the shouting matches," as one manager remarked. More generally, decision making in new product development is made more efficient and effective, as this comment shows:

In the past, engineering and marketing would argue about a product. Or 3 months into development, marketing would simply say, "Well you really have to improve this. We found out from Customer B that this is the most important feature." And the engineer would say, "But I've been doing 3 months of development not going in that direction—that's going to add time to the program!" And then when you get to the end of that 3 months the manufacturing people say, "I can't make it that way. You are going to have to change it." Instead, now we have marketing, manufacturing, and engineering all together deciding on the goal from the beginning. It's more of a trust and a team-building kind of thing. We traveled together and went to all these customers together. And we had conversations following it so that we trust each person's opinion more. *(R&D manager)*

Note also that the need to coordinate different functions is not restricted to technology firms. The following quote from a financial services executive suggests that it is a more general concern in BTB markets:

This company is functional in nature. In the health care business, you have claims people, administrations people, the managed care people. If those people are not in the game, there is no game. They will not be motivated to try to understand the customer perspective, and they will fail.

Building Customer Relationships

A third basic argument for having engineers and manufacturing people visit customers has to do with the need to build strong relationships with customers. Recall that one of the distinguishing features of BTB markets is long-term buyer-seller relationships. As part of the general move toward a strategic focus on customers, more and more firms are looking for ways to strengthen their ties to customers. In this connection, although relationship maintenance is and always will be a core function of the sales force, there appears to be a limit to how much relationship building the sales force can accomplish on its own. The managers I interviewed claimed that customers wanted their vendor contacts to extend beyond the sales force:

I think that the customer gets a chance to see that there's a real person back there. The customer gets to verify that there's someone concerned with his needs who can do something about it. If they continually deal with the salesperson . . . the customer feels like he's dealing with only a salesperson. *(R&D manager)*

TABLE 1.1. Conceptual Summary of Benefits of Customer Visits

Specific Features of Visit Methodology	Nature of Information	Outcomes for the Firm
1. In-person visits		
– Firsthand experience	Credible	Heightened motivation to respond
– Customers encountered in the flesh	Vivid, compelling	Increased potential for change
– Interactive	Detailed, complex	More thorough understanding
– Flexible	Novel	Heightened possibility of innovative solutions
– Observation	Contextual, nonverbal	Deeper understanding
2. Cross-functional teams		
– Jointly planned	Complete, relevant	Protection against partial understanding
– Jointly conducted	Consensual	Heightened commitment and responsiveness
– Multiple perspectives	Triangulated	Decreased bickering among departments
– Participation of technical staff	Technical	Better marketing-R&D integration

By definition, a salesperson cannot have the specialized knowledge of technology that an engineer possesses. In the case of highly technical products, the customer wants to have contact with vendor personnel who are intimately familiar with, and have decision-making power over, the core product technology:

> You are establishing a sales contact that I don't think any sales person can do in the same way. Because here you have the actual designers, the people who dictate what the product is going to be like and how it is going to work, visiting you and asking for your input. I think that makes a huge difference. *(marketing analyst)*

In short, the firm that seeks to be customer focused must not restrict customer contact to the traditional channels. The sale force cannot monopolize it, and research specialists cannot own it. Rather, the people who need customer input have to participate in getting it.

Better information, greater motivation to respond, and improved customer relations are the results that you can expect (see Table 1.1).

NOTES

1. See Cleland and Bruno (1996) for more information on combining shareholder and customer value.

2. For the early development of the marketing concept, see Drucker (1954) and Levitt (1960). For a summary of current thinking, see Day (1991) and Jaworski and Kohli (1996).

3. The first definition can be found in Narver and Slater (1990, p. 1) and the second in Kohli and Jaworski (1990, p. 6; see also Jaworski & Kohli, 1993). The work of these authors plus that of myself and others has been sponsored by the Marketing Science Institute (MSI), 1000 Massachusetts Avenue, Cambridge, MA 02138, (617) 491-2060. MSI is a consortium of more than 50 blue-chip firms that attempts to facilitate productive interaction between business academics and the business community. The area of market orientation is a central topic for MSI that continues to receive research funding, and the interested reader should contact MSI for an update on more recent publications.

4. See Deshpande and Webster (1989) for more on marketing culture, and Kotter and Heskett (1992) for a more inclusive discussion of the relation between corporate culture and performance.

5. Narver and Slater (1991) discuss conceptual reasons and provided evidence for why a "market-back" approach is superior to a top-down approach.

6. See Jaworski and Kohli (1996) for a review of this work.

7. A copy of the application guidelines can be obtained by writing to: Malcolm Baldrige National Quality Award, National Institute of Standards and Technology, Route 270 and Quince Orchard Road, Administration Building—Room A537, Gaithersburg, MD 20899.

8. I owe this example to Bill Siefkin.

9. The source of these and other quotes is a study sponsored by the Marketing Science Institute, as described in Exhibit 1.1. Quotations have been edited for style, and ellipses have been removed for readability. Sources were invited to check the manuscript for accuracy prior to publication.

10. See Deshpande, Farley, and Webster (1993). Their data are from Japan; they are in the process of replicating the research in other countries.

11. A vast amount of evidence on new product success and failure has accumulated over the past two decades. See the books by Cooper (1986) and Souder (1987), along with citations in those sources and more recent ones such as Griffin and Hauser (1992). The *Journal of Product Innovation Management,* sponsored by the Product Development Management Association and edited by Thomas Hustad at Indiana University, regularly reports empirical studies of new product success and failure.

12. See Utterback (1974) and also Bonnet (1986) for a discussion of similar findings reported in other studies.

13. See Jaworski and Kohli (1996) for additional insights into the value of seeking a market orientation.

14. A fuller treatment of this idea is given in McQuarrie and McIntyre (1990b).

15. Although there is a vast literature on the topic of "the learning organization," for present purposes the best points of entry to that literature are Barabba and Zaltman (1991) and Slater and Narver (1995).

16. I use the term *decision maker* here for its broad applicability. Whereas often the decision maker will be a manager, sometimes it will be an engineer, as in the case of design decisions, or a staff member, as in the case of program or policy details.

17. Other writers have also pointed out the value of personal visits. See Shapiro (1988) for a case study, and Bailetti and Guild (1991) for an empirical study. The approach of Von Hippel (1986, 1987), although it differs in many respects, also relies on personal visits.

18. See Daft & Lengel (1986) and Daft, Lengel, and Trevino (1987).

19. I got this idea from Dougherty (1988). She in turn adapted it from the work of the sociologist Douglas (1986).

20. See Moorman (1995) for a discussion of recent work concerning the utilization (or lack thereof) of market research findings.

21. See Deshpande and Zaltman (1982, 1984, 1987).

22. For more on interfunctional communication, see Maltz and Kohli (1996).

23. See, among others, Gupta, Raj, and Wilemon (1986), Griffin and Hauser (1996), and Ruekert and Walker (1987). There is a large and growing literature on this topic. More recent studies can be found through examining such journals as *Research Technology Management, Industrial Marketing Management,* and *Journal of Product Innovation Management.*

24. See Souder (1987).

25. See Tushman (1979) and Tushman and Nadler (1986).

CHAPTER TWO

The Customer Visit in Practice
Some Examples

The procedures described in this book have been used at a wide variety of leading firms. Before offering a step-by-step guide to planning, conducting, and analyzing customer visits, it may be helpful to describe existing practice and to give some idea of both the range of activities and their perceived value. This chapter begins with a discussion of customer visit activity at Hewlett-Packard (HP), where I have the most extensive data, and continues with briefer profiles of other firms, some studied as part of the MSI research described in Exhibit 1.1, others encountered as part of my consulting practice.

HEWLETT-PACKARD

Two studies were conducted in 1990 and 1991 in cooperation with Corporate Marketing Education (CME) and Corporate Engineering

(CE) at HP (see Appendix B for a description of the methodology used). The CE study examined how customer visits were used in new product development whereas the CME study examined the perceived value of a wider variety of visit efforts conducted for diverse purposes. (See Exhibit 11.1 for other pertinent findings from the CME study.)

New Product Development

A total of 54 development projects that included customer visits were examined. The typical visit program included visits to 10 to 40 customer firms by a two-person team that included one engineer and one product marketer. In most cases, the visit programs were conducted early in the development process. Most visit programs also made an effort to select the customers visited according to a sampling plan and to follow up the visit program with additional market research. On the other hand, projects that included a substantial number of visits to international customers, or to competitor's customers, were in the minority.

The study revealed a high level of enthusiasm for customer visits on the part of the R&D project managers interviewed. When asked what advice regarding customer visits they would give to a new project manager, typical comments included, "Do more of it," "Do it earlier," "Get as much customer contact as possible," "Go see the customers yourself," and "Take all project team members." Interestingly, about two-thirds of these project managers clamed that at the time (early 1990), their customer visit program had been unusual within their business unit for its degree of structure and sophistication. However, nearly 70% of these same managers claimed that this structured, programmatic approach to visits was now becoming the norm. It appeared that the practice of customer visits, believed to have very old roots at HP, began to enter a new phase as the 1990s began.

Perceived Value of Visit Programs

The CME study, completed by more than 200 people, asked respondents to describe a customer visit program in which they had participated over the past year. Several questions addressed the perceived value of this visit program. Specifically, 47% characterized the visit program as extremely valuable, and another 49% felt it had been fairly valuable. In terms of specific outcomes, 90% stated that the visits had had a direct impact on the products and services offered to customers, and 88% felt that the visits had led to greater customer satisfaction. A high proportion (76%) stated that they had gained some unexpected or surprising information as a result of the visits. A substantial number of the visit programs described by respondents corresponded to the procedures described in this book; namely, they had stated research objectives, used a sampling plan to select customers to be visited, conducted the interview with the aid of a discussion guide, assigned different roles to team members, and had a structured reporting process.

OTHER FIRMS THAT
CONDUCT CUSTOMER VISITS

In 1989 I was still unsure of how generally applicable the programmatic approach to visiting customers was. For all I knew, it could be a unique outgrowth of the organizational culture at HP. A primary purpose of the research sponsored by the MSI was to discover whether there were other firms that made it a practice to visit customers in a systematic way.[1] By the conclusion of that study it was clear that the practice was quite widespread, although the frequency and sophistication of visit activity varied widely. The following brief vignettes provide some additional examples of how customer visits are used and the range of contexts in which they have been found to be appropriate. Note, however, that these vignettes should not be taken as summary statements concerning how visits are done at Company X, but rather as an account of some things that one part of Company X does on occasion.

John Fluke Manufacturing Co., Inc.

Fluke, based in Everett, Washington, is a leading supplier of handheld and other test and measurement instruments used by electrical manufacturers. Of all the firms in the study, it is the most similar to HP, being an electronics manufacturer that sells instruments to business customers in markets where the potential customers number in the hundreds or thousands. In fact, Fluke directly competes with several of HP's test and measurement divisions. As at

HP, customer visit activity for purposes of market research and product development appears to be a widespread and entrenched practice at Fluke. A typical program involved several dozen visits conducted by teams consisting of a product planner and a development engineer. Samples were chosen according to a plan and a discussion guide was used to structure the interview. Also notable were early efforts to database customer visit reports.

At Fluke, there was a strong commitment to conducting customer visits in Europe and Asia as well as in North America. These programs were undertaken even when a local translator had to be used. People felt that the value of firsthand observation and the opportunity to watch body language and observe the work site outweighed any logistical impediments. An interesting observation by one product planner was that visits to Japan had become easier and more productive over the past 6 years. In fact, contrary to impressions from other interviews, this individual did not believe the cross-cultural barriers to effective customer visits to be particularly significant in this instance.

IBM

A manager in a software business at IBM described a large customer visit program. In this program, teams were formed that consisted of one manager from IBM and one consultant from a leading management consulting firm. These teams visited roughly 40 IBM business customers in the course of the program and interviewed two or three individuals. They used a discussion guide to structure the interviews and wrote a formal report. The purpose of the program was to generate a possible segmentation scheme for a complex software protocol. The visits suggested that customers' attitudes toward risk might be a key segmentation variable. Participants contended that alternative market research methods would have been unlikely to uncover this particular segmentation variable or assess its importance.

Raychem

The division of Raychem discussed here manufactures heat-shrinkable closures, tubing, and connectors for use primarily in the telecommunications and cable television industries. There were several examples of programmatic visits. These represented a new development that had been stimulated by corporate involvement in

QFD and associated techniques for TQM. Of particular note was the inclusion of manufacturing team members along with marketing and R&D. Team visits to customers were seen as an important means of implementing a total quality approach, and managers spoke favorably of such visits as an example of a new way of doing business.

CIGNA

At CIGNA, organized customer visit programs are a recent but increasingly common phenomenon. These programs typically have established research objectives, a sample of several dozen customers, a discussion guide, and cross-functional participation. Several of these programs had the explicit goal of making the customer more visible to CIGNA staff normally isolated from customer contact. In other words, over and above the research value and the relationships they established with individual customers, these programs were intended to instill or maintain a customer focus among the business unit's decision makers.

Milliken

Milliken's drapery and fabric unit is situated further back on the value chain relative to a firm like HP or Fluke. As a supplier of material in bulk to manufacturers (who subsequently sold to retailers, who then sold to consumers), this business naturally faced different challenges. In fact, a high proportion of the business consisted of custom work for one or a very few customers, rather than standard products sold to multiple market participants. Hence, the normative model of sampling from a population of customers (see Chapter 5) for the purpose of constructing a program of visits was less applicable here. On the other hand, new business development, in which there might be many potential customers for a particular textile innovation, more closely conformed to the model. In fact, research scientists at Milliken were accustomed to going on tours of potential customer sites in an attempt to understand emerging needs or assess possible reactions to design initiatives from Milliken.

Du Pont

As was the case with Milliken, Du Pont's electronic materials business lay far back in the value chain, with the business functioning as a supplier of materials to manufacturers who themselves might be component manufacturers several levels removed from the ultimate user of the electronic equipment. What was particularly notable in the interviews at Du Pont was the involvement of research scientists, and not only development engineers, in direct customer contact. As was the case at Milliken, research scientists played a key role in business development efforts, and a series of customer visits was a common feature of their efforts. Customer contact for research scientists might take a number of forms beyond a personal visit to the customer site. For instance, a Du Pont scientist might serve on a committee set up by an international standards body. Scientists employed by key customers would also serve on this committee. Relationships forged here and at scientific conferences led to a number of benefits. These included (a) the ability to arrange customer visits that included key technical personnel at the customer site; (b) enhancement of Du Pont's credibility in technical discussions with customers, leading to clearer information from the customer on their needs and product performance; and in general, (c) improved access to the customer, such as the ability to pick up the phone and get a quick answer on a technical issue. In the opinion of these Du Pont scientists, there could be no substitute for direct contact between research scientists and technical customers. In fact, not only could marketing personnel not serve as a channel for this information, but in all likelihood, key technical people in the customer organization would not bother to participate at all unless Du Pont scientists were on the visiting team.

Sun Microsystems

In the early 1990s, Sun wanted to understand problems associated with a customer's first encounter with the company, from the point where the shipment of computers first arrived until the system was up and running. This effort was spearheaded by the quality function, based on perceptions that the first encounter was often more problematic than it ought to be. Cross-functional teams were organized and more than 50 visits were conducted worldwide. The visits yielded a variety of insights that would be difficult or impossible to obtain in any other way. These ranged from the impact of the packaging used, to international differences in desk layout and office configuration, to subtle problems with the usability and installability of various pieces of equipment. Because solutions to many of these problems cut across departments and functions, the cross-functional makeup of the visit teams proved crucial in securing a response to identified problems.

Apple Computer

In the mid-1990s, the Display Products Division of Apple Computer wanted to explore the potential for an entirely new product category that would expand the division's offerings. The goal of the program of visits was to discover unmet needs that present products did not satisfy, to describe customer requirements that the new product would have to meet, and to explore the fit between Apple's core competency and these requirements. More than 30 visits were conducted in the United States and Europe. A product manager from the marketing function coordinated the visits, and a wide range of scientists and engineers participated (the new product solution was much more than an incremental change or twist on an existing offering). Information gained from these visits was combined with secondary and other market research to assist division management in making a decision about whether to invest in that market.

SUMMARY

This chapter shows that there are no insurmountable barriers to conducting an organized program of visits. Whatever the costs in terms of time and money, quite a number of leading firms have found it worthwhile to engage in this activity. A program of visits can be conceived, designed, and executed within 6 to 12 weeks. If multiple teams are used, no individual need be away from his or her desk for more than 1 week. Most important, the benefits, as developed in this chapter and the preceding one, are reported by managers to be orders of magnitude greater than the costs.

NOTE

1. Portions of the chapter appeared previously in McQuarrie and McIntyre (1992) and are reproduced here by permission of MSI.

CHAPTER THREE

A Typology
of Customer Visits

Most of this book focuses on the programmatic approach to customer visits. However, there are actually a wide variety of activities that can be subsumed under the heading of "customer visit." This chapter describes the various alternatives and briefly discusses how to maximize the value of each of the nonprogrammatic types.[1] The underlying point of view is that much can be gained even from nonprogrammatic visits, despite their limitations relative to a true program of visits. The next chapter will discuss in more detail the rationale for moving beyond ad hoc approaches to more systematic procedures.

As shown in Table 3.1, we can distinguish ad hoc from programmatic visits, and within the ad hoc category we can also distinguish among outbound, inbound, and neutral site visits. Ad hoc visits generally occur one or two at a time, whereas programmatic visits require that a dozen or more visits be executed according to a plan. In an outbound visit, you travel to the customer, whereas for an inbound visit, the customer travels to you. Neutral site visits take place at a trade show, a standards meeting, a convention, or the like.

TABLE 3.1 A Typology of Customer Visits

Category or Type of Visit	Description	Possible Application(s)
Programmatic visits	A dozen or more visits planned as a set and dedicated to research	Explore key factors determining customer satisfaction and dissatisfaction
Ad hoc visits	Unplanned, occurring in isolation one or two at a time	Any customer contact; generally triggered by a need to sell, tell, or fix
Outbound	Employee travels to the customer site	Troubleshooting visits, strategy presentations, assisting sales rep to close a key sale
Inbound	Customer travels to the vendor site	Invite customer to visitor center for a day of presentations
Neutral site	Encounter occurs at third-party site	Explore perceptions while at a trade show
Hybrid, emerging forms		
Customer council	Regular meeting with executives from key customers	Brainstorm possible strategic alliances
Extended on-site visit	Vendor employee spends more than a day on site with customer	Quality engineer spends a week at customer factory to better understand materials flow during manufacturing
Customer workshop	Day-long meeting with a group of articulate, knowledgeable customers	Brainstorm possible enhancements to next generation of existing product
Contextual inquiry	Customers are observed while they use the product in the course of normal business	Identify ways to improve visual interface of a software product
Store visits	Vendor employees spend a day in a retail outlet answering customer questions	Generate improvements to channel marketing strategy
Listening booths	Executives answer questions in a special area at trade show	Identify intangible factors that raise or lower customer satisfaction
Customer panel	Group of customers discuss topics in a room off the floor of a trade show	Explore customer perceptions of competitive offerings

In summary, any time an employee from outside the field sales and support organization encounters a customer, a visit can be said to occur. However, it seems best not to use the term *visit* for an ordinary encounter between a customer and an employee in sales or support—here, *sales call* or *service call* would be more descriptive terms.

OUTBOUND AD HOC VISITS

At a typical firm, a tremendous number of customer contacts occur every year across all managerial and professional levels. In most cases, market research is not the driving factor that motivates these visits. Rather, sometimes you visit to *sell,* other times to *tell,* and others, to *fix.* For example, and with reference to the various job roles that constitute the audience for this book, a product manager may be called to a customer site to help a sales rep close a deal (sell); an R&D project manager may be invited to make a presentation on the firm's future technology directions (tell); or a lead engineer may travel to a customer site to help untangle a particularly nasty failure (fix). Whatever the primary agenda, each of these customer contacts also provides an opportunity to *learn.*

The distinguishing feature of all ad hoc visits is that however many may accumulate over time, these visits were not planned or constructed as a set. They simply happened, driven by the concerns of the moment. "We really need you in Chicago—Acme has been asking some tough questions, and someone from the factory has got to make an appearance." In addition to being unplanned, ad hoc visits take place in isolation. You don't know what visits your colleagues are about to undertake and they don't know what visits you have made. Although the total volume of visits is often quite large, on current practice they do not accumulate—they do not become a data set.

The basic advice with respect to ad hoc visits is to find ways to leverage these customer contacts for learning purposes. Recognize that this visit activity is already budgeted; it is going to take place regardless. If it could be made less isolated, and a plan put in place in anticipation, then you would gain a very powerful intelligence-gathering tool. The end of this chapter gives some specific advice in this regard. First, we review the other major types of nonprogrammatic visits.

INBOUND AD HOC VISITS

An inbound visit occurs whenever the customer comes to visit you. In small firms, these inbound visits take place haphazardly in a variety of settings, including managers' offices and whatever conference room is available. By contrast, larger technology firms almost always have a visitor center set up and the bulk of inbound visits will be hosted here. Typically, the visitor center is a suite of meeting rooms surrounding an exhibition space. For large technology firms, there is a constant stream of customers wanting to hear about the firm's technology and strategic directions, or just desiring to strengthen the relationship. Hence, the institution of the visit center grew up to facilitate the hosting process. The annual volume of visits to the visitor center for any sizable firm can easily run to the hundreds or even thousands.

Most visits to the visitor center are set up by the sales force. The purpose is some mix of a desire to extend VIP treatment to an important customer, a need to overcome doubts so as to close a deal, or a desire to impress upon the customer the exciting new developments on tap. Because the visitor center is at the vendor's site, it becomes possible for the sales force to place in front of the customer a greater variety of key people at a higher managerial level. It is far easier for a director to spend an hour at a building across the way then to get in a car or on a plane to spend that same hour at the customer site.

Unfortunately, because the sales agenda is primary, most firms do little to take advantage of the substantial market intelligence potential presented by the visitor center. What happens instead might be called "death by slide show." The pressure is on to tell the customer as many positive things as possible. As a result, the agenda quickly fills up with one presentation after another. Of course, the presenters take questions, so that some dialogue results, but the basic format of the day remains one of vendor talks, customer listens.

What makes the underutilization of the visitor center particularly sad is the incredible cost-effectiveness, in terms of both time and money, of customer contact achieved via the visitor center. By contrast, even occasional outbound visits are both time-consuming and expensive. Focusing now on engineers in particular —a crucial component of the core competency of any technology firm—realistically, how many outbound customer visits can the typical engineer make in the course of a year? In particular, consider design engineers who are not managers. In the course of performing their tasks, each such engineer must make countless choices about what would be the better or worse solution to a design problem. Ideally, these choices will be made with constant reference to a mental model of customers' needs and priorities. However, when customer contact is minimal or absent, a very different reference point is often used: Engineers may gravitate instead toward what is technically challenging, constitutes an interesting problem, or might impress esteemed technical peers. Such solutions don't always sell!

Given these constraints, the challenge for management might be phrased as, What is the most cost- and time-effective means to increase the number of productive customer contacts on the part of engineering staff? In many cases your visitor center will emerge as an enormously underutilized source of market intelligence with the potential to provide a very cost-effective way of making customers more visible throughout the organization. Unfortunately, in too many cases every minute of the visit is scheduled with an unremitting parade of presentations and exhibits, forcing a relatively passive role on the customer, and making dialogue the exception rather than the rule.

Try this instead: Set aside 1 hour where the presentations stop. Move to a different room where the seating is arranged for dialogue rather than one-way interaction. Label this part of the agenda as *customer feedback, exchange of views,* or *customer issues.* Make it clear at the outset of the hour that this portion of the day has been set aside to listen and learn. (It will help if you advise customers in the invitation letter as to the topics you hope to cover.) Signal the change of pace by having a different person host this session. Most important, arrange for key technical people who work on projects relevant to this customer and market segment to be present. The goal is to begin the hour by asking one or two perennial questions (see following sections), and then to let the conversation develop as it will.

Firms that have tried this even once have told me that customers liked this part of the day best—in fact, it almost always runs over the hour scheduled. A moment's thought shows why. Consider yourself: Do *you* like to sit still and be talked at for an entire day? Of course not. You are an experienced manager and a skilled professional, and you have a great deal to contribute about topics within your domain. What makes you think your customers are any different? To cement the gains, schedule these feedback hours immediately after lunch, when presentations are in any case deadly. If nothing else, they will reenergize the customer for the presentations that follow.

To make better use of inbound visits to the visitor center is in some ways more challenging than taking advantage of occasional outbound visits, because more people, in more dispersed parts of the organization, have to be coordinated if the effort is to succeed. The sales team responsible for inviting this customer has to agree to release an hour on the agenda. The staff of the visitor center has to be informed of the particular interests of this customer, has to have the means of identifying relevant engineering and technical staff, and has to be empowered to invite and cajole their attendance. Directors of engineering have to see the benefits of this exercise and agree on the number and frequency of contacts to which they will commit engineering staff. Finally, marketing management may have to champion this change to make it happen.

If all of these people associated with visitor center activities could be coordinated, then at a minimum your firm would be able to increase the number of meaningful customer-engineer contacts by several hundred relative to last year—for no additional travel cost whatsoever! Customers will get more out of the visit, engineers will expand their reference group to include a wider range of customers, and you will obtain a new stream of ongoing market intelligence.

HYBRID AND EMERGING VISIT TYPES

The occasional, ad hoc customer visit on the one hand, and the program of a dozen plus visits on the other hand, comprise the bulk of the activities that can be subsumed under the heading of "customer visit." However, these two formats do not exhaust the set. There are also other types of visits, some fairly common and others quite rare in my experience, that have a more specialized application. To put these hybrid and emerging types in context, note that programmatic visits are fundamentally interviews: face-to-face encounters where one person asks a series of questions of another. Ad hoc visits, to the extent they are harvested for market intelligence, also become interviews. By contrast, many of the hybrid and emerging forms discussed in this section are distinguished by being something more than, or something different from, interviews. Others represent time or cost-effective means of conducting something, either an interview or a mini-interview. Each has specific benefits as developed later in this chapter.

Customer Council

Many technology and BTB firms find it useful to set up Executive Councils (Sun Microsystems is an example). Companies that use distribution channels find it useful to convene Dealer Councils (Apple Computer and Hewlett-Packard are examples). A council will often meet quarterly. Members of the council are executives from key customers or channel partners. Depending on the purpose of the council, these customer executives may have broad business responsibilities or more focused technical responsibilities. Historically, IBM has made heavy use of the latter kind of council.

In all cases, the purpose of the council is straightforward: to get feedback and share perspectives. A typical council session will last all day. In addition to the information gathered, there is a secondary gain in terms of stronger customer relationships. Perhaps the key benefit of councils relative to other types of customer visits is the potential for synergy through group interaction. In this respect, councils resemble focus groups, but are distinguished by a caliber of respondent almost impossible to recruit for a focus group, a lengthier session, and more in-depth discussions.

Best practice in council management can be simply stated: The council sessions stand or fall as *meetings*. Of course, too many business meetings, particularly all day meetings with more than a dozen participants, are bad meetings: boring and frustrating. Here are a few suggestions for improving customer councils:

- Pay careful attention to seating arrangements. A U-shaped table allows customers to both face one another and to face a presenter. You will get much more interaction among customers with this arrangement then when everyone faces forward, or when people surround a narrow table and can't easily see people to either side of them.

- Have customers *do* things. Some firms have experimented with workgroup software on laptops; others have customers come forward and make presentations. Either way, you get a much livelier group. If you restrict customers to an audience or discussant role, the councils lose a great deal of energy.

- Consider hiring a professional meeting facilitator.
- Slave over the agenda. When it's too crowded, or too vague, or the time boundaries are poorly set, attendees get alienated.
- Make sure that the topics for discussion are relevant and engaging, *from the perspective of the customer.* The temptation, of course, is to select the topics that are of most interest to you, the vendor.

An overarching rule is that presentation should be minimized and discussion maximized. At the end of the day, it has to be clear to council attendees that these issues needed to be discussed *and* that a group had to be physically convened for this discussion to bear fruit. Otherwise, you have wasted their time.

The customer council has several distinctive advantages. It is more focused on relationships than most customer visit techniques. Because customers will attend regular councils, these relationships are built over time. Moreover, these relationships are forged between top management of the vendor and customer firms. Hence, the customer council makes a great deal of sense in circumstances where a relatively small number of customers account for a large proportion of sales, or drive the market toward new technologies, or are otherwise influential.

A customer council also benefits from group process. A topic discussed by a group of customers will develop in a fundamentally different way than a topic discussed with an individual customer. In groups, diverse views can be challenged, elaborated, and differentiated. Multiple overlapping perspectives become evident. Topics that might be very difficult for an individual to address may benefit from the stimulating effect of the comments of others.

Groups both integrate and differentiate, unify and polarize. This basic human dynamic offers a number of benefits to the vendor (as an aside, this dynamic is one reason why the focus-group technique has always exercised a certain fascination).[2] Because groups integrate, the customers in the council meeting will, metaphorically speaking, reproduce for the vendor's inspection a kind of distilled essence of "what it is like to be your customer." If the vendor were instead to encounter the same group of customers one at a time over a period of weeks or months, it is less likely that this same quintessence of customer perspective would emerge as clearly. Groups also differentiate—once customers have found common ground, they can set about exploring their differences. In complex market situations this differentiation can be extremely important. The simple fact is that many times, different customers desire different things; preferences are not homogeneous. The risk in encountering customers individually is that the most recent or most articulate customer comes to dominate the vendor's view of "what the market wants." In a council meeting, opposing views are instead set against one another and can be developed in depth.

The final benefit is the length of time one has the customer's attention, in conjunction with the relatively small investment of time on the part of the vendor participants. An entire day allows much more information to be exchanged than a 1- or 2-hour meeting. The council meeting often occurs at the vendor site, although it may take place at a conference center. In either case, the amount of time invested by the half-a-dozen vendor participants is far less than would be required to encounter the same number of customers, for the same amount of time, one by one at their own sites. The customer council is thus attractive on simple grounds of efficiency—the amount of information gained relative to the amount of time invested.

However, customer councils are not without risks and a downside. Meetings of this sort are notoriously hard to pull off successfully. All day, large group meetings easily descend into a mind-numbing procession of presentations alternating with a boring rehash of stale issues. Group process also cuts both ways. Crowd control can be very difficult in these circumstances. If a few obstreperous customers unduly dominate, then the entire day may be largely a failure. Even with good crowd control, any group discussion suffers from the inability to focus in depth on any single customer and develop the complexity of their specific situation. Another limitation is that councils usually only include only executive-level personnel—fine for discussion of certain kinds of strategic issues, but not so useful for exploring product-related issues, inasmuch as these executives may be influencers but not users. Lastly, the customer council is not field research—one does not encounter the customer in context, on his or her own turf.

Extended On-Site Visit

It is not unusual for engineering, manufacturing, or quality personnel to undertake to spend a week at a customer site. This most typically occurs when the vendor's product is used as part of a complex manufacturing or physical distribution process (although in principle, the same approach could be used to study the delivery of services, at, say, a Department of Motor Vehicles). The practice, I believe, was inspired by the literature on TQM. The idea is that by spending an extended period on site in a mix of observation and conversation, a kind of learning can take place that would be impossible to duplicate by any other means.

This approach is akin to anthropology—one goes to "live with the natives" in order to understand all aspects of their business operation and corporate culture. This comparison to anthropology reveals much about the requirements for success in extended on-site visits. Here, the fundamental research skill will be participant observation. In a very real sense, the anthropologist is the measuring instrument in anthropological research. For extended site visits to yield the most value, the visitor has to be a keen observer, have a lively curiosity, be able to quickly win the confidence of strangers, and possess an integrative intelligence. This is a tall order, compounded by the fact that the visitor is most likely to be a relatively junior engineer.

On the plus side, if the visitor is a junior engineer—or anyone new to the vendor or unfamiliar with the product category—the downside risk is fairly low, so long as the visitor is not personally obnoxious or clumsy on the order of The Three Stooges. Regardless of whether any strategically valuable information is acquired by the vendor firm, the individual visitor is going to gain much from this immersion experience. The thought world of the customer will become more apparent, and the visitor's ability to think like a customer in future decision scenarios will be enhanced. Experiences and insights gained during the extended stay are likely to be formative and to stay in memory for a long time.

To take best advantage of an extended on-site visit, give serious thought to how you will record the multitudinous perceptions and insights likely to occur over the course of a week. As always, a clear set of objectives is necessary. If your goal is only the vague "to better understand the customer," you will have difficulty translating this goal into a specific observation strategy or an analysis plan. By contrast, if your goal is more specific—"to describe the customer's manufacturing process step by step, and identify obstacles and problems our technology can solve"—you are much closer to the level of implementation.

The following list of tools and techniques may prove useful across a variety of specific extended on-site visit efforts:

- *Process map.* A flowchart showing inputs, outputs, and transformation points provides a framework for integrating observations. This visual representation is a crucial step in making it possible to communicate what has been learned to others. Without it, you may drown in data.
- *Roles and Requirements.* A thumbnail sketch of the responsibilities and requirements of each job role involved in the manufacturing process provides a framework for integrating data from the many conversations that will occur during the week. Different job roles will have different requirements, and keying quotes and comments to particular job roles helps you keep straight who wants what.
- *Themes.* Data reduction is one of the biggest challenges facing anyone who conducts an extended visit. Your notes will be too voluminous to share, and even the process map and role list can quickly grow very complex. Hence, a useful discipline is to compose a brief account of the "big news"—your own personal "top 10" list of key insights. An example of a theme might be *interrupt and resume.* That is, you might observe again and again that workers must interrupt a task before completion, perform some unrelated duty, and then take up where they left off. You might further observe that the attempt to resume the task often fails, causing the worker to start over from the beginning, with a consequent reduction in productivity, increase in errors or waste, or both. Once identified, such a theme can guide the vendor's efforts to add value through product innovation.

In summary, the great strength of the extended on-site visit— enormous depth and detail on a single customer—is also its great weakness. Most visitors will conduct, at most, two or three such visits. Hence, one learns a great deal about a very few customers when using this approach. Under some circumstances, the strengths outweigh the weaknesses. This would include situations where a small number of customers make up the bulk of the market, where the customer process does not vary much across customers, or where other research efforts will provide breadth to balance the depth offered by extended on-site visits. By contrast, if customer processes vary considerably, the market is highly segmented, or little other research on customers is being conducted, then extended visits may be misleading, and constrain the vendor's vision of the marketplace rather than enhance it.

Customer Workshop

Often, the inspiration for customer visits is the hope that customers will offer creative new ideas that the vendor can profitably exploit. This goal is particularly common among engineering teams. Just as often, this hope turns to disappointment. The engineer conducting visits for this purpose soon discovers customers to be, on the whole, an uncreative sort, lacking in vision, and narrowly focused on tweaking existing technology and solutions. Sometimes the response to this disappointment is to seek ever more novel or extreme ways of phrasing questions, in the hope that one gambit or another will unlock the buried creativity of customers: "What is your dream for product X?" "In an ideal world where cost was no object, how would you . . ?" But generally, these gambits fail as well, as the customer sticks doggedly to what he knows, which is what already exists, and not what the engineer was after at all.

There are two lessons to take away from such encounters. Perhaps the most important is to realize that solutions are the responsibility of the vendor, not the customer.[3] Put more strongly, the customer is the authority on what the problems are that demand a solution; but for any such problem, only the vendor can decide what form a profitable solution might take. In other words, expecting the customer to hand you a solution, on a platter as it were, for the price of spending an hour or two in conversation, is an error of judgment. It is not impossible to find a profitable solution this way, just unlikely.

The second lesson, more germane to the topic of this section, is that changing the wording of questions is a very weak stimulus insofar as changing the idea productivity of customers is concerned. There are very good reasons why customers may seem uncreative with respect to generating profitable new ideas for you, the vendor, in the context of an hour-long interview. Simply put, it is not their job, and they probably have not spent much time or effort thinking about these matters prior to the interview. Although you can't make idea generation their job, you can change the time and circumstances of your interaction with them, so as to create an environment more conducive to creativity. This second lesson provides the inspiration for a customer workshop.

The insight underlying the customer workshop is that customer idea productivity can markedly increase under the following conditions: Customers are selected carefully, put into a group, given more time, and motivated. A concrete example comes from an effort that took place at a software subsidiary of Sun Microsystems. The goal was to generate enhancements for an existing software product. About a dozen key customers were identified as candidates for participation in the day-long workshop. The incentives for participation were first, the opportunity to influence development of this important software product (all customers were dependent on the product to some degree); second, the opportunity to learn from what other customers were doing; and third, the fact that all travel expenses were paid. The workshop itself was organized as an idea-generation or brainstorming exercise. Customers were given plenty of opportunity to interact with one another and with programming staff responsible for the software. All customer participants made presentations of their suggested enhancements during the afternoon. The consensus of the programming staff was that more than enough ideas had been generated to justify the time and cost, and the perception was that the customers found the exercise worthwhile as well.

This example suggests why the customer workshop can be more effective than ordinary customer visits and how it has to be structured. First, the very fact that the customer is going to spend an entire day on the topic changes everything. This is now a big deal, and the motivational picture changes accordingly. The odds that a significant new idea may be generated are now much better, as a result of increased motivation combined with more cognitive resources being available. Second, putting customers together allows for synergy as customers build on each other's perceptions. Although groups are not necessarily the most effective format for brainstorming, groups are particularly effective at helping individuals with topics that might be too hard to deal with in a one-on-one interview. I don't mean hard emotionally, but hard cognitively—that is, information difficult to retrieve or cover thoroughly without the cuing effect of listening to others make the same attempt. Third, having fellow customers present is important because it increases engagement with the process.

Although I have not encountered very many examples of the customer workshop, I think it is a promising technique and encourage you to explore its application in your own situation. It seems most likely to succeed when the product is complex, when it plays an important role in the customer's operation, and when individual customers have significant expertise, if not in the product itself, then in its effective application. The fundamental insight, again, is that if you want customers to be creative, it takes more than an hour-long interview.

Contextual Inquiry

The contextual inquiry procedure emphasizes the observation potential of outbound customer visits. It was developed to assist in the design of computer software, in particular, the user interface.[4] The distinguishing feature of contextual inquiry is that product designers watch customers using a product at the customer's place of work. Contextual inquiry can thus be thought of as a field approach to usability studies. As part of contextual inquiry, designers discuss with users what they just did or what just happened. The basic idea is that so much of a user's product experience is tacit or taken for granted that it cannot be effectively vocalized or discussed unless the user is placed in context, that is, examined while doing their job. Moreover, in contrast to usability testing, the presumption here is that the designers do not necessarily know which tasks are important, or very much about the nature of these tasks; hence, the need to observe customers in context, doing what they will, as opposed to observing them perform assigned tasks in the usability lab. Like all the specialized techniques discussed in this section, contextual inquiry emphasizes a particular activity (observation) from among the many that comprised by customer visits, and focuses on a particular research task (interface design) and a particular research user (product designers).

In terms of procedure, designers first meet to identify areas of interest and uncertainty with respect to product design. This should culminate in a list of activities to observe and events to notice. Customers are then recruited to participate as in any customer visit program. Typically, a team of designers will go to a customer site, fan out, and each spend an hour or two with a user in the user's cubicle as the user performs work using the product of interest. Several such site visits will be made, so that a dozen or more observations accumulate. These experiences then become inputs to the remainder of the product definition activities, and are analyzed similarly to any qualitative study.

The specific technique just described emerged at Digital Equipment in the 1980s. It is ideal for topics such as design of the visual interface of a product, where the user is unlikely to be able to retrieve and discuss failures and shortcomings unless actually engaged in the use of the interface. Contextual inquiry also shares in the strength of any observational technique: It gets beyond the customer's self-report. Furthermore, like any field research technique, it also takes designers out of the laboratory and places them in the customer's world.

The key weakness can be highlighted as follows: How would you react if someone watched you work *and* interrupted you with questions as they saw fit? How much work would you get done, and how representative of your actual work experience would this vignette be? Rather than being approached as a total solution, contextual inquiry might be thought of as one of many good things that can be done during a customer visit and as something that you ought to at least try if you haven't yet.

An important benefit of discussing approaches to contextual inquiry is that it raises the questions of what form an *anthropological* approach to customer research might take. By contrast, most customer research has historically been psychological, social-psychological, or sociological in inspiration. Controlled experiments, usability testing, and conjoint analysis build on the idea of a psychological laboratory as pioneered in Germany a century ago. Customer visits, focus groups, and some survey research build on social psychological concepts developed in the early decades of this century. In turn, survey research in general and much secondary research build on sociological ideas dating back many years. By contrast, the distinctive methodology of anthropology has been ethnographic study and participant observation. Specifically, anthropologists perform their studies by going to live with the natives in their village. They converse, they observe, *and* they participate in the life of the village. None of the traditional techniques of market research quite correspond to this anthropological model.

From this perspective, contextual inquiry is only the tip of the iceberg. Live-in visits, as discussed earlier, also represent an implementation of fundamentally anthropological ideas. The anthropological approach is distinguished, then, by the intensity of its engagement with a small number of customers. Adaptations of the basic anthropological approach can be expected to proliferate as vendors seek to get ever closer to customers and to more thoroughly instill the customer perspective in key employees. Contextual inquiry is one example of how to proceed.

Store Visits

Both Apple and Hewlett-Packard have experimented with store visits where engineers will spend a day at a retail store such as CompUSA. The engineers will demonstrate products and assist store salespeople in answering customer questions. The purpose is to provide a concentrated exposure to real customers. Much can be learned about the kind of explanations that satisfy customers, the applications that customers contemplate, and the sorts of issues and concerns that come up as part of the buying process.

In effect, the store visit mimics, in the context of retail products, what happens at a booth at a trade show devoted to BTB products. A concern for many technology companies, as retail channels become more important to their business, is the distance that that channel structure introduces between the firm and its customers. The store visit is intended to close that gap.

The strength of the store visit is that it puts engineers face-to-face with a large number of ordinary customers in a concentrated period of time. These ordinary customers are likely to be very different in concerns and outlook from the technically knowledgeable engineer. Because customers are encountered at the cusp of purchase, their minds are unusually focused on product issues, enhancing the relevance and usefulness of conversations. Purchase facilitiators and purchase inhibitors may emerge with particular clarity. The experience is likely to leave engineers with vivid memories of real customers and assist in divining the underlying motivations that technical solutions must address.

The weakness of store visits is that customer contact will often be fragmentary or fleeting. Although there may be some opportunities for extended dialogue, for the most part there will be no time for a sustained pursuit of any line of inquiry. It may be very difficult to draw together 8 hours of scattered impressions into any coherent picture or model of customers and what they are trying to accomplish by using the product.

Listening Booths

This technique has been used by executives of Sun Microsystems at trade shows. The idea is to set up an area within an exhibit and label it as a *listening booth*— a place where customers can sound off or add their two cents. Although any employee manning a trade-show exhibit should of course be listening as well as talking, the primary task at most exhibits is to tell and sell. Hence, it is desirable to set aside some space, label it differently, and staff it with executives. Listening booths are similar to store visits in their profile of strengths and weaknesses. On the positive side, they provide an opportunity to receive a great deal of input, in a concentrated period of time, from customers whose minds have been focused on product issues and vendor comparisons. On the negative side, it can be difficult to integrate all of this input, and the lack of control over which customers participate forestalls any purposive comparisons across customer types. It may also be difficult to control the agenda of each miniconversation, as one is vulnerable to being waylaid by individuals with a great deal to say but not much to add.

Customer Panel

The customer panel represents a different way to take advantage of trade shows and conventions. Here, one reserves a suite with a big-enough seating area to handle a small group. Out on the trade-show floor, the team members recruit customers to participate in the panel. A financial incentive or significant gift, similar to those used in recruiting for focus groups, is typically necessary. A big advantage of this approach, relative to store visits or listening booths, is that customers can be screened to match a specification. This can be as simple as only addressing people who have just left a competitor's booth, or as complex as a structured series of questions.[5] Customers who pass the screening are invited to attend one of the panels scheduled for later that day or the next.

The goal is to recruit anywhere from 3 or 4 to 10 or 12 individuals for the panel. Once the panel convenes, it can be considered a group interview. Unlike a standard focus group, however, in most cases the vendor's own personnel will moderate the groups. This offers real efficiencies in terms of dollar cost and planning time, but does pose risks. Bias is always a danger, and in a larger sense, moderating a group discussion is more demanding, by at least an order of magnitude, than conducting a one-on-one interview.

Virtually any topic that could be covered in a focus group or field customer visit can be discussed in a customer panel. Another strength is that because of the draw of the trade show, one can recruit both a caliber of customer and a diversity of customer types that would be difficult to duplicate in any other fashion without a much greater expenditure of resources. On the negative side, the customer panel is essentially a poor man's focus group, in which customers are encountered outside any organizational context, and removed from actual usage of the product. It is also fair to worry whether the fevered atmosphere of a trade show might unduly influence the tenor of panel discussions—perhaps by emphasizing product experiences, rather than the customers' business situation and task demands, which are often more crucial to understand and more distant from the vendor mindset.

SUMMARY

The hybrid techniques discussed in this section do not exhaust the possibilities for face-to-face contact with customers—they only represent instances that I happen to have encountered. Curious and energetic managers can be expected to continue to devise time- and cost-efficient ways of gaining direct personal experience of customers. For instance, if seminars and training are an important part of your total service to customers, you should be thinking about how these contacts might be used to harvest data with broad relevance to your business strategies.

As a general rule, all the hybrid techniques provide value because they minimize one or another type of cost, while yielding a reasonable amount of information. However, when the goal instead is to maximize the quality of information obtained, hybrid techniques, and ad hoc visits generally, fall short. For that purpose, a program of visits is most appropriate, as discussed in the next chapter. However, ad hoc visits have their place, and better management of ad hoc visits is one of the ways that a firm commits to becoming a learning organization. In any case, there may only be two to three formal customer visit programs in a year within a given business unit, and that is probably not enough customer contact. Finally, the key to maximizing the value of ad hoc visits is to solve the challenge of converting casual contacts into actual data. The next section discusses how to do this and is broadly applicable to all the ad hoc visit types.

HOW TO HARVEST DATA FROM AD HOC VISITS

To leverage your ongoing ad hoc visits, you must:

1. Agree on a small set of perennial questions
2. Log customer profiles
3. Share and discuss profiles regularly
4. Build and maintain a database of profiles

Ultimately, you must resolve that every customer contact is an opportunity to gather market intelligence, and act accordingly.

Agree on Perennial Questions

A perennial question is an open-ended query designed to start a discussion on some topic of enduring interest. It should be a question that could be asked of virtually any customer with whom you have a few spare minutes. An example might be, "What factors led you to choose our product?" This question invites the customer to lay bare their choice process, and may lead to a fruitful discussion of competitor strengths and weaknesses, brand image perceptions, possible future product revisions, and so forth. There are always many candidate perennial questions, as shown in Table 3.2. The important thing is that your team select or devise the one or two questions that make the most sense for you, today. The perennial questions may change over time, but should always represent a query that you would like to direct to as many customers as possible.

Articulating perennial questions is a practical step toward realizing the goal of becoming a learning organization. A good perennial question starts a discussion, opens avenues for exploration, and provides an opportunity to probe for details and clarification. These questions act as an invitation to the customer to give us their perspective on fundamental strategic questions. The goal is not to tabulate the customer's response on a clipboard, but to enter into their world for a brief space and to see matters through their eyes.

It is quite likely that you and your colleagues are already asking customers questions of this sort when the opportunity presents itself. Perennial questions are the natural expression of a healthy curiosity. The crucial step, however, is to get everyone on the team to ask *the*

TABLE 3.2 Examples of Perennial Questions Organized by Business
Challenge

Product Development

1. If you could change any one thing about this product, what would that be?
2. Are there any tasks you have been unable to perform with this product?
3. What does this product *not* do, that it *should* do?

New Product Positioning

1. Who do you suppose is our target customer for this product? How would you describe this person?
2. If you had to compare this product to something else, what comparisons come to mind?
   a. Be prepared to prompt with an example: "If this were a car, would it be a sports car or a station wagon?"
   b. Who are the major competitors for this product? What is the biggest advantage this product might have relative to competition, and what might be its biggest disadvantage?

Customer Satisfaction Assessment

1. What is the most difficult aspect of working with us as a vendor?
2. What business problems have you been unable to solve with this product?
3. What do you *like* most, and what do you *dislike* most, about this product?

Business Development

1. What business issues are keeping you awake at night?
2. Who is your customer when you use this product, and what do they demand from you?
3. Is there anything your customers are demanding from you that you are unable to supply using existing technology?
4. Within this category, what is the most exciting product you have heard of recently? What makes that product so exciting?

Purchase Process

1. In this category, how do you decide which product to buy?
   a. (Follow-up): Please describe a recent purchase step by step—*who* was involved, *what* factors did they consider, *how* did the chosen product emerge as the best choice?

Competitor Analysis

1. Who do you see as the major players in this category?
   a. (For each one): Compared to us, what is the major advantage this competitor enjoys? What is the major disadvantage?
2. (If aware): Have you considered buying [competition product name]? What factors incline you to buy it, and what factors give you pause?
3. If you had to point to any one thing that prevents you from buying [competition product name], what would that be?

same questions. Only then can the real power of a perennial question emerge.

When asked of a single customer in isolation, the answer to a perennial question means little. True, it does educate the person who asks the question, helping them to update their mental model. The answer may also assist in dealing with that specific customer. But as a data point, a single answer to an isolated question is really very weak. We don't know how idiosyncratic this customer may be, how well or poorly informed they are, how initially favorable or unfavorable their stance toward us may be, and so forth. The situation is very different when a dozen team members ask the same questions of a dozen different customers. Idiosyncrasies begin to average out and trends and patterns can appear.

Again, I am only asking you to change one thing: Use the ad hoc visits that already occur, rely on the curiosity that already motivates team members, but get everybody on the same page. Schedule a meeting at the beginning of the quarter. Hash out what the perennial questions are to be, and get buy-in from everyone.

Although the costs are low, the obstacles remain real. Leadership is required to identify perennial questions and motivate visitors from across the business unit to ask these questions. For example, here is the process recently followed at a division of CIGNA. The corporation as a whole was committed to becoming more customer focused, and this direction was supported from the top. A new marketing executive at the division began to encourage specific activities, including customer visits, that would bring the division closer to its markets. From its beginning, this effort was cross-functional in scope and directed at encouraging non-marketing managers to be more involved with customers. Presentations and workshops built commitment across the division to the idea that improving customer visit practice was both feasible and desirable. A key moment came when a good chunk of the division's management made a public commitment to one another to each visit a certain number of customers over the next fiscal quarter. Between the managers present and their direct reports, it was clear that well over 100 ad hoc customer visits could be expected. Following that meeting, participants suggested a variety of candidates for the perennial questions to be asked by everyone during these visits. Marketing staff collated, organized, and distilled these questions, which were then recirculated for approval. Marketing staff also designed a customer profile form, using an electronics forms package, for capturing answers to the perennial questions (see following section). In addition, several business teams undertook a more systematic program of customer visits in order to make a more intensive examination of issues involving repositioning parts of the business to meet changing conditions.

Log Customer Profiles

You take a giant step when you unite everyone on the team behind a small set of perennial questions. To get full value from these questions, however, you have to take the next step and capture customers' answers in a form that can be stored and shared. The key idea is to think in terms of developing *customer profiles*. The structure of each profile is straightforward, consisting of a header page combined with insightful commentary. The header information changes slowly if at all; it consists of descriptive data on the customer's business, along with data on how long they've been a customer, the nature of their purchases, the amount of these purchases, and so forth. This information generally already exists in some kind of corporate database. In fact, historically, such header information—objective, "hard" data, predominately numerical combined with brief text—has been the only kind of customer information collected into a database.

What customer visits allow one to do is to enrich these descriptive data in the header with the kind of insights that can only come about through direct encounters and sustained dialogue with customers. A typical profile will fit on a single page and include three things: (a) answers to the perennial questions asked of this customer; (b) additional insights vis-à-vis unmet needs, areas of satisfaction and dissatisfaction, or key customer requirements; and (c) a brief statement of your personal takeaway from this visit. In other words, the profile seeks to capture the learning that occurred for the visitor. The very fact of the existence of the profile encourages visitors to take a more systematic approach to conducting the visit and assessing what was learned. The request for a profile validates the importance of the visit and reinforces the point that this particular visit is part of a larger marketing intelligence effort.

Table 3.3 gives an example of how a customer profile might look when completed. It is very brief and focused, which is important if you expect individual employees throughout the group to actually

TABLE 3.3 Example of a Customer Profile

Header

Customer	Application
Acme Propulsion Systems	
14873 Jetplane Avenue	Test components prior to assembly
Big Valley, Nevada	
Products installed	**Who we talked to:**
6A-1695 oscilloscope	Joe Smith, VP Quality
3M-3901 logic tester	Sally Jones, Manager, Final Assembly

Body

Question 1: How would you compare our strengths and weaknesses relative to the competition?
  - Customer said we were more innovative, more likely to introduce new functionality.
  - Criticized us on the dimension of usability—said we kept changing the interface across products and product versions, driving up their training costs.

Question 2: Is there anything we do that makes life difficult for you?
  - Criticized our billing system—said we "nickel-and-dimed them to death." Didn't like having every separate part of the system individually priced. Joe complained that too many, too complex invoices made it hard to track total system cost. Wasn't asking for a discount, just wanted a single package price to make their accounting easier.

Personal takeaway
  - These people were really impressed by our technology and pace of innovation.
  - Sounded like we put them through a lot of unnecessary grief, though, in terms of our day-to-day working relationship.
  - Maybe those segments where we have been losing market share represent areas where innovative technology is less important, so that the difficulties of working with us loom larger, and cost us business?

fill these out on an ongoing basis. You want something that can be filled out in 10 minutes or less while waiting to board an airplane flight. If you make completion of a profile too onerous, the whole endeavor will quickly sink of its own weight.

The ability to work with profiles of this sort has been significantly enhanced by the dramatic changes in business information systems that have occurred since the first edition of this book was published. The combination of easy-to-use desktop database packages, the spread of computer networking in general and corporate intranets in particular, the proliferation of laptop computers, and the development of search technologies stimulated by the Internet make it far easier to effectively log and maintain hundreds of customer profiles (see following section).

Share and Discuss Profiles

The next step is to make sure that the accumulating profiles are read, shared, and discussed. If this does not happen, the number of profiles logged will slowly fade away as people lose motivation. Try scheduling a review meeting about 3 months after profiles begin to be logged. Prior to that meeting, make hard copies of all the profiles thus far accumulated and distribute them to all participants. Request that everyone read everyone else's profiles in preparation for the meeting. As a result, for the first time, each person sees what other people have been hearing from customers. You may discover that something you heard, but dismissed as an exceptional or idiosyncratic case, in fact cropped up in other profiles as well. Conclusion: Something is happening in the marketplace.

The general goal of the meeting is a creative response to the customer data in the profiles. For instance, you want people to,

- *Spot trends*—If five different customers made the same comment, something is going on. This is the kind of pattern recognition that logging profiles should stimulate.
- *Define segments*—The combination of header information with commentary may reveal why you do well in some markets and poorly in others. Better target marketing efforts should result.
- *Identify problems*—Repeated complaints become very obvious and can now motivate change.
- *Glimpse opportunities*—New product ideas, low cost enhancements, and new applications should be plentiful.

Continue to schedule these meetings until people have internalized the habit of sharing profiles, commenting on each other's profiles, and using profiles to guide day-to-day decisions. When these activities become self-sustaining, you have a customer-focused organization.

Database the Visits and Profiles

The final step is to store a record of the visits and profiles in some kind of database. For example, if you are familiar with a PC database such as Microsoft Access, you could design a data-entry form corresponding to Table 3.3 in 30 minutes or less. That form can be stored in a database on a corporate Intranet. Anyone on the team with a laptop computer, perhaps after checking their e-mail by remote, can then call up the form and complete a profile for the ad hoc visit they conducted that morning. A month later, another team member can do a key-word search on all the accumulated profiles, seeking, for instance, all mentions of competitor X, or all profiles for customers engaged in a certain application, and so forth.

Even a simple record of who visited who, and when, would be invaluable in planning future ad hoc and programmatic visits. With such a record, anyone contemplating a customer visit could easily discover when this customer was last visited, who did the visit, and what issues emerged. Similarly, as more and more profiles accumulate, it becomes possible to do more interesting analyses of customer issues. Moreover, managers planning programmatic customer visits can review profiles to determine likely candidates for inclusion.

A few years ago, leading firms such as Sun Microsystems began to store customer visit reports on the network where they could be accessed online. Some firms have also experimented with semi-intelligent e-mail systems that provide templates for planning customer visit programs, examples of past customer visit efforts, and a repository of completed reports. Moreover, both Sun and Hewlett-Packard, among others, have taken steps to make secondary market research available on-line at individual managers' desktops. In time, customer visit profiles will become an integral part of these on-line market intelligence systems. These and other kinds of computer technology show great potential for assisting firms in immersing themselves in the world of customers.

NOTES

1. Parts of this chapter originally appeared in McQuarrie (1995). Reprinted with permission from *The Customer Visit,* published by the American Marketing Association, McQuarrie, 1995.

2. See Chapter 11 for further comparison of the focus group technique to customer visits.

3. For a somewhat different perspective on the role of vendor and customer with respect to innovative solutions, see Von Hippel (1987).

4. See Holtzblatt and Beyer (1993) for more information on contextual inquiry.

5. Any good book on focus groups (e.g., Goldman & McDonald, 1987; Greenbaum, 1998) can be consulted for ideas on how to construct a screener.

CHAPTER FOUR

Planning a Program of Visits

WHY A PROGRAM OF VISITS?

In a program, customer visits are carefully planned so as to maximize the amount and quality of information gained. As suggested in the previous chapter, much of the customer visit activity that goes on today is not programmatic at all, but can only be described as opportunistic or ad hoc. Even when a set of visits is deliberately undertaken, there is considerable variance as to how much planning goes into these visits and how well the visits are executed. As a result, many of the visits that are undertaken are not terribly productive.

The key to conducting an effective program of visits is to have a clear idea of what you are trying to accomplish together with an articulated process for achieving that goal. Specifically, a program of visits will have the following:

- Written objectives
- A sampling plan that describes specific types of customers to be visited
- Visit teams whose composition reflects the objectives
- A discussion guide that links objectives to the actual conduct of the interview
- A procedure for analyzing and reporting results

All of these issues have to be addressed before the first visit occurs. This kind of advanced planning helps you to leverage the value of what often proves to be a considerable investment of time and money.

Good planning is also the only means of averting certain uncomfortable or even disastrous situations within the interview itself. Perhaps because of a widespread, albeit implicit, understanding that customer visits are best viewed as an exploratory research procedure, historically there has been a tendency to approach visits in an opportunistic, unplanned, or casual fashion. Hence, although customer visits are not uncommon in American business, carefully organized visit programs remain the exception rather than the rule. However, I would argue that effective exploratory research demands just as much care and discipline as confirmatory research. Hence this book, which is designed in part to motivate the interested reader to conduct visits in a more programmatic manner.

PROBLEMS WITH NONPROGRAMMATIC VISITS

There are two types of nonprogrammatic visits whose limitations are of particular note. These represent the kind of nonprogrammatic visits that are most likely to be perceived as a tempting shortcut relative to the approach developed in this book. The problem with these shortcuts is that research is best considered a "jealous master." Hence, mixed agendas, where you want to do research and accomplish some other goal at the same time, almost always create problems. If you want to gather high-quality market information, then from time to time you are going to have to mount a program of visits exclusively dedicated to research. Instead, the following mixed agendas are all too common.

Sales Support. Here an engineer or someone from product marketing is sent out to help a field sales representative close an important sale. The primary agenda is to support the sales representative by making factory expertise available on the spot.

Troubleshooting. In this case, a customer experiences a problem with the product that could not be resolved through telephone support or local field expertise. Technical experts, typically from R&D or manufacturing, travel to the customer site to conduct a more in-depth investigation in an attempt to resolve the problem.

Before criticizing the attempt to combine a research agenda with a sales or troubleshooting agenda, I want to reiterate that *every* visit holds some potential for learning and discovery. In fact, as noted in the previous chapter, the single most cost effective step that most firms could take to improve their customer research effort would be to do a better job of harvesting information from the never ending stream of ongoing ad hoc visits including sales calls, troubleshooting visits, and much else.

Nonetheless, there are several reasons why sales, troubleshooting, and other nonprogrammatic visits tend to fall short of what a program can accomplish. Consider, for a moment, the state of mind you would want a customer to experience if your primary agenda was research, or learning about customers. As you interviewed that customer, you would hope that he or she felt relaxed, comfortable, and at leisure to think about your questions. Ideally, the two of you would approach the interview in a cooperative spirit, and there would be a high degree of trust. In addition, you would make every effort to eliminate bias from your questions and from the interviewing environment. Finally, you would conduct a sufficient number of interviews to be reasonably confident that your findings accurately reflect reality. The fundamental goal would be to discover the truth, whether pleasant or unpleasant, familiar or strange.

The question to ask about any nonprogrammatic visit is whether it satisfies this standard. Generally, the answer will be no. I can't speak for you, but when someone is trying to sell *me* something, I put myself on guard. I don't want to volunteer too much information because, like most people, I have a vague understanding that professional salespeople are taught strategies for using such volunteered information to close the sale. I don't want to prematurely commit myself, I don't want to limit my freedom to ultimately say no, and for all these reasons, you would find it rather difficult to conduct basic research on my needs and perceptions as long as I think you are trying to sell me something. The dynamic just described thus places limits on what can be learned in the context of sales support visits. Although a sales encounter is not an impossible arena in which to do research, it is decidedly not the optimal setting.

The problem with troubleshooting visits is somewhat different. If I'm having some difficulty with the system I bought from you, I want you to solve that problem, *now*. At some level I'm agitated, displeased, and nervous. I certainly don't have much patience for answering questions that are remote from the problem at hand. That has to wait until after you've solved my problem! Thus, for very different reasons, a troubleshooting visit is also a far from ideal setting in which to do research.

Finally, a problem shared by virtually all nonprogrammatic visits is that typically too few are performed to give confidence in the results. Moreover, each visit follows its own course as dictated by its primary agenda, which tends to minimize the commonalities across visits. This lack of thoroughness and the unsystematic character of what is done make it impossible to describe these types of visits as *research.* It is certainly true that ongoing efforts to be alert to signals from the marketplace should include making use of these visits and other sorts of customer contact; but to do research requires that you meet a higher standard.

OBSTACLES TO PROGRAMMATIC VISITS

If past seminar experience is any guide, at this point some of you will have recognized the logic of the argument for programmatic visits devoted to research, but regretfully concluded that pragmatic considerations must override this logic in your own case. You may specifically object that:

- The customer will not permit you to simply conduct research visits, but will demand a presentation from you or insist on other forms of interaction during your visit.
- Travel to the customer is so expensive that only one person can be sent and each visit must accomplish as many tasks as possible.
- In your case, the tasks of research, sales development, problem resolution, relationship building, and so forth do not seem readily distinguishable.

In response to the first objection, it *may* be feasible to have multiple purposes in mind for a single visit, provided that you observe two precautions. The most important is that you conduct the research interview first, prior to making any kind of slide presentation. Once you have begun to convey your own ideas, you have muddied the waters as far as discovering the customer's true perspective is concerned. The second precaution, if you must pursue multiple agendas, is to segregate research in time and space. You may be able to accomplish certain sales development goals, as well as research, in the course of a single visit, but it is unlikely that you can do a good job of both at the same time.

My response to the second objection tends to be a little more hard nosed, with one exception. If, in fact, your revenue and profit on a certain product is minuscule, then, indeed, you cannot afford to do programmatic research and you must make do with whatever intelligence you can gather on the run. If, on the other hand, the product in question accounts for substantial revenues, then my reaction is one of suspicion: Do you in fact believe in the value of customer research? The issue ultimately reduces to one of pay now or pay later; pay now, in the form of an adequate budget for customer research, or pay later, in the form of failed products that do not meet customer needs.

The third objection requires a more subtle reply. It may be that your business situation lies outside the boundaries of where the customer visit technique is most effective. In particular, you may be in a *customer partnering* situation. The hallmarks of this situation include:

- You have an extremely small number of customers in total—less than half a dozen, and perhaps only one or two.
- You are fundamentally a supplier of raw material or components to a manufacturer, as opposed to a vendor that sells a product to end users.
- You have frequent, ongoing contact with your customers.

In customer partnering, visits solely for the purpose of research may be neither possible nor wise. In general, the customer partnering situation is sufficiently distinct to demand its own body of frameworks and techniques that overlap only in part with those discussed in this book. Although you may find parts of this book helpful, I would acknowledge that ultimately your situation requires its own distinct treatment.

In summary, you either believe in the value of customer research, or you do not; your profit margins are either adequate to support research, or they are not; and customer visits are either appropriate for your situation, or they are not. I hope this discussion has stiffened your resolve to conduct customer visits in the most effective way possible; remember that the alternative to discovering customer needs and understanding sources of customer dissatisfaction can be quite grim, both for the responsible managers and the firm itself. Going forward, global competition will not be kind to firms that only make a half-hearted effort to understand customers.

APPROPRIATE AND INAPPROPRIATE APPLICATIONS

Most customer visit programs will be conducted in the context of either *new product* development, or *new market* development, or initiatives to improve *customer satisfaction*. A few customer visit programs will come about as part of a larger program of market research. Here, customer visits play a role similar to that classically assigned to focus groups, enabling a preliminary exploration of key issues in order to generate hypotheses to be investigated further using other market research techniques (e.g., a large sample survey, or a conjoint analysis—see Chapter 10 for more on this point).

The key to distinguishing appropriate from inappropriate uses of the customer visit technique is to examine carefully the stated objectives of the visit program. Here is a specific example of the kind of objective that can be fulfilled through customer visits:

1. Identify emerging customer needs not met by current versions of our product.

This sort of objective would make sense during the product planning effort for a new version of an existing product, and it is well suited to the capabilities of programmatic customer visit research. A couple of dozen visits to selected customers will likely unearth unsuspected product shortcomings, clarify what customers are trying to accomplish by means of the product, and reveal specific opportunities where improved product functionality could be profitably pursued. The power of face-to-face interaction, along with the illumination occasioned by field visits to the customer site, enable an in-depth investigation of unmet needs.

Another example of a suitable objective would be,

2. Describe customers' purchase decision models and procedures for qualifying and selecting vendors.

This objective is also well suited to the capabilities of programmatic customer visit research. In many cases, BTB products are purchased via some kind of group decision. An outbound customer visit provides the opportunity to interview two, three, four, or more individuals at each customer site, together or singly. Extended face-to-face interaction allows very complex social and organizational processes to be teased out. In fact, it might be difficult to pursue this objective using any other market research technique. The complex contingencies characteristic of this kind of purchase process do not lend themselves to survey research, and in a typical focus group only one individual from any given customer would attend, making it difficult to see how job roles interact around purchase decisions.

Although both of these objectives are appropriate for customer visits, they are quite different. And that is really the point of insisting on a programmatic approach to customer visits in which objectives are drafted, debated, and refined in advance of any visit. That is, to achieve Objective 1 demands the participation of key design engineers. It will require recruitment of customers who have substantial experience using the product. The specific questions asked will in turn be focused quite differently than in the case of Objective 2. In the second example, the issues are more related to marketing and business development concerns, and the participation of engineering staff may not be necessary. A wider range of job roles will have to be recruited at the customer site, probably at a higher managerial level. Questions will be much less focused on the product and the application, and more concerned with the customer's business strategy and corporate culture.

Although customer visit programs can serve a wide variety of objectives (see the end of this chapter), there are clear boundaries beyond which customer visits will no longer be the appropriate research technique. Consider, for example, these two research objectives:

3. Test which of several possible product configurations will be preferred by customers.
4. Forecast potential sales to be expected from each of three possible segments identified as candidates for market expansion.

Both of these objectives are extremely relevant across a range of strategic planning scenarios—and neither of them can be effectively

---

SIDEBAR 1

Pitfalls, Traps, Dangers, and Risks *Experience has shown that there are many ways to fail or fall short while attempting to execute a program of customer visits. Boxed inserts throughout Chapters 2, 3, 4, and 5 will highlight the more important of these threats. These are intended both as a check on excess enthusiasm, and as a set of reminders and cautions that the program coordinator can consult at various points in the execution of a program. On a more positive note, Appendix B offers a planning checklist that encapsulates the process set out in these chapters.*

---

addressed by a typical customer visit program. Chapter 10 will discuss the limitations of customer visits and the need for other kinds of market research in more detail. Here, it is sufficient to note that each of these new example objectives requires a much larger sample than the typical visit program, along with procedures that can estimate numerical quantities with precision.

Thus, for Objective 3, customer preference for each configuration is going to be operationalized as a number of some kind, and a statistical test will have to be performed to determine which configuration earns the highest score. Customer visits, in almost all cases, never yield precise numerical estimates of this kind. This objective requires instead a market research procedure such as conjoint analysis, in which a large sample of customers rate many possible permutations of product features, allowing mathematical estimation of the optimal feature bundle.

For the forecast objective, a survey of some kind is in order, in which a large sample of people drawn from each of the three segments would rate their perceptions of the firm and its competitors, as well as their interest in various product offerings. A statistical comparison of the segments would then allow an estimate of the potential revenue that might be gained from each.

In summary, a program of visits will generally be much more illuminating than ad hoc visits can ever be. On the other hand, no

TABLE 4.1   Seven Step Procedure for Planning a Program of
Customer Visits

Step 1	Set objectives
	– Indicate the kind of information you want to collect
Step 2	Select a sample
	– Describe the types of customers to be visited
	– Estimate the required number of customers
Step 3	Compose the visit team(s)
	– Identify individuals from different functional areas who should participate in the visits
Step 4	Develop the discussion guide
	– Generate the topics and questions to be covered in each visit
	– Organize topics into a sequence and set priorities
Step 5	Conduct the interviews
	– Specify roles for team members
	– Seek a loosely structured interaction
Step 6	Debrief after each interview
	– Assess whether any changes need to be made to the interviews
	– Begin process of analysis
Step 7	Analyze, report, and store visit data
	– Heed limitations of qualitative research
	– Disseminate reports to interested parties
	– Archive reports in customer database

matter how carefully planned the program, what you have is still only a set of interviews, a kind of qualitative research—one market research technique among many—and in no way a panacea. An important part of planning customer visits is thus a matter of examining your research needs to determine whether customer visits are the right market research technique at all. This question will be taken up again in Chapter 10; the remainder of this chapter assumes an affirmative answer, and begins to lay out the planning process in detail.

A SEVEN-STEP PROCEDURE FOR PLANNING CUSTOMER VISIT PROGRAMS

Table 4.1 lays out a structure for planning a program of customer visits that will be adequate for purposes of research. The remainder of the book is organized around each of these steps. Because a

---

SIDEBAR 2

Problem: Unsuitable Objectives *Time and budget pressures consistently drive organizations in the direction of asking too much of customer visits. In technology and BTB firms during the 1990s, the problem can often be traced back to middle management. Top management has gotten the word on customer focus, and the troops have taken top management at its word; but managers who succeeded under the old system may nonetheless refuse to fund the necessary research. They expect instead that a few customer visits can resolve any and all research questions. Sometimes these managers think of $10,000 as the most anyone would ever want to spend on market research, whereas in fact it is close to the floor. Many market research objectives require $50,000 to $500,000 to be fully addressed (particularly, those that involve test, selection, or prediction). Expecting too much of visits, and the consequent disappointment, can in the worst case discredit the whole enterprise of market research.*

---

program of visits begins with the articulation of objectives, this chapter will develop that topic.

SET OBJECTIVES

The crucial first step is to write out explicit research objectives. A helpful discipline in devising such objectives is to begin the statement with an action verb. This keeps the objective from being vague, flabby, or impossible to attain, and makes it clear that some action must be taken before the objective can be achieved. For best results, you should always include these objectives in the memos and overhead slides that you use to present, discuss, and prepare for these customer visits.

Several useful things happen when objectives are stated in advance of visiting customers. First of all, this forces you to make choices. If you are a typical manager, you are fighting fires everyday, you are subject to conflicting pressures and unexpected demands, and you must make too many decisions on too little information. At any given point you will always have a long list of information gaps and areas of ignorance. However, one of the surest paths to failure in research is trying to do too much. Even more dangerous is not having a clear direction. As you struggle with the task of putting down on paper, in a few sentences, what you are trying to accomplish, you are forced to grapple with these issues. If you are new to this, you probably won't like your initial attempt at stating objectives. Some will be too vague, others too narrow, others clearly impossible with the resources at hand. The point is that, however painful this process, it is far less painful and costly than having to rework the program at a later point, or worse, discovering at the end of the program that you have gathered lots of information that you don't need and can't use.

HOW TO IMPROVE THE
STATEMENT OF OBJECTIVES

One of the things I learned following publication of the first edition is how difficult it can be to hammer out a small set of objectives on which the core team can agree. That is, during consulting sessions I had the opportunity to work with teams planning a specific upcoming visit program, helping them to resolve issues surrounding objective setting, sample selection, questions construction, and so forth. Two phenomena recurred again and again in these sessions: First, the initial statement of objectives, forged by the project lead, was almost never accepted without demur by other teammates. Second, regardless of whether the project lead had read the first edition of the book, the initial statement of objectives seldom had the necessary crispness and focus that experience has shown is required if tough choices are to be made down the line.

Table 4.2 gives an example of how a conventional statement of objectives, quite comprehensible and perfectly adequate for any ordinary business memorandum, can be transformed into a set of more focused statements that can effectively guide choices concerning other aspects of the visit program. The firm planning the visits makes data acquisition hardware and software. The product is used by manufacturers inspecting the quality of their products and func-

TABLE 4.2 Example of How to Construct Clear Objectives for Visit Programs

Situation: This firm manufactures data acquisition hardware and software. The product family allows data from a variety of sensors (heat, vibration, frequency, etc.) to be collected and analyzed. The primary users are manufacturers inspecting products for quality control.

Initial Statement of Objectives	Objectives as Rewritten
1. "Gather information by interviewing customers in a structured manner to create actionable user need-based market segments. Quantify volume and business opportunities within segments."	1. Identify and describe key segments based on common benefits. Define criteria for success in each segment.
2. "Understand 'what it takes' for us to expand our data acquisition business to small- to medium-sized industrial manufacturing companies conducting product design verification with limited resources to integrate their system platforms."	2. Generate linkages between current customer frustrations and present or future VXI functionality. Define the limits of VXI extensibility to these customers.
3. "Understand how the customers' current frustrations and missed opportunities translate into future data acquisition solutions that may include lower-priced VXI-based[a] system platforms, system integration tools and services, and necessary linkages with customer-based data analysis software."	3. Identify areas of synergy between our two strategic business units

"VXI" refers to an industry standard for data interchange.

tions by collecting and analyzing data from a variety of sensor devices. The left panel in the table shows the first draft of the objectives, the right panel shows the final version. The overall strategic situation suggested a need to segment the market and find opportunities for new business development based on these segments. Commentary on how the statement of objectives evolved follows.

Looking at the left panel in Table 4.2, note the verbs that begin the sentences in the first attempt: *gather, understand, quantify.* The first two are unhelpful from the standpoint of making decisions about what questions to ask in the visit (too vague), whereas the latter is inappropriate for customer visit research generally (which is rarely able to estimate quantities). The remainder of each sentence is more promising—the business goals of segmenting the market, spotting opportunities, and targeting specific kinds of customers come through clearly. We can quibble about the wording—*actionable user need-based segments* could be clarified by a restatement free of jargon—but the basic thrust of what the team wants to accomplish is apparent. Nonetheless, there is work to be done if these objectives are to serve their purpose as a basis for decisions concerning program design.

In the rewritten example, note the verbs: *identify, define, generate.* These are action verbs that promise certain deliverables. For instance, *identify* means we will produce a list with commentary that names some set of phenomena, in this case, potential segments. Moreover, in this second attempt, the target customers have been stated separately, thus unburdening the old Objective 2 (often a good idea). Old Objectives 1 and 2 have been combined into new Objective 1, whereas old Objective 3 has been restated in a simpler form as new Objective 2. The simplification is valuable because it highlights the idea of linkages between customer problems and a core technological competency of the firm. The new Objective 2 is thus going to be much more effective in suggesting what kinds of topics to pursue in the interview, where to probe customers for additional information, and the like.

The new Objective 3 has no parallel in the first set. It emerged that afternoon during discussion. Essentially, the firm had two SBUs that made data acquisition products with different capabilities, using somewhat different platforms, and historically targeted at different applications. Members of both SBUs were present along with a higher-level manager to whom both reported. Both marketing and

R&D representatives were also present. It became clear during discussion that the effort to seize the business opportunities believed to be present was going to be more successful if areas of synergy could be found between the two SBUs' product capabilities. Articulating this as an objective insured that this topic would receive due consideration in the visits.[1]

Generalizing from this example, there is a small set of verbs generally applicable across the objectives of many kinds of customer visit programs. This set includes the verbs *identify, define, describe, explore,* and *generate.* There may be other verbs that also correspond to the capabilities of customer visits—I don't wish to be doctrinaire on this point—but each of these verbs combines a concrete focus on a specific kind of information while remaining generally applicable, and, most important, hews to the boundaries of what the visit technique can and cannot accomplish. Here are more examples of how these verbs can be fleshed out into objectives:

- Identify unmet customer needs
- Identify new market opportunities
- Explore likes and dislikes concerning the current product offering
- Explore how customers perceive the intangible aspects of the product, its delivery, and support
- Describe the role played by the product within the customer's operation or business strategy
- Describe the customer's decision model and process for choosing among vendors
- Generate possible explanations for observed market trends
- Generate alternative ways of segmenting the market

As these examples make clear, the important rule to observe in deciding whether to do customer visits is this: Would you benefit from a preliminary, exploratory, discovery-oriented research procedure? Note that objectives that rest on words like *identify, explore, describe,* and *generate* properly come early in the decision process. These kinds of objectives lead to information that lays the groundwork for narrower, more specific, and final choices (see Chapter 10).

There are, of course, many other kinds of information needs or research questions that may concern you. However, to the extent that these objectives are concerned with confirming, proving, choosing, or testing an idea, they tend to be unsuitable for customer visits.

Specific verbs that do *not* match the capabilities of customer visits would include *test, select, evaluate, rank-order, measure, forecast,* and *track.* Of course, these tasks are very important to business success. And they do correspond to the capabilities of other market research techniques. But these tasks require large samples and quantitative precision of a sort that is foreign to the nature of customer visits. Here are some more detailed examples of the kinds of objectives that *cannot* be achieved through customer visits alone:

- Select which of two product concepts is more likely to succeed in the market
- Evaluate the revenue-generating potential of adding a new feature to the product
- Forecast potential sales to be gained from entering a new market
- Test and compare the profitability of two alternative marketing strategies

An explanation of why customer visits are not suitable for such questions would take us far afield, and is reserved for Chapter 9. Suffice to say that such objectives logically come late in the decision process and demand a size of sample and a degree of precision that is impossible to attain with a few dozen interviews. These objectives are best pursued using some other research technique.

A final category of verbs is neither clearly appropriate, like *identify,* nor clearly inappropriate, like *measure,* but simply unhelpful. *Understand, learn,* and *gather information* are easily spotted as too general to be helpful, once this chapter has been absorbed. However, a trickier case is presented by a verb such as *validate.* Can customer visits validate something? Well, what does *validate* really mean, anyway? That's the first problem, and as good a warning sign as any. Just for the fun of it, try innocently asking the next businessperson who uses *validate* in your presence just what they mean by this term. A struggle to respond suggests that this verb may not be terribly useful to research planning.

In fact, *validate* can refer to one of two tasks, one of which is appropriate for customer visits and the other of which is not. On the one hand, *validate* could mean, "Explore the extent to which customer perceptions of this issue coincide with our own." Customer visits can definitely help here—an in-depth, extended discussion will clarify both which perceptions are shared, when they are shared, and why they may not always be shared. On the other hand, *validate* could mean, "Test whether our hypothesized explanation is correct." It is doubtful that customer visits can adequately test whether an explanation is correct. Customer visits could provide supporting evidence or a dissenting view; but isn't that evidence or that dissent, to the extent it emerges at all, going to come about through a thorough *exploration* of the topic? Moral of the story: Beware of verbs that obfuscate rather than clarify what you are trying to accomplish by means of the visit program.

BENEFITS OF STATED OBJECTIVES

Stating objectives helps you, the program planner, directly; but this step also helps you indirectly, as a result of the impact these stated objectives will have on two important groups: (a) your management and (b) your associates. With respect to the first of these audiences, as a result of reading this book you are likely to have a better grasp of the strengths and limitations of customer visits than the person(s) who will pay for this program. More bluntly: If you work in a technology company, and your management was trained in engineering, you probably have to deal with people who hold unrealistic expectations about the knowledge that can be acquired through customer visits. Being scientists by training, they expect hard numbers and conclusive data from any activity labeled as "research." Because customer visits may also be the only market research technique with which they have much experience, you may discover that management expects or assumes that you will present confirmatory objectives similar to those pointed out elsewhere in this chapter as highly problematic. This is a recipe for failure.

Experience suggests that you are going to get hurt if you proceed in good faith to conduct visits for the purpose of exploration and discovery, even as management expects you to bring home confirmatory evidence and hard data. You will be hurt worse if you have to torture the valuable but limited data you do obtain from customer visits to match the unrealistic expectations of management. Hence, one of the most important reasons to state objectives in writing is to make sure that management concurs with the proposed visits as you conceive them; or, if they do not, to give you the opportunity to either educate management about the distinctive but limited contribution

---

SIDEBAR 3

Problem: Too Many Objectives or Conflicting Objectives
Time and budget pressures also lead to the attempt to do too much, or to combine research and other objectives. An organization that is new to the idea of customer focus, or has skimped on market research in the past, may attempt to answer too many questions at once or impose too many agendas on a single visit. Effective visit programs tend to have at most two or three research objectives. It is the responsibility of the program coordinator to control the tendency to overburden the visit program. Firms that fail to sufficiently empower their program coordinators will suffer accordingly.

---

of visits, or press for the resources necessary to do the kind of research that could yield confirmatory data. Instead, what I have seen on numerous occasions is that people are given a budget appropriate to a limited, exploratory study, even as management expects results that could not be fully achieved with a budget 10 times as large and a time frame twice as long. That's not fair to you; management owes you a budget commensurate with expected results (or at least an honest statement to the effect of, "I know this is impossible, but I have no choice but to ask you to attempt it").

The above paragraphs address the situation typically faced by a product or project manager. If you are a manager of managers, then your world is even more one of conflicting imperatives: many worthwhile projects and initiatives, and not enough funds to support them all. Focusing now on your needs and your situation, it is important that you insist on a clear statement of objectives from the people competing for the funds at your disposal. In fact, given a competition for limited funds, I would suggest that you reward those who present the clearest and most appropriate objectives. This is one practical step you can take to improve the sophistication of your firm's customer visit activity.

Returning to the product or project manager (this is the level where most visits are planned), stated objectives also help you with your associates in other functional areas or departments who will be affected by, or will want to make use of, the results of the visit program. Recall one of the rules of organizational politics: No buy-in at the beginning equals no buy-in at the conclusion. It is really quite easy for an excluded bystander to reject or deny the results of a customer visit program. The objection will typically take the form of, "You visited the wrong people/asked the wrong questions." This same person, had he or she been given an opportunity to influence the design of the visit program, might have become one of your strongest supporters; but, frozen out at the beginning, is just as likely to become a foe. On a more positive note, because visits will involve people from different functions, and cover a variety of topics, it is unlikely that you, working in isolation, can come up with an optimal set of objectives. Hence, you should welcome input from peers and associates. Although it adds to your workload in the beginning, it can save you an enormous amount of grief down the road. Make it a rule: Anyone who will be expected to act on the visit data will be given a voice in the articulation of objectives. More pointedly: If marketing expects R&D to participate fully in the visits, and use the results, then program objectives must be devised and debated with R&D, and not decided on by marketing alone.

Explicit, agreed-on objectives also help you make choices and tough decisions as the program proceeds. Your objectives will help you resolve such questions as (a) which customers to visit, (b) who should conduct the visits, and (c) what questions to ask. Objectives are also critical in shaping the analysis of visits. Interviews, as one manager remarked, can be like "drinking from a fire hose." Without clear objectives, it may be very difficult to make sense of the wealth of input received from customers.

NOTE

1. My thanks to Steve Johnson for this example.

CHAPTER FIVE

Selecting Customers to Visit

The process of sample selection is among the most difficult parts of the planning process. The key point to remember is that the selection of customers to visit is a make-or-break activity for the visit program. If you don't succeed in talking to the right customers, your excellence in all other aspects of the planning process will scarcely matter. Hence, the first law of sampling in customer visit programs is garbage in, garbage out. In other words, talking to the wrong people is not going to help you achieve your goal of achieving market-driven quality in the form of successful new products. In this context, *wrong* means visiting customers who are neither relevant to nor appropriate for the objectives you have set.

The second law of sampling is that, all other things being equal, bigger samples are better than smaller samples. I want to caution you against the use of *tiny* samples consisting of three, four, or five customer firms. As always, *something* can be learned from such a tiny sample; but please don't call it a program of visits. The term *program* suggests a threshold of 10 to 12 visits (this refers to the number of firms visited, not the number of individual customer employees interviewed). When you visit a dozen or more customers, patterns emerge, themes develop, and you become more confident in your results as you hear certain things again and again. The implicit assumption in the remainder of this section is that you are going to visit between one and three dozen customers as part of your program, with the exact number a function of your particular objectives. The more complex the issues under study, or the more heterogeneous your customer base, the larger the sample required.

SIDEBAR 4

Problem: Sample Too Small *The difficulty again reduces to time and money. Common sense suggests that complex market structures, diverse customer needs, and global sales all require more than a handful of visits if a solid understanding is desired. The Hewlett-Packard Corporate Engineering (CE) study—a showcase sample from a leading practitioner—nonetheless indicated that roughly 30% of the projects examined visited 10 or fewer customers. Again, research has shown that a relatively small increase in sample size, to the level of 20 to 30, is all that is required for effective exploratory research*

The third law of sampling is that although larger samples are better, in the case of customer visits you rather quickly reach a point of diminishing returns. I get very suspicious when I hear about plans for a program of visits to 60 or 100 customers. I suspect that this is a manager who really wanted to do a survey or other form of quantitative research for the purpose of confirming or disconfirming a hypothesis, but found that there was no money left in the market research budget, whereas there were funds remaining in the travel budget (true story!). Because the customer visit program is an exploratory procedure designed to uncover new insights, it is seldom necessary to visit more than a few dozen customers.

There are two exceptions to this cap on the number of visits needed. First, there are cases where a firm needs to conduct a worldwide program of visits. Here, sample sizes on the order of 50 to 60 are advisable: allocating 15 to 20 visits to North America, 15 to 20 to Europe, and 15 to 20 to Asia Pacific. Second, there are a few research objectives that demand a larger than normal sample size. If you are conducting customer visits as part of a once-in-10-years overhaul of your fundamental business, or if you intend to redo your segmentation analysis from scratch, then it may also be necessary to visit 40, 50, or 60 customers.

However, it always sets off warning signals when I hear a client contemplating such a large program. If you are considering such a large program, please think carefully about two questions: Do you actually want or intend to do preliminary, exploratory research—or are you driven to a large sample size because you want something that customer visits really can't deliver? Second, even if you are clear about your intent to conduct exploratory research, are you best off spending a large amount of money on customer visits alone, or might you be better served by spending a reasonable amount on customer visits, and expending the remaining funds on follow-up research using some other technique, so as to nail down some of the insights generated by the visits? As a later section on costs will show, the amount you would spend on a 60-visit program could equally well support a perfectly good 30-visit program plus a solid phone survey that would fix the exact frequency of key customer responses, or a conjoint analysis that would certify which of two price-performance configurations was most preferred by customers. Much of the time, you would learn more from the combination of customer visits plus some other technique than from conducting a very large visit program.

Until recently, this injunction to cap the sample at 30 visits had only the status of a rule of thumb. Now, however, work at MIT has provided empirical and mathematical support.[1] This work showed that a sample of 30 customers could be expected to identify 90% of all the needs that might exist in the total population of customers; that a sample of 20 would probably identify 80% to 85% of needs; and that a sample of 12 might uncover 70% to 75% of needs. Although this work is limited by certain assumptions (that customers visited are a random selection of the population and that the population is homogenous), it provides reasonably strong support for the expectation that a good customer visit program need only visit a couple dozen customers.

COST

Given a target of 12 to 36 customer visits, you can estimate the likely costs of your visit program. If you live in a large urban area and your firm has hundreds of customers located nearby, then the out-of-pocket costs could be negligible: auto mileage, some food, copy charges, and so forth. The more common case is that out-of-town air travel is necessary. A rule of thumb for estimating such travel costs (assuming domestic travel in the United States, circa 1997) is $1,500 to $2,000 per person per week. This covers airfare, hotel, rental car, and food. Next, assume that in a typical week a team can visit 6 to 8 customers (two per day for 3 to 4 days). Finally, because visits should ideally be team visits, assume that two people will do the traveling. Hence, a small customer visit program will probably cost between $8,000 and $12,000 in travel expenses; a larger program, limited to the United States, will cost between $16,000 and $24,000; and a large international program of visits might cost $35,000 to $60,000.

The most important cost factors are the amount of air travel required and the number of people on the visit team. It is going to be much more expensive to visit 12 customers across 12 different cities then to visit 6 customers in each of 2 cities. Similarly, although it is often desirable to have three people on the visit team, the addition of a third person has the potential to raise travel costs by 50%. The question naturally arises as to which is better: more visits by a smaller team, or fewer visits by a larger team. The answer depends on whether the overall budget permits a relatively small or large sample. For instance, if given the choice between visiting 12 customers with a team of three, or 20 customers with a team of two, I would visit the 20 customers; but given the choice between visiting 24 customers with a team of three, or 36 customers with a team of two, I might visit the 24 customers. It is particularly advisable to choose the larger team size in situations where there is a history of disharmony between functional areas. In that case, you want as many people as possible to receive input directly and in concert.

In summary, out-of-pocket costs for customer visit programs are moderate relative to the cost of some other types of market research. A four-group focus group study in industrial markets will often run

$30,000 to $40,000. A phone survey may cost anywhere from $2,000 to $500,000, depending on number of questions, sample size, and difficulty of locating respondents; $75,000 to $125,000 is typical for a national probability sample of 1,000 to 2,000 respondents, and $2,000 to $10,000 is characteristic of more limited, local surveys. A simple marketing experiment will run $20,000 to $30,000 or so, with more complex designs doubling or tripling those amounts. Nonetheless, in absolute terms, customer visit travel costs can quickly mount into the tens of thousands of dollars.

In short, if you can afford to do market research at all, you can probably afford to do visits. But, you ought not to fall into the habit of thinking of customer visits as "quick-and-dirty" research. In fact, it would be better, overall, to think of visits as somewhat expensive but very valuable.

DEVISING A SAMPLE FRAME

Construction of a sample frame is an intermediate step between the basic decision to visit customers and the phone call to a specific customer requesting cooperation. A sample frame describes the basic parameters of the types of customers who will be considered for inclusion in the research effort. For example, in the computer industry you might construct a frame based on three distinctions: between large and small customers; among applications centering on wide area, local area, or other types of computer networks; and among customers whose primary computing application involves manufacturing, distribution, or financial services.

Careful attention to specifying the sample frame is important for three reasons. First, it insures that the people actually visited correspond to the objectives set for the project. Second, it provides a disciplined way to think through the question of which customers are relevant to your objectives. Absent a sampling frame, you might unknowingly include customers who don't have much to contribute, or (more likely) unintentionally ignore or exclude a group of customers whose input ought to have been gathered. Third, a sample frame is a key feature that distinguishes programmatic from nonprogrammatic visits. Without a sample frame, you may find yourself visiting customers for all kinds of dubious reasons: this one is the salesman's favorite customer, this one lives in the same city as the next trade

---

SIDEBAR 5

Problem: Convenience Drives the Selection of Customers to Visit *It is difficult to discover new things if you always visit a small coterie of favorite customers. Although it is often more time consuming to arrange visits to new and unfamiliar customers, and may increase your travel costs, you must visit the right people or else the visit effort is wasted. A particularly subtle trap comes about through concentrating one's visits on so-called national accounts, A-list customers, or very large customers. The rationale, of course, is that these people account for a substantial fraction of your sales. But why is this so? Is it because these are the largest users of this product category in the world, or is it because your product has become tailored over the years to the needs of a subgroup among large users? Might there also be large users who are small customers of yours (because your product is not quite right for them)? If so, then the most rapid expansion of sales might come from visiting and learning from customers who aren't buying very much from you today.*

---

show, this one always sounds friendly on the phone, and, worst of all, this is a customer we have always visited.

Step One: Review Segmentation Scheme

There are four steps in devising a sampling frame. The essential first step is to review whatever segmentation scheme your firm now uses.[2] Table 5.1 gives an example of a very simple segmentation scheme that might be used by a medical equipment manufacturer. This firm distinguishes between type of medical organization, type of application for the equipment, and domestic U.S. versus European customers. There are a total of 32 cells (4 organization types x 4 applications x 2 locations). Each cell defines a specific customer subgroup whose needs, preferences, or responses might be different from the rest.

TABLE 5.1 Example of a Sampling Grid

					TYPE OF MEDICAL ORGANIZATION			
TYPE OF APPLICATION	Urban Hospital		Rural Hospital		Teaching Hospital		Doctor's Office	
	USA	Europe	USA	Europe	USA	Europe	USA	Europe
Infant Care	1	2	3	4	5	6	7	8
Minor Surgery	9	10	11	12	13	14	15	16
Major Surgery	17	18	19	20	21	22	23	24
Trauma	25	26	27	28	29	30	31	32

The basic idea of a segmentation scheme is an enormously flexible tool. Do not be misled by the example in Table 5.1 into thinking that all segmentation schemes have to distinguish applications, differentiate organizations, or separate domestic and international customers. *Any* variable that groups together like customers and distinguishes unlike customers may be useful and appropriate. You should also not fall into the trap of thinking that a segmentation scheme must be limited to two or three variables (of course, it becomes difficult both to visualize and to draw *n*-dimensional segmentation schemes!). As a final caution, do not fall prey to "chart-itis." The goal is not to completely and elaborately capture, in diagrammatic form, all the complexity of your customer base. Rather, the goal is to remind you of the most important distinctions within your customer base, as a prelude to drawing up the sample frame for your visit project.

It is possible that your firm, or at least your division, has no segmentation scheme. In that case, you will have to apply common sense to the task of differentiating your customer base. With or without an existing segmentation scheme, the purpose of this initial step remains the same: to remind you of important sources of diversity within your customer base. It is unlikely that your customers are all unique or that your customers represent a homogenous population. Most likely they fall into a number of distinct groups, several of which will need to be included if the visit program is to succeed.

Step Two: Focus on a
Few Types of Customers

The second step in devising a sample frame is to decide which types of customers need to be visited as part of the visit program. The underlying assumption here is that *you never have enough money to visit every type!* Here you might object that the typical sample size is 24 to 36; there are only 32 cells in the example in Table 5.1; so, what's the problem? The difficulty is that, if you went to compare any two cells (types of customers) during the analysis, then you need to visit three to six instances from within each cell. If you were to only visit one customer per cell, you would have no way of knowing whether the answers to your questions are typical for customers of that type, or idiosyncratic to the one instance that you happened to visit. Only when you have visited several instances per cell is there any hope that common themes will emerge. Given this rule of thumb, you can see that to include all the cells in Table 5.1 within a customer visit program would require 100 visits or more. This might make sense during a fundamental overhaul of a business plan, but even there, the cost would be so high that you would have to examine other, potentially more profitable uses for the money. Again, in most cases, a predisposition to make 70 or 100 visits is a signal that you ought to reexamine your assumptions that a customer visit program is the most appropriate market research tool for your purposes.

How then do you go about the task of selecting a few types of customers for inclusion in your sample frame? Here is where the labor invested in refining your statement of objectives begins to pay for itself. Generally, you will select two to five distinct types of customers based on their relevance to your objectives. To return to our medical equipment example, suppose the research objective is to explore needs for a new type of patient monitor at the high end of the product line (i.e., a high-priced instrument with sophisticated capabilities). You might then determine, based on information you already have, or on logical grounds, that the bulk of the market for such monitors will be in large urban hospitals and in teaching hospitals. In addition, the sophisticated capabilities of such a monitor are only required during major surgery or in cases of multiple trauma. However, both the domestic and European markets, within the constraints just outlined, are of substantial size. Hence, you would select eight cells for your sampling frame (cells 17, 18, 21, 22, 25, 26, 29, and 30 in Table 5.1), representing two types of hospitals (urban and teaching), two applications (major surgery and trauma), and two geographical regions (the United States and Europe). This would suggest a visit program comprised of 24 to 48 visits, which would require a budget of approximately $25,000 to $60,000.

Step Three: Check Feasibility

The third step is to check your newly devised sample frame against the practical constraints of time and money that you face. If you only have $10,000, then the sample frame just described is not feasible. In that case, you have to revisit your objectives. Can the objectives be scaled back in some way, so as to reduce the size (hence, the cost) of the sample frame? If the answer is no, then the next step is to point out to responsible management that the available budget does not match the agreed-on objectives. If neither the objectives nor the budget can be relaxed, then it is time to get creative with the design of the sample frame.

The two basic modes of creative tinkering with the sample frame are (a) deleting cells from consideration and (b) collapsing two or more cells together. With respect to cell deletion, you might decide that you are only going to visit domestic hospitals. In today's global market that is a risky decision, but it may in some circumstances be an intelligent risk. An even better choice might be to eliminate the domestic teaching hospital cells, on the grounds that you already have a great deal of contact with this type of customer, making it unlikely that you will learn anything very new (most medical equipment companies work closely with selected teaching hospitals that are affiliated with universities and that, because of their sophistication, are regularly consulted in the course of normal business). With respect to collapsing cells, you might decide that major surgery and trauma applications are sufficiently similar to group them together into a single cell that might be labeled *high mortality risk*. Of course, whenever, because of budgetary constraints, you collapse or eliminate cells that you initially thought were important, you are compromising and taking risks. However, taking intelligent risks is one of the many ways that you earn your salary as a manager.

SIDEBAR 6

Problem: Sample Too Homogeneous *Hewlett-Packard, like many technology firms, derives more than half of its sales revenue from outside the United States. Yet, only one quarter of the projects examined in the CE study included a substantial number of international visits. Similarly, only about one quarter of the projects included visits to competitors' customers. There is no reason to expect that customer needs are the same worldwide or across existing and potential customers. Exploratory research that does not reflect the structure of the overall market in which a firm competes is likely to contain serious gaps and omissions. Again, the choice is stark: You either pay now, in the form of larger and more diverse samples, or pay later, in the form of disappointing sales.*

Adjusting the Sample Frame

Before going on to the fourth step in developing a sample frame, I want to address some misapprehensions that may have resulted from the discussion thus far. Referring again to the medical equipment example, you might have concluded that the sample frame should always take the form of what in statistics is called a *complete factorial design*. That is, in the initial example, all three factors were completely crossed, so that a 2 (type of hospital) by 2 (type of applications) by 2 (geographical market) design was the result (completely crossed means that every level of each factor is matched with every level of every other factor). Such designs, although common, are not required in the case of customer visit programs.

Here is an example of how the same medical equipment company, given a different research objective, might have constructed a different sampling frame. Suppose now that the research objective is to understand areas of satisfaction and dissatisfaction with the existing equipment, in contexts where staff availability is insufficient or lower than optimal (we may presume that prior market intelligence has indicated that the equipment is being used under such contexts). A fresh look at the segmentation scheme in Table 5.1 might now suggest that staffing is mostly a domestic U.S. issue (due perhaps to the spread of managed care), and that trauma in urban hospitals, newborn care in rural hospitals, and minor surgery in doctors' offices (cells 3, 15, and 25) all represent situations where there is too much to do and too few people to do it. Hence, the sample frame would now consist of three cells. The fact that these three cells are, as it were, plucked out of the macrosegmentation scheme according to no regular or simple rule is immaterial. All that matters is that these types of customers be judged focally relevant to the research objectives at hand.

A second caveat concerns where to start when drawing up a sample frame. I have sometimes observed a tendency to "cut to the chase" and go directly to the target cells for the current visit program without laying out the larger segmentation scheme first. In the running example, this would mean that you started by listing urban and teaching hospitals and major surgery and trauma applications, without ever laying out the complete grid in Table 5.1. This approach is problematic for two reasons. First, it lends itself to tunnel vision, making it easy to neglect or ignore possibly relevant customer groups. Second, it makes it hard for colleagues to constructively critique your selection of customer types for inclusion in the sample frame. It's much easier for other people to point out holes in your thinking if they can see your sample frame within a larger context. Yet another problem is the attempt to do too much, leading to an overelaborate segmentation scheme and sample frame. Most of the time, you would be well advised to use no more than two or three dimensions to create your sample frame. Quite often, of course, there will be a half dozen or more relevant dimensions. Good advice in this situation is to select the two or three most important dimensions to construct the sample frame and to address the remaining dimensions during the subsequent recruiting process. All you really need to do is insure some variety in your ultimate sample with respect to these additional subsidiary dimensions. For instance, in our medical equipment example, there may be reason to believe that, in addition to the dimensions included in Table 5.1, hospitals constructed within the last 10 years have a different infrastructure that facilitates a different equipment mix in the operating room and hospitals in the Northeast follow a different medical tradition than elsewhere. Rather than adding these factors as additional dimensions to the grid in Table 5.1, you need only make sure that the sample as ultimately recruited contains some hospitals from the Northeast and some from elsewhere, and some newer and some older hospitals. I would not spend any time worrying about getting an equal number of urban, trauma cell customers and rural, intensive care customers from the Northeast, and so forth (i.e., a completely crossed design). You don't need that level of precision for the sort of exploratory research we are discussing. In any case, it's probably impossible to obtain that precision during real-world recruiting for customer visits.

A fourth problem to beware of is what might be called unimaginative segmentation. For instance, in many BTB markets, the customer's industry (i.e., standard industrial classification [SIC] code) is the starting point for all discussions of segmentation. And, of course, a difference in industry often implies different applications, different operating environments, and so forth, making industry a serviceable starting point for differentiating customers. But there can never be any guarantee that industry differentiation is the optimal starting point, or even relevant at all, in your particular situation. There is no imperative to start with or include industry, application, domestic versus international, or any other time-honored distinction.

The only imperative is that your sample frame clarify the distinctions that really matter among your customers with respect to the research objectives at hand.

In one incident in my experience, a team began by differentiating five industry segments, and then brainstormed half a dozen other possibly relevant distinctions. We placed the industry distinction as a column variable on a white board and began to try to complete the grid using one or two of the other distinctions. After 40 minutes we had gotten nowhere—none of the other variables was plausible as a second dimension overlaid on the industry dimension. The team began to question whether the industry differences were even important at all.

As discussion proceeded, the team's view of the situation recrystallized around one of the other distinctions. It became apparent that a four- to five-node tree diagram (see below) provided a more effective representation than a grid based on industry. Specifically, what mattered was whether customers used outside system integrators or not; and if they didn't, whether they used software from a key competitor or not (I have simplified matters somewhat for the sake of this discussion). Under each of these nodes, it appeared that a subset of three to four industries might be relevant and worth differentiating. The moral of this story is that you should heed any unease you may feel concerning your first cut at sample frame construction. Put the initial effort aside for a little while and let your subconscious mull it over. Then take a fresh look, possibly experimenting by trying to rebuild the sample frame starting with a different dimension. Finding the most illuminating differentiation of customers is well worth the extra effort.

Along these lines, here are some less customary starting points for defining groups of customers for use in constructing the sample frame.

Lost Leads. A lost lead is a customer who expressed an interest in buying your product, but who ultimately bought from someone else instead. These people may offer a great deal of insight into subtle problems with your offerings. Because they invited you to bid, your offering must have been relevant to their needs. Yet, because they gave the business to someone else, you must not have had the best offer. Much can be learned about how you stack up against competitors and about the strengths and weaknesses of your total offering (product plus intangibles) from visits of this kind.

Lapsed Customers. These are people who used to buy from you but no longer do. Why did they leave? To which competitive offering did they migrate? What gave that product its advantage over your own? A sample of lapsed customers could provide crucial insights during an assessment of customer satisfaction.

Power Users. In any market, there are some individuals who are ahead of the curve. These people may be more innovative in their product usage, in a better position to extract more value or more diverse benefits from product usage, or simply highly skilled. Although it can be dangerous to visit only power users (in Silicon Valley, there are many tales of products designed for power users that never sold in any volume, because they left the general user cold), a subsample of power users may provide a useful contrast to the main sample.

Competitor Customers. Although it is much harder to find and recruit these people, visits to competitor customers can be particularly illuminating. You are likely to gain a fresh perspective, along many dimensions, regarding the strengths and weaknesses of your product.

Channel Partners. Channel partners can distill the responses of a wide variety of small end users, who may be relatively invisible to you but with whom they work every day. Difficult to set up, but potentially rewarding, are joint visits where you and a channel partner collaborate to visit customers further down the value chain. For manufacturers of raw materials, who are several levels removed from the ultimate user, this may provide considerable insight into new ways to add value.

Internal Customers. An important target for visit efforts may be your own field staff. It is a rare program of customer visits that would not benefit from a dozen phone "visits" with people in the field sales organization and customer support function. These people have a lot of customer contact, but as often as not, no one at headquarters or in product marketing ever gets around to exploring their views. It's

worth your while to try out questions and solicit input from these
people about what the burning issues are for customers.

A final bit of advice is that a grid is only one of several repre-
sentational devices that can be used to portray the diversity of your
customer base. Here are some additional examples of designs that
may be more appropriate in specific situations:

1. *Crossword-puzzle grid.* Sometimes a number of cells in a grid
simply do not exist—that is, the combination of the row and column
dimensions is logically impossible or extremely scarce. For instance,
you might have five industry segments as the columns, with the rows
distinguishing (1) high production volume and mission critical application, (2) high volume only, and (3) low or medium volume. One
can imagine an industry where the low or medium volume condition
simply doesn't exist, making it an empty cell.

2. *Tree diagram.* In a consulting session for visit program design,
I always start the sample discussion by trying to elicit a grid. If that
grid starts to turn into a crossword puzzle, I begin to question
whether a tree diagram might be a more effective representation of
distinctions among customers. An example is given in Figure 5.1 for
computer graphics software. In general terms, a tree diagram will be
superior to a grid whenever second-level distinctions are not parallel
across each first-level distinction. With respect to the computer
graphics example, the distinctions that elucidate the corporate department segment are quite different from those that matter in the
specialized business segment. A tree diagram also allows different
segments to have either more or fewer additional levels of differentiation. In the example, the specialized business and corporate segments have two additional levels, whereas the other segments only
have one.

3. *Set of profiles.* Sometimes there really is only one meaningful
dimension along which customers can be differentiated. This may be
because there are only four distinct applications, and application
drives everything else; or because previous research has worked up
a small set of customer portraits that encompasses the major distinctions among customers. A vivid example of customer portraits can
be found in the "Not by Jeans Alone" videotape.[3] In 1980, Levi

Computer Graphics Software Market

Segment 1: Corporate	*Segment 2:* Specialists	*Segment 3:* Freelance professionals	*Segment 4:* Individuals
• Service bureaus	• Copy centers	• Artists (illustration)	• Hobbyist
• Inhouse ad agency	• Ad agencies	• Industrial design	• Home office
• Design or documentation	• Architects	• Graphic design	• Educators
• CAD CAM design	• Publishers		
• Large format	• Engineering		
• Small format	• Civil		
• Structural	• Structural		

Figure 5.1. Example of a Tree Diagram Approach to Sample Frame Construction

Strauss conducted a large segmentation study that broke up men's clothing buyers into five groups, including the Classic Independent (wool blend clothing, conservative, buys from specialty shops, very concerned with looking good), the Trendy Casual (partygoer, dresses for the opposite sex), the Mainstream Traditional (polyester, shops department stores with wife, conventional tastes), and so forth. When such a set of portraits exists, it will often be the logical starting point for differentiating customers.

Step Four: Define the Job Roles to Be Included

The final step in constructing a sample frame is to define the job roles of the people you wish to interview at the customer site. You cannot visit Boeing or Procter & Gamble; you have to visit *individuals* at Boeing or Procter & Gamble. Selecting the right individuals— not by name, but in terms of job roles—is just as crucial as selecting the right types of customer firms. In fact, there is probably no more disappointing feeling, across the whole spectrum of customer visit activity, than traveling at considerable time and expense to a distant city, sitting down at a conference table, and realizing within the first 5 minutes that you are talking to an individual *who cannot help you.* That is an unrecoverable error that no amount of interviewing skill can correct. Only good advance planning can solve this problem, by preventing it from occurring in the first place.

To help with this step, you should sketch out a model of the buying process for your product. In developing this model, you can draw on the basic insights into organizational purchasing that can be found in any marketing textbook.[4] Specifically, most BTB buying decisions involve multiple parties who play different roles and bring a distinctly different mindset to the examination of your product. A distinction that is almost always important in technology markets is that between the technical user and the managerial decision maker. The first of these actually uses the product on a day-to-day basis, is intimately familiar with its application, and can probably give quite detailed feedback regarding specific features and capabilities. The managerial decision maker, by contrast, often cannot answer such specific questions very well. However, this person probably has more of a big-picture view and can discuss how your product fits into the overall business plan of the customer organization. This person is also more likely to have an impression of how you compare to other vendors with whom you compete. The user may only be familiar with your product, and quite unable to compare vendors.

For this part of sample planning, the marketing members of the team ought to be able to identify specific job roles relevant to your objectives. Some consultation with the field sales force will often be helpful as well. The field sales force necessarily works from some kind of model of the purchasing process in the course of day-to-day selling efforts, whether tacit or explicit, and should have some sense of the different people who have to approve of your product before it can be purchased.

Here is an example of how job roles might be elaborated and considered in the context of a specific product. Suppose that you sell some kind of computer networking product. Because it is a computing product, the MIS director, and computing professionals generally within the customer firm, are logical choices of people to interview. However, because computer networking often involves leased phone lines and has other telecommunications aspects, the director of telecommunications is also a logical participant. Hence, you would want to set up interviews with both of these people at each customer firm that you visit. One caveat: If you only visit MIS directors at some firms and telecommunications directors at other firms, then any contrast between those firms will be confounded with the contrast between job roles. Hence, it is important to be consistent in your contacts across firms.

Returning to our medical equipment example, we can envision at least four distinct job roles whose views might be worth eliciting. On the one hand, there are the surgeons and other doctors who use the results of patient monitoring to make decisions on patient care and treatment. Then there are the nurses, who may actually have much more hands-on involvement with obtaining and using the output from the monitor. There may also be medical technologists, who perhaps install, maintain, or directly use the equipment. Finally, there are hospital administrators, who may set overall technology strategy for the hospital, have crucial budgetary authority, or have the power to include or exclude vendors from consideration. The satisfaction or dissatisfaction of any one of these parties, or the match of your product capabilities to the needs of any one of them, may be a critical factor in market success.

You might object that you really have no idea as to who is involved at the customer site, or how the purchase process develops. In fact, you remark, this ignorance is part of the reason you are thinking about doing customer visits in the first place! Two responses come to mind, depending on whether you are currently selling a product to this customer population. If you are, and you have no idea who is involved in buying your product, then your marketing problems run deeper than the question of what kind of research to do. (I would suspect in particular that there is poor coordination between your department, wherever you are, and the field sales force; or that you market exclusively through distributors). However, in most situations where you are tempted to say, "I just don't know," it is probably the case that somewhere in your organization, knowledge of purchasing roles does exist. Hence, your first task is to locate and obtain this knowledge. A series of phone calls to half a dozen salespeople (or other customer contact personnel) is a good place to start. If this doesn't help, a few phone calls to friendly customers, exploring the question of participation in the purchase decision, is the next step. If these initial steps produce widely varying information, it may be worthwhile to conduct a pilot test involving visits to several nearby customers during which a range of customer personnel are interviewed, giving you a chance to see which job roles might be crucial to the main program of visits.

If you don't sell products to this customer population at present, then the difficulty of determining relevant job roles is more pressing. For instance, perhaps you are expanding into a new market or industry where you currently have no presence. I would again try to draw on existing knowledge within your organization, exploratory phone calls to potential customers, and pilot testing. It might also be helpful to break the visit program down into two or three phases. In the first phase, comprising half a dozen interviews, you would be fairly inclusive, inviting a number of different types of customer personnel to participate. In subsequent phases, you would concentrate on a smaller number of roles found to be most relevant to your research objectives.

By the way, one of the arguments for sending cross-functional teams to the visits is that single-function teams (e.g., all engineers) tend to seek out and visit only those customer personnel whose role and outlook correspond to their own. This leads to engineers visiting engineers, which produces conversations rich in technical detail but prone to neglect of larger considerations. The result is technically excellent products that don't sell because they don't satisfy the needs of the nontechnical constituency within the customer firm. The better approach is to have cross-functional teams visit several individuals at the customer site, each of whom represents a different function and has a unique perspective to offer.

In summary, it generally adds little to the cost of a visit program to include two, three, or four individual customer employees during the visit process. Most costs are fixed (e.g., airfare), and the additional input from a range of customer participants comes virtually for free. Because most BTB products and services must satisfy multiple people at the customer firm, it is a rare customer visit program that can be restricted to interviews with single individuals.

Recruit Customers

Once the sample frame has been completed, the actual process of recruiting customers to participate in the visit program can commence. The first step in recruiting is to obtain a list of customers who match the parameters set forth in the sample frame. Depending on your organization, there may be several sources for such lists. In most BTB firms, you will begin by contacting the field sales organizations in a handful of regions, providing a description of the objectives of the visit, and asking for names of customers in that region who might be appropriate.

There are several reasons for starting with the field sales organization. Often, this will be the only part of your firm that can actually supply a list of, say, rural hospitals doing newborn care in Texas, complete with contact person and phone number. Even more important, in the typical BTB firm, the field sales organization "owns" customers in its region, meaning that it controls contact with and access to these customers by other parts of the firm. Hence, you have to get the field's permission to visit a customer at all. A final reason for starting with the field is that they can do so much to either facilitate or inhibit the success of your project. If the relationship between "factory" (where engineers and product managers reside) and field is poor, or not managed properly, any number of unfortunate things can happen.

For instance, failure to interact effectively with the field in arranging customer visits may lead to what one seminar participant described as the *set-up*. The set-up works as follows: First, a factory person innocently calls up a field sales rep looking for names of customers in the region. Whereupon, the field person thinks to himself, "They ought to visit Smith; he's really upset, he's been beating on me for months, and it's basically the factory's fault anyway." All smiles, the field person offers Smith as just the right customer to visit. Factory person hangs up, happy that recruiting proved so easy. When the day to interview Smith arrives, the factory person shows up ready to do research, and instead gets blown away by Smith, who's loaded for bear. No amount of skill in interviewing may be sufficient to overcome the set-up; it has to be prevented in the first place.

The point of this story is that the more thoroughly the field is briefed and the more effective your communication is as to why the visits are being done and what the result will be, the greater the likelihood that the field will offer you a good set of names from which to begin recruiting. In this regard, I suggest that you briefly explain the sampling frame and the specific types of customers you are seeking. I would also indicate to the field that you are most interested in customers who are neither very happy nor very unhappy. Customers in the middle, or who have had mixed experiences, generally produce the most valuable interviews. Very happy customers may not have much to say, or much that is new and surprising; very unhappy customers have a lot to say, but much of it will not be directly relevant to your research agenda.

In some organizations, the field may not be the best or only source of customer names matching your sample frame. Product marketing, or some other internal organization, may maintain a good database on customers with enough descriptive information for you to do a sort and generate a list of names. Sad to say, in my experience very few BTB marketing organizations possess any kind of customer database beyond a simple list of billing addresses. As software technology improves, and as more businesses come to understand that it is far easier and less expensive to retain existing customers than it is to find new ones, customer databases should become more common and grow in sophistication. When they do, the ability to execute customer visit programs will be enhanced.

In certain cases, where you are expanding into a new market, introducing a new product for which there are no existing customers, or seeking to talk to customers of competitors, neither the field nor any other part of your organization will have the names you need. Here recourse must be made to outside lists. These might include membership lists for professional societies, lists of trade-show attendees, or lists of firms participating in industry forums, standards-setting organizations, and the like. If the idea of searching for and then winnowing through such lists leaves you cold (perhaps for the very valid reason that time or staff is lacking), then you might want to use the services of a commercial market research firm. The activity of recruiting people for participation in market research (whether this be focus groups, interviews, etc.) is a core competency for most such firms. For a fee, a market researcher will agree to locate and even schedule people for visits who match the specifications that you lay out. Note, however, that the more information you can give the recruiter to work with (e.g., a list), the lower the fee charged.[5]

Since the first edition was published, I have observed an increased use of outside recruiters to find and schedule customers for visits. There are at least three reasons why this might be so:

1. It is not getting any easier to reach people on the telephone.
2. Persuading people to take an appointment is a specialized skill.
3. Recruiting can take an enormous amount of a product manager's time, time that might more productively be spent elsewhere, or that simply isn't available, given the press of other obligations.

More generally, there may be more recognition that market research is a specialized area of expertise, that it costs money to do it well, and that outside recruiting and similar expenditures are investments in success. The spread of outside recruiting may also be seen as part of the maturation of customer visit activity, as it moves from something indistinguishable from the ordinary day-to-day activities of a product manager to a strategic weapon in the firm's arsenal of market-intelligence gathering procedures.

On the assumption that you will do the recruiting yourself, and that you have obtained a list from some source, the next step in recruiting is to begin calling up people and securing their agreement to participate. You should not delegate this task to the field. Certainly, the field may usefully prepare the way for you with a prior phone call, but you cannot afford to give up the control that delegating recruiting altogether would entail. The field always has its own agenda, and it is not necessarily your agenda. If you want to maximize the productivity of the interviews in your visit program, you need to conduct these phone calls yourself. In a sense, you are qualifying these customers as well as recruiting them. If, instead, you use an outside firm, then you need to invest time and effort in the development of a screener, so that the recruiters' phone force can attempt to do some of this qualification.

Besides retaining control of the visit agenda, the other reason to do the phone calls yourself is that getting an agreement to participate is only one of three important tasks to be performed during these phone calls. A second and very important task is to find out, from the first person you call, who else you might have called instead. That is, there is no reason to believe that the name supplied by the field or dredged up from the database is exactly the right person to interview. Instead, think of the person you first reach on the phone as your entry point to the customer organization. As a member of that organization, they are probably more familiar with how it works than is the salesperson. Your goal is to enlist the person who answers the phone as your ally and informant. Hence, after introducing yourself and briefly describing what you are trying to do, you want them to indicate whether there might be a better person to contact. This process may have to be repeated; you should expect a chain of phone calls. Sooner or later you will reach the right person to interview. In addition to securing their cooperation, you also want them to indicate other people in their organization whom it might also be appropriate to include. Ideally, your contact will agree to enlist their participation for you. Not only does this economize on your labor, it is probably more effective anyway.

The final task to be performed during these recruiting calls is to adjust the customer's expectations of what will happen during the visit. A customer visit dedicated to research probably remains a novelty for most customers. Customers are used to sales calls, technology briefings, troubleshooting, and the like, but they may not be accustomed to a research interview in which the vendor's primary objective is to listen and learn. You want to be very clear that the purpose of this visit is to listen to customers in order to better understand their needs.

A useful device for managing customer expectations is to send a confirmation letter once the visit has been arranged. The confirmation letter reminds the contact person of the day and hour of the visit and reiterates the basic purpose. Attached to the confirmation letter should be a brief agenda consisting of half a dozen broad and general topics or questions. What the confirmation letter does is make it very

---

SIDEBAR 7

Problem: Decision Makers Do Not Participate *Most of the key advantages of on-site personal visits disappear if the people who conduct the visits have no power to act on what they hear. Of course, even though a wide range of people may be affected by the information uncovered in a particular set of visits, not everyone can participate in every visit. The program coordinator has two important responsibilities in this connection: to think carefully, in light of the research objectives, about who should be on the teams; and, to make sure that people who must heed the results, but will not personally participate, have been given an opportunity to influence program design. Note that the Corporate Marketing Education study showed that visit programs where the people who had to use the information were given an opportunity to influence program design were perceived as yielding greater value to the organization.*

---

plain that you are not coming to give a presentation, and that you are not coming to sell; instead, you are going to arrive prepared to discuss certain topics with the customer. Please recognize that most people don't like to show up for a meeting (to you it's a visit, to the customer it's a meeting) whose purpose is vague or obscure. This is part cynicism (will my time be wasted?) and part genuine anxiety (I don't know how to prepare myself). The brief agenda plays an important role in assuaging this uncertainty.

The questions that typically occur at this point are these: Why should the customer bother? Why should they give you the time? The answer to these questions hark back to an important characteristic of BTB marketing. Although there are certain respects in which BTB marketers are handicapped relative to consumer marketers, there is one very important advantage that BTB marketers do have: your customers' *need* for you to succeed. More precisely, although customers may not care whether *your* firm succeeds, they do need for one or more vendors in your industry to succeed. Customers need better computer systems, better networks, better instruments, and so forth, if their own businesses are to prosper. As a BTB marketer, you are selling products that assist your customers in conducting their business (if your products do not actually perform any useful function for customers, then, once more, you have larger problems than are dealt with in this book). Hence, in BTB marketing you have the opportunity, during recruiting and visits, to tell what I call "the market research story": We are visiting you today so that we can supply better products for you tomorrow. As one quality manager remarked, "Customers appreciate it. Especially if you are not just trying to peddle something. You generate good will when you visit. Invariably both parties learn something."

This is the fundamental fact that makes customer visits possible: A case can be made that it is worth the customer's while to make time available in the hope of providing input that will shape your future direction in an advantageous way. Moreover, when you are visiting at the managerial level, visits from vendor personnel are simply part of most managers' jobs. Managing relations with vendors of important products is one of the things these people are paid to do. Interestingly, although customer motivation has often been questioned during seminars, generally other people present will be quick to respond in terms of their personal experience of customers' willingness and even enthusiasm for participating in visits. Again, it is a rational decision on the customer's part. This holds true both in new product development and in the case of more general objectives, as the following two quotes show:

> The customer's perception is that new product development is a mystical process that they don't understand or have control over. They buy the product if it suits them, but they have no influence on designing it. We made the customers feel they were an extension of our development team. We were including their opinions and allowing them to mold this product into whatever shape would work best for them. And the tie that was created by doing that was invaluable. *(market analyst)*

> We would go to lunch or sit down and have a cup of coffee and donut with 25 employees. They were shocked that we wanted to talk to them. People said, "Insurance companies never come out and talk to us, this is really unusual, why are you guys doing this?" And when we asked them things like how can we make the health care system work better

for you, a lot of them just said, "Well, we don't know but just the fact that you are out here talking to us is unbelievable." If we could convince the top 20 people in our business that they have to do that, that spending time in meetings with our own people is in some cases far less important then it is to go out and sit down with customers and just talk. *(marketing manager)*

Nonetheless, I will readily acknowledge that in certain situations you may encounter some difficulty in securing the participation of exactly the people you want. For instance, you may wish to interview people who don't normally interact with vendors. In a telecommunications context, you may want to speak with the "craft" (the craftsmen who actually install wire and cable) and not just system planners, who are white-collar workers far removed from field installation activities. As another example, you may wish to visit competitors' customers, who necessarily have less motivation to interact with you. My basic advice again is to remember the market research story, believe in it yourself, and find a way to adapt it to overcome resistance. At the extreme, you may have to offer a quid pro quo. This typically takes the form of some kind of review of industry trends, update on future products, product strategy briefing, and so forth. Although not ideal (you would prefer that the whole visit focus unambiguously on research), such a quid pro quo is fine as long as you observe the rule mentioned earlier: research interviews first, briefing second.

Finally, let me acknowledge one situation where the persuasive tactics just offered may not succeed. This refers to a situation where there has been a history of poorly planned or ineptly executed visits to a particular customer. Because time is a precious resource, customers on the receiving end of this kind of visit may understandably get fed up, and refuse to participate any further. Even more difficult is a situation that may arise in large and highly decentralized firms. Here, numerous parts of the organization, for independent and valid reasons, have targeted a particular customer firm for visits, with the result that that customer is used up and no longer has any interest in being visited. This outcome is particularly depressing if the most important project happened to come late in the stream of visits. The solution again is good planning and coordination, so that this precious and limited resource—the time and insights of key customers—is used to best advantage. Sophisticated firms also expect their sales force to "meter" access to customers so that they don't become overwhelmed.

SPECIAL CASES IN SAMPLE SELECTION

Small Market Size

There are two instances where the general advice concerning sample frame construction has to be adapted. One occurs when the customers for your product or service are internal customers—for example, other divisions within your firm. Perhaps you manufacture integrated circuits that a number of other parts of your firm incorporate into a variety of electronic products. A second special case occurs when the total number of customers for your product is very small—fewer than two dozen, say.

These two special cases are similar in that it is possible to conduct a census rather than construct a sample. That is, it is financially feasible in these two cases to visit every single one of your customers. And, in most cases, that is exactly what you should do. Because you are conducting a census, rather than sampling from a larger population, the problem of generalizing from customer visit data is greatly altered. In many cases, you will be able to draw definitive conclusions and perform confirmatory research, in contrast to the strictures imposed in Chapters 9 and 10.

Still, caution is in order. Yes, you have visited 100% of your customers, but have you visited the right individuals at each customer? The choice of which job roles to contact becomes particularly crucial here. When there are a small number of high-volume purchasers, the number of people in the customer organization who have some influence over the purchase often grows correspondingly large. Hence, the systematic omission of a few job roles might seriously skew your results.

International Visits

A third special case involves international visits. Let me first assure you that the idea of visiting customers is a globally relevant procedure, and not something peculiar to North America. I have taught seminars in England and Germany and others have taught this material in Singapore and Japan. Attendees have come from Finland, Spain, France, Italy, Austria, and elsewhere. In fact, some managers stated that overseas visits were among the most productive they had done:

> I hate to admit it, but if I had to rank order the quality of visits it would go: Japan, Germany, U.S., every time. When we talk to a Japanese engineer, they are the expert on this tiny bit of the process only, but they are extremely knowledgeable. Not only about their products and process, but your products and your process and your competitor's products and process. They go into the *n*th degree of gory detail: why it's strong, why it's weak, what they want, want they don't want, and to be honest, it's a pleasure to get so much information. It's usually bad news but it's a lot of information. *(product manager)*

Of course, conducting international visits is much more challenging. All of the logistics become more difficult (and expensive), plus there is the problem of cross-cultural communication.

Here are two specific pieces of advice to improve your international visits. First, recognize that close cooperation with the local field becomes even more crucial. In many cases, someone from the field will serve as a translator during your visits. In all respects, you want to rely on the local office to preserve you from faux pas and misunderstandings. For example, I have twice heard the following story from managers who visited India. Attempting to explain something to the Indian customer, the visitor noted that the customer shook his head from side to side. The visitor then tried explaining the matter from another angle. Again the customer shook his head. After several more attempts to explain, the visitor gave up. Later, he ruefully discussed the incident with the local field person in attendance, who laughed and said, "No, no, you were doing a great job giving multiple explanations—hereabouts that particular head gesture means 'yes very good—I've got it'!" Such tales are legion, and any internationally traveled businessperson can recount one. As a result, you should never attempt to visit an overseas customer without the field or other local personnel being present.

Here is another example, from an engineering manager who has visited Asia extensively:[6]

The protocol for visits varies from place to place depending on local custom. There is a definite way to drink tea there, having a very broad discussion, and it helps to know it, lest you look uncultured or boorish. The time spent in this way can be quite long but not unproductive. This is an East Asian trait in general—they give the background first as a way of being polite or humble. What is actually happening is that the Chinese want to get to know you as a person so that they can decide if they want to do real business with you.

The second bit of advice is to be even more careful about team composition (see next section). Americans are among the least formal and status-conscious peoples. In other cultures, sending a visitor of the wrong level (i.e., too junior relative to the customer) can be a serious error. One scientist told me that when he visits U.S. customers, he is introduced as "Jack," but when he visits German customers, he is introduced as "Herr Doktor John Smith"—the sort of individual who ought to have been sent out to talk to this important German customer! In general, participants in European seminars have complained that American visitors don't always make adjustments to European ways. These include, among others, a more formal style of dress and a more diffident or critical way of responding to vendors. As one participant remarked, for an understated British customer, "Not bad" would be about as positive a comment as "That's pretty neat" would be from a Californian.

Despite the difficulties of cross-cultural visits, my firm belief is that global firms have no choice but to attempt them. You have to make the effort, whatever the obstacles.

SELECT TEAM MEMBERS

Your objectives should shape the choice of who will participate in the visits. The cardinal rule is simple: The people who have to use the information that will result from the visits should be involved in gathering that information. The benefits of customer visits outlined in Chapter 2 presume that this rule has been observed. It is the experience of encountering customers firsthand that gives the customer visit technique much of its power. If you delegate this firsthand encounter to a subordinate, a superior, a specialist, or an outsider, that power is diminished. Hence, if the objectives of the visit program concern product design, engineers must participate; if the objectives focus on satisfaction, people from the quality function must participate; and so forth.

The second rule in putting together a visit team is to ensure that each team contains people from different functional areas. One of the unique benefits of customer visits is the triangulation and cross-fertilization that occurs when people from different backgrounds with diverse agendas jointly encounter customers. As mentioned, such jointly conducted customer visits help to serve the larger goal of promoting better harmony and a common vision across functional areas within your firm. In the course of a visit, program members of the visit team are going to eat meals together, drive around together, discuss customers together, and so forth. The people who make up the team may not otherwise work together closely on a day-to-day basis and the visit program thus helps to integrate

---

SIDEBAR 8

Problem: Key Influentials Participate in Only One or Two Visits *One of the most dangerous things you could do is have a general manager or similar high-level manager participate in only one or two visits. If these happen to be the strangest and most divergent customers in your installed base, too bad: This manager heard it all firsthand, and these visits are going to dominate his or her understanding. This is where the vivid and compelling quality of the customer visit becomes a two-edged sword. A good rule of thumb is that anyone who participates in the program should encounter a minimum of four to six customers. In the course of six visits, certain customers will directly contradict what others have said. As a result, participants will be forced to grapple with the complexities of customer response, rather than retreating into simple certainties.*

SIDEBAR 9

Problem: Failure to Coordinate Visits With the Field Sales Organization *A substantial number of firms who attempt to adopt the customer visit technique will shipwreck on this reef: an inability to forge a compact between field and factory as to their respective roles when the factory comes to visit customers. Here are some diagnostic questions to ask about customary practice in your organization. Does the factory respect the sensitivities of the field personnel (who have to live with any fallout after the factory person returns home)? Does the factory obtain a previsit briefing from each customer's sales rep to learn where the land mines are and what skeletons are locked away? On the other side, does the field accept that bringing the factory on site can in itself reflect favorably on them in the eyes of customers?*

Does the field allow the factory to do research, or does the field insist on harvesting short-term sales gains from every encounter? As one seminar participant remarked, the typical sales rep can talk faster, louder, and more articulately than the typical factory engineer. The sales rep has to be willing to let go if visits are to function as research.

In all too many cases, the questions just listed will be answered in the negative. After all, whereas market research may be complex, organizational politics is truly complicated! The executive reading this book must recognize that organizations that fail to manage the factory-field interface will not get full value from their customer visits. I say executive because there is little that an individual product or project manager can do to turn matters around; this situation has to be addressed at the top.

---

functions within the vendor organization even as it brings the vendor closer to customers.

In most visit programs involving more than a dozen visits, it will be necessary to use more than one team; it is just not feasible to expect two or three people to drop their other responsibilities and spend weeks and weeks visiting customers. For a 36-visit program, there might be as many as six teams, each of which will visit a total of six customers. As a result, each member of those teams need spend only 1 week on the road, and the firm benefits because a large number of people get firsthand contact with customers.

If you are going to have multiple teams, certain other steps have to be taken to insure positive results. First, it is important to set a floor on participation. If a person is going to participate as a team member, then they ought to visit a minimum of four (preferably six) customers so that they can get a sense of the complexity and range of customer reponse. Another useful step in the case of larger projects is to appoint a program coordinator. This person is responsible for devising the set of objectives, coordinating recruiting, composing the teams, briefing the teams, and coordinating data analysis and reporting. Some kind of briefing for the teams is particularly important in a large project. The coordinator should restate the objectives, discuss the kind of customers to be visited, explain which interview topics have the highest priority, and caution teams about any topics that ought not to be broached (e.g., "Remember that next year's new product launch has not yet been publicly announced and should not be mentioned."). True, all this information has doubtless been put in a memo that has been circulated in advance; nevertheless, there is no substitute for the opportunity the oral briefing provides to answer questions and allay concerns.

NOTES

1. See Griffin and Hauser (1992).

2. A segmentation scheme is simply a way of organizing customers into subgroups that differ in some important respect. See Kotler (1994) for a basic discussion with examples, and see Bonoma and Shapiro (1983) for ideas on segmenting industrial markets.

3. Part of the Enterprise series, available from Learning Corporation of America, New York, 1981.

4. See, for example, Kotler (1994), Chapter 8.

5. Check the *Marketing News*—the bimonthly newsletter of the American Marketing Association (call 312-993-9517)—for occasional directories of market research firms. Firms that recruit for focus groups are a good bet.

6. My thanks to David Zawadzki of Xerox for this and other illuminating tales of customer visits overseas. Chan-Herur (1994) can be consulted for advice on specific cultures across the world.

CHAPTER SIX

Prepare a Discussion Guide and Construct Good Questions

DATA CAPTURE TOOLS

The purpose of a discussion guide, and the reason you must carefully construct questions for it, is to capture effectively data from the visits. You should also give careful consideration to the use of two other data capture devices: tape recorders and cameras. Virtually any research-oriented program of visits should consider tape recording, whereas there are a few types of programs where cameras may be very important. This advice only applies to research visits; rarely, if ever, would a customer expect to see a sales call, service call, or presentation tape-recorded. This advice is also limited to North America—cultural norms elsewhere may argue against a tape recorder.

The idea of tape-recording even a research visit is always controversial in seminars. Won't the tape recorder inhibit customers and undercut learning? My views on this matter are as follows. First, you must always ask permission, and if permission is refused, heed that refusal. Second, most of the people you will visit have been tape-recorded before in similar contexts. Third, although an individual may be initially mindful of the tape, in my experience, once an interview is launched people soon forget about it. Fourth, a tape recorder can contribute significantly to the task of data capture. Seldom will you or anyone else listen to all the tapes accumulated over a program. Rather, any program will contain a handful of very rich, illuminating, or complex interchanges. It is these moments that require review and that motivate use of the tape recorder. Similarly, verbatim quotes are very powerful in visit reports (see Chapter 8). Customers always speak more vividly than visitors dare. Particularly when you must deliver bad news to management, it helps to have the customer be the messenger! Tapes serve to retrieve these quotes. More generally, referring to the tape of a particular interview can be useful in resolving disagreements among team members and clarifying the analysis of particular topics. In summary, tape recorders are only a convenience; you can conduct a successful program of visits without them. But, on balance, you will capture more information with a tape than without.

Cameras cannot be recommended as universally as tape recorders, but may bring important benefits to particular programs. For instance, a printer team from one firm conducted a series of visits to home offices and small businesses. They discovered that space in such offices was extremely limited. Conventional printer design, which had the power cord coming out the back, caused problems—two or three precious inches were lost as the printer had to be placed some distance out from the wall to accommodate the power cord. The visit team documented this problem with photographs, and new versions of the printer were designed with the power cord on the side.

In general, a camera is advisable when the physical context of your product is of interest. A picture can save you much laborious description, while having greater impact. Recognize that on balance, a Polaroid process camera will be less threatening to customers—they can satisfy themselves as to the triviality, to them, of the pictures you are taking away. In any case, allow plenty of time for gaining permission to bring a camera; this process is more onerous in the case of cameras than tape recorders. And, of course, you must expect that more security-conscious customers will flatly refuse you permission to use a camera or tape. Nonetheless, it does little harm to ask.

RATIONALE FOR USING
A DISCUSSION GUIDE

Have you ever participated in a meeting that was boring, dull, a waste of time? Of course you have! Bad meetings generally result either from the lack of an agenda or a chairperson who fails to exercise leadership. A good interview requires the same things as a good meeting: a feasible agenda and appropriate leadership. The discussion guide serves as an agenda for the visit (a discussion of leadership in interviews is given in Chapter 7). Without a discussion guide, your interviews will tend to suffer from digressions, lack of continuity, and excessive variability.

It is generally useful to prepare the discussion guide using an outline format. You might think of the discussion guide as a kind of roadmap to the interview. It tells you what has to be covered in the 1 or 2 hours at your disposal. It indicates a sequence for the interview, gives the priority level for each individual topic, and helps you to stay on track and use the time well. The discussion guide also assures some minimum level of consistency from interview to interview, and keeps you from inadvertently omitting a topic. Finally, the discussion guide helps to coordinate the efforts of multiple teams in a larger

---

SIDEBAR 10

Problem: The Discussion Guide Becomes a Questionnaire
There can be a tendency to obsess over the discussion guide, causing it to grow ever longer and more detailed. People with technical backgrounds tend to be most comfortable with precision and exactitude, and may end up creating an over-elaborate discussion guide. Remember that the guide is best thought of as a rough agenda or as a collection of conversation starters. It is not necessary to worry or slave over the wording of every item. Two to four pages is about the right length. Too much elaboration suggests either anxiety about the value of qualitative research or the attempt to satisfy too many objectives in a single visit.

project. It makes certain that all the teams are really engaged in the
same research program.

EXHIBIT 6.1

Sample Discussion Guide:
New Product Development

I. Introduction
   1. Orientation questions: nature of customer's application,
     how much and what kind of equipment owned
   2. General business issues: factors driving purchase of this
     equipment, upcoming changes in the business,
     and so on
II. Perceptions of Current Offerings
   1. Problems in buying, using, and supporting existing
     solutions
   2. Limitations and shortcomings of existing equipment
III. Desired Project Enhancements
   1. Probe for underlying needs and driving factors
   2. Get specific examples of desired functionality
   3. Probe for relative importance of each need; tie back to
     fundamental task
IV. Product Support
   1. Probe for issues surrounding product functionality:
     support, training, documentation, ordering, and delivery
V. Wrap-up
   1. Summarize and probe for additional insights
   2. Allow customer to raise own issues

In designing a discussion guide, you have to consider three aspects.[1] *Topics* correspond to the Roman numerals in a conventional
outline format, and represent the half-a-dozen major content areas
that will be covered during the interview. For instance, if you were
exploring satisfaction with a test instrument, the topics might include
reliability, performance, support, and documentation, among others.

Within each topic you will have one or more specific *questions*. For example, under reliability, you might explore such questions as "Has the instrument ever failed while in operation?" or "What kind of problems have you experienced in using the instrument?" A final, less obvious component, is the *sequence* of topics and questions. As discussed in the next section, this sequence ought not to be left to chance or whim.

TIPS FOR PREPARING AND WORKING WITH A DISCUSSION GUIDE

1. The discussion guide is the link between your research objectives and the actual dialogue that takes place during the interviews. As with the statement of objectives, it is a good idea to circulate early drafts of the discussion guide to responsible management, peers and associates, and prospective team members for their comments and suggestions.

2. The structure of the discussion guide needs to balance generality and specificity. If it is too vague and high level, it won't help you to navigate the rougher and more tumultuous interviews. If it is too specific, it will cramp your style. Remember that your guide is only a guide, not a script. If you make your guide too elaborate, specifying every last detail, you will undercut your interview performance! Think of the guide as a set of prompts and reminders. You want something that you can glance at now and then within the interview. If you have to read directly from your guide in order to execute the interview, then you have gone astray.

3. The arrangement of topics in the discussion guide should promote a smooth flow of conversation. Ideally, one topic will lead logically to the next. As will be discussed in more detail in the next chapter, the discussion guide should "ramp up," starting with a few safe and easily answered questions, and moving on to the more difficult and challenging. The importance of constructing a logical flow among topics can best be illustrated in the negative. If you fail to develop a good flow, the customer is more likely to feel confused. He or she may feel jerked about, unable to gather their thoughts for

a considered answer. The more confusing and helter-skelter the interview from the customer's perspective, the greater their fatigue and the less likely they are to go the extra mile for you. In devising a logical flow of topics and questions, use the following three rules of thumb:

a. Start with the familiar and work out to topics more remote from the customer's immediate concerns. For example, first ask about the present, and even the past, before exploring the future.

b. Begin with general issues before getting very specific. It takes time to build rapport with customers, and plunging immediately into very technical details is likely to put people off. In any case, you want to discover the overall frame of reference before attempting to nail down details.

c. Within each topic area, begin with open-ended questions and finish up with closed-ended questions. These two types of questions are elaborated in the next chapter. Open-ended questions leave the customer free to choose answer categories, whereas closed-end questions ask customers to pick an answer from a list you supply. It is important to begin topics with more open-ended questions so as to minimize the biasing effect on your preexisting notions. Open-ended questions open up a topic; closed-ended questions bring closure on specific points.

4. Pilot test the guide with one or two easily reached, safe, and familiar customers. Perhaps your 1-hour guide really requires 3 hours to execute; or perhaps what you thought was a 2-hour guide is easily handled in 45 minutes. The learning curve as regards assembling a discussion guide is very steep: One or two pilot tests will generally lead to a much more effective discussion guide. In the pilot test, clumsy transitions and errors of omission will quickly become apparent.

5. Be flexible in applying your guide within the interview. Sometimes newcomers to the customer visit method, especially quantitatively trained individuals such as engineers, operate under the misapprehension that George Gallup, Louis Harris, and other pollsters are their role models. Hence, they attempt to execute the discussion guide in exactly the same way in each and every interview. Instead, remember that you are conducting a series of loosely structured, exploratory interviews with the goal of discovering and understanding customer needs. You should expect that each interview will

be somewhat different. Whereas all the basic questions should be covered in each interview, how these are handled will vary, sometimes dramatically. At the extreme, you may encounter a customer who wants to discuss the topics on your guide in a different order. So? What do you care? It was your responsibility to envision one feasible discussion flow and to write that out as your guide. If a particular customer drives toward a different flow, you should be flexible enough to accommodate them. All you care about is that somewhere during the interview all essential topics get addressed in sufficient depth.

6. Remember that less is more in the case of discussion guides. As you invite associates to give input, the guide may come to resemble a Christmas tree, hung with all manner of side issues and nice-to-know subtopics. Part of the program coordinator's responsibility is to keep the discussion guide within bounds. The addition of unrelated topics, or the attempt to combine what should have been two different research programs into one, can only impede and undercut the interviews. If you want simple answers to a wide variety of questions, you probably should be doing a survey instead of customer visits. The unique advantage of a face-to-face interview is the opportunity to probe a few topics in depth. Your discussion guide, in keeping with your objectives, should concentrate on those few essential topics.

7. Know your priorities. Inevitably a guide will contain some topics and questions that are less important than others. Each team leader should be briefed on the priority of individual topics. Sooner or later, you will find yourself in a chaotic interview, or an interview that has been interrupted, or one that has proven to be exceedingly rich on an unsuspected topic. The consequence in all of these cases is that, due to time limitations, something has to be dropped. You want this item to be a low-priority topic and your discussion guide should help you make this decision on the fly.

A PROCESS FOR TEAM
PREPARATION OF A DISCUSSION GUIDE

Here is some step-by-step advice for a program coordinator designing a substantial program of visits involving several teams and half-a-dozen or more participants. First, draft and circulate the research objectives, as described earlier. Once the objectives have been firmed up, convene the key players among the participants for a brainstorming session in a room with a large whiteboard or several flipcharts. The goal is to generate a large number of possible topics and questions relevant to the research objectives. Next, the program coordinator needs to sit down with this fund of topics and questions and hammer out a possible sequence. The coordinator will discard, combine, and add topics as needed to satisfy several constraints: the key information needs as indicated by the research objectives, the amount of time you expect to have available with customers, the need for a logical flow, and last but not least, the political sensitivities and team dynamics that surround the project.

This draft discussion guide should then be circulated among all participants for comments and feedback. The program coordinator then processes this information to produce a second draft. This draft may or may not benefit from being recirculated for comments at least among key participants (it depends on how messy the revision of the first draft proved to be). Next, the draft can be pilot tested on a safe local customer. In many cases, after the pilot test, the discussion guide achieves a kind of final form. Individual teams will tend to elaborate it as the visits progress; all teams will tend to streamline the guide a bit as visits and experience develop; but all teams should commit to the guide as the basic structure of each and every visit. If you confront a particularly confusing or challenging situation, it may make sense to schedule the visits in two or three waves, with a gap in between. After the first wave, the teams can be convened for a critique of the process thus far, and this may suggest a number of changes and refinements to the discussion guide and other aspects of the program.

Remember, the discussion guide is not a questionnaire, and it does not have to be executed in lockstep each and every visit. All that is important is that each visit correspond to the topics encompassed by the guide, which is only to say that each visit should address the research objectives that motivated the program. Ultimately the interviewer himself or herself is the measuring instrument; the discussion guide is simply a convenient set of advice and reminders for the interviewer, an opportunity to envision how the interview might best develop to address the research objectives.

CONSTRUCTING GOOD QUESTIONS

Your goal in developing questions is to strike a balance between preparation and spontaneity, consistency and improvisation. On the preparation side, there will always be certain questions that are central to your research objective and that will probably be asked, with little variation, in each and every interview. These questions can be worked out in advance, and you should certainly spend some time experimenting with the best way to word them. But—and this is important—you should not, and must not, fall into the trap of thinking that you must always ask each question at the same point in each interview, using exactly the same words each time. Such uniformity in question delivery is properly a characteristic of survey research, and is neither necessary nor desirable in a qualitative interview. In survey research, an essential component of the success of the national polling organizations such as Gallup and Harris is precisely the discipline and training of their workforce, which enables them to execute what, for all intents and purposes, is the identical ordering and wording of questions across all of the 1,500 people contacted. In customer visits, you are attempting something very different. You *do* need to think about better and worse ways of phrasing your questions, and you should always strive to avoid obviously bad wording (see following sections). However, it is not necessary, and in fact not optimal, to attempt to ask a given question exactly the same way in each interview.

Many of the best and most illuminating moments in customer visits will occur when you venture into uncharted territory. The customer will say something unexpected, the conversation will veer off into an unanticipated direction, or, less positively, you will encounter resistance or reach an impasse. It is at this point that you must come up with an unrehearsed question that seizes the advantage or releases the blockage. This is where the ability to improvise becomes crucial. The basic rules of question construction, as set out in the following paragraphs, need to be internalized sufficiently that you can act on the spot. You have to be prepared to veer away from the guide and do something more useful.

The second reason spontaneity is necessary is that every customer whom you visit will have his or her own cognitive style, unique vocabulary, and distinctive outlook. Moreover, each interview will take an idiosyncratic course as you explore the answers to initial queries. To succeed you have to be flexible, adapting your approach, sequencing, and choice of words along whatever lines prove productive. For these reasons, excessive rigidity would be an indication that someone is not well qualified to be a moderator. Returning to the other end of this polarity, a minimum degree of consistency across visits is required if the interviews are to deserve the name "research." The way to balance these two criteria is to make sure that all essential questions do get asked, in some form, in each and every interview, while allowing yourself substantial freedom in terms of the point at which each question will be introduced and the way it will be phrased. After all, the employees who will be sent out on customer visits are far more highly paid than those who conduct polls for Gallup or Harris (including equipment, benefits, and other support costs, companies in Silicon Valley during 1997 might budget the cost of a single engineer at upward of $175,000 per year). It is both fair and appropriate to expect more from these visitors than the rote delivery of questions prepared in advance, even as we require of them that each and every interview address a basic core of questions.

WORKHORSE QUESTIONS

There are a small number of questions that are widely applicable to a great variety of customer visit situations, and examples are given here. As a preface, let me reiterate the importance of asking open-ended questions. Although I wasn't present at your last customer visit, if pressed about potential shortcomings, I would bet that you asked too many closed-ended questions and not enough open-ended questions. This is one of the most common errors I have observed. All *yes-no* questions, and all multiple choice questions, are closed ended—you supply the answer categories along with the question. Two examples: "Do you want your printer to print on both sides of the page?" and "Do you prefer to buy at large computer stores, small hobbyist stores, or through the mail?" By contrast, an example of an opened-ended question would be, "What are you looking for in your next printer?" A closed-ended question, when asked too early in a questioning sequence, closes off avenues of discussion and steers the conversation along a preordained path. Such questions find their proper place at the conclusion of a topic, when you need to pin down an answer. Recognize, however, that much of the real work in the interview is performed by open-ended questions that invite the customer to structure the discussion. Open-ended questions thus form an important component of the distinctive advantage of customer visits considered as a research technique.

Identify Task Demands. It is all too tempting in visits to focus immediately and directly on product specifications. Thus, you might be inclined to ask, "How many megabytes do you need this instrument to transfer per second?" Instead, you would be better off beginning with an analysis of task demands. What kind of data are being transferred? Where do the data come from, and where do the data go? Who produces the data and who consumes it? In other words, what business purpose does transferring the data serve, and what are the criteria for success that apply to that business purpose?

The point here is that the customer's business purpose is fundamental, not the product specification. The product will be purchased if it satisfies a business purpose, otherwise not. Hence, the most important thing is to understand the business purpose—the task the product supports—and how this purpose articulates with product functionality. Laying out the task demands, and anchoring the discussion there, is the most effective approach to understanding how product specifications may have to evolve. Again, I was not present at your last customer visit, but a very typical flaw is asking too many product-focused and not enough customer-focused questions. A focus on task demands, first, and product specifications, second, is one concrete way in which you give meaning to the quest for a market-focused business strategy.

Understand Product Context. Virtually all computer-related products must do their work as part of an assemblage of other products. Hardware is hooked up to networks, software runs hardware, one piece of software must speak to another, and so forth. The same sort of cross-dependencies often obtain in the case of noncomputer products. It follows that your product will succeed or fail in part based on how well it fits into the matrix of surrounding products. Thus, understanding product context is yet another example of a questioning strategy that is focused on customers. To you, your product is the be-all and end-all. To the customer, it is just one of several tools assembled to accomplish some business purpose.

Identify Unsolved Problems. Many customer visit programs are motivated by the desire to identify customer needs that could be profitably filled. It would seem natural, therefore, to ask some question such as, "What are your needs with respect to this product?" The problem with this phrasing is that it presumes that customers carry around in their heads a list of needs that they can easily access when prompted. In actual fact, perhaps only product developers carry around need lists in their heads!

A more powerful approach to identifying unmet needs is to ask something like, "What problems have you been unable to solve with this product?" Customers most definitely carry around an inventory of complaints, shortcomings, frustrations, obstacles—and the energy to discuss these in depth! This approach to identifying needs through a discussion of unsolved problems places the burden of insight on the vendor. Based on the customer's problem description, you must infer the nature of the underlying need, and then relate this inferred need to the various technologies at your disposal. Multiple competing inferences may be possible, and each step in the chain of reasoning is vulnerable to blockage. So be it. It is an illusion to suppose that you can visit customers and have them hand you the specifications for the profitable product you ought to be building. It isn't that easy.

A summary statement on this issue would go something like this:

- The customer is the authority as to the problems they are trying to solve.
- The vendor is the authority as to what form a profitable solution to that problem might take.[2]

Of course, once in a while a customer may toss off a useful and valuable solution that you can easily implement. By all means, take advantage of these suggestions. But recognize that most of the time, the highest and best use of the customers' time is to have them explain the problems encountered as they attempt to do their job using your product.

Identify Likes and Dislikes. When there is an existing problem or solution, customers almost expect you to ask this question. Asking what they like and what they dislike is an efficient means of unpacking their experiences. Also, you earn points by asking about dislikes and listening in an unflinching and receptive manner to the answers.

The like-dislike question is treated very differently in customer visits as compared to its usage in surveys and questionnaires. In surveys, you attempt to quantify the strength of the positive or negative reaction to each item in a list. These items may then be summed, or factor analyzed, or otherwise treated statistically. The list of items is determined by you and constitutes a kind of closed-ended question. In customer visits, the like-dislike question functions as an open-ended question. The goal is *to identify* what is liked and what is disliked, to understand *in depth* what exactly is being approved or disapproved, and to *explore why* an aspect is liked or disliked. You want to understand the qualities that characterize customer responses, not fix their quantities.

Probing is particularly crucial in the case of the like-dislike question (the next chapter discusses probing in more detail). After the customer volunteers one like or dislike, it is important to follow up and ask whether there is another. As you can imagine, sometimes vendor personnel shrink from this additional probing in the case of dislikes! Your goals with this kind of question are to discover likes and dislikes that are new to you and to better understand the meaning of the likes and dislikes with which you are already familiar. Thorough probing is required to achieve this goal.

Force Trade-Offs. Often customers will express a desire for two pieces of functionality that conflict. This is one of many good reasons to include technical people on the visit team—technically knowledgeable visitors are more likely to realize that yes, we can solve this problem for the customer—but only by degrading performance in this other area! The question becomes, which desire is more important to the customer? It is a good idea to attempt to force trade-offs in this situation. Much can be learned as the customer thinks out loud about whether advancing on one front is worth a setback on another. You may gain further insight into the customer's hierarchy of preferences and primary motivations.

Sometimes the customer will vigorously push back and refuse to make a trade-off—he or she demands that the product accomplish both aims equally well. You know that this is not technologically possible. What should your takeaway be: (a) that the customer is an impossible person, or ignorant; or (b) that this customer's resistance might indicate an opportunity for technological innovation? To follow up on this point, imagine visits paid to printer users in the early

1980s. Very likely, some of these customers would have demanded both print quality (then only available from daisy wheel printers), and print speed (then only available from dot matrix printers), refusing to compromise on either count. As we all know, when later the laser printer became possible, it swept the other partial printer solutions away in part because it eliminated this trade-off. Moral of the story: Don't cavalierly dismiss customers who refuse to make trade-offs.

Push for Priority. A good open-ended question, especially one concerned with future products, may easily produce a dozen or more responses. The customer may indicate he wants this, he wants that, also this other thing, and on and on. Once you have elicited all of the responses that the customer has to offer, it is appropriate to ask about the relative priority placed on each problem or wish. However, given a dozen or so responses, it will *not* work to ask the customer to rank order these from 1 to 12. Most people can't maintain a mental rank ordering of that level of complexity, nor can they apply one on the fly to a dozen freshly generated items. Two common workarounds are,

> "Of all the things you mentioned, what are the top three or which three are most important?"
> "If you had $100 to spend on all these desires, how would you allocate the $100 across them?"

The first of these is simpler, and it is perfectly adequate for determining what is critical and what is not. The second is more powerful because it yields more information, in that it gives both a rank order and information on the distance that separates ranks (a response of "$50 on A, $40 on B, and $10 on C" indicates not only that B is more important than C, but also how much more important it is). However, the second version presumes both a high degree of involvement on the part of the customer and a precise habit of mind. Either version will work much better if you have brought along a supply of 3" × 5" cards on which you note the individual problems or desires elicited in the first part of this questioning sequence. Having the customer move these around on the table as they settle on a rank order will facilitate the task.

Whenever you push for priority, your next question should always be some version of "why"—why is X more important than Y to this customer? There is little point in using customer visits to generate an average rank order of problem importance across customers—the small sample size and nonrandom character render such averages dubious at best. The point, rather, is to explore the motives that led this customer to rank the items in this way. The request for priorities simply provides another route for exploring this customer's thought world. Thus, it is not uncommon for customers to produce a "top three" containing one or more items that were not even mentioned during the open-ended elicitation (these might be more abstract concepts produced as the customer struggles to make sense of his own replies). Ultimately, just as the presence or absence of certain problems helped to define this customer's world, so also the relative importance of certain items carries information about the customer's worldview. And that worldview is what you are after on these visits.

SPECIALIZED QUESTION STRATEGIES

These next few questions will be relevant to some investigations, but not to most. They are useful enough, often enough, to be worth discussing here, and may stimulate you to think of even more specialized questions germane to the particular project you are considering.

The Critical Incident Technique. Consider the following question, which was proposed as part of an investigation of hand-held "personal information appliances." The project team reasoned that frequent business travelers would be a primary target for this handheld product, and proposed to visit a sample of these travelers and ask questions such as,

> "When you first arrive in a strange city, what kind of information tends to be lacking?"

At first glance, this may seem to be a reasonable sort of open-ended question, one that would allow the customer the freedom to mention virtually any kind of missing information. On closer inspection, however, it can be seen that this is really a very difficult question. It requires the customer to go into long-term memory, pull together that category of events known as *first-time arrivals,* focus in on the particular aspect referred to as *missing information,* and then extract from that assembly a typical instance. This is very hard cognitive labor!

Using the critical incident technique you would rephrase the question as follows:

> "Think back to the last time you arrived in a strange city—were you missing any piece of information?"

The preface, "Think back to the last time . . ," is characteristic of the critical incident technique. It focuses the customer on one specific and relatively recent event, making information retrieval easier. You can then follow up with one or two more probes of this sort ("How about another time you visited a new city?"). At that point, the whole category and its various aspects have been cued up in memory, and a question such as "In general, what kinds of information have been lacking?" will now work well. The critical incident technique is very flexible and can be applied to many targets ("Think back to the last time your system crashed—what process did you go through to bring it back on line?"). Consider using this technique whenever you want to discuss a whole category of past events in some detail.

The Image Question. A question that won't be effective with every customer, but that may sometimes be useful in helping people vocalize tacit reactions, is to ask about the images they might have in some situation. For instance,

> "You've just received the disks needed to upgrade your network operating system to the next version. What images might be passing through your mind as you opened the package?"

When it works, this question will unearth responses such as, "I wondered if this upgrade was going to require another all-nighter like the last one"—vivid, emotionally charged recollections. It has to be used with care, however; some customers will give you a look that says "What kind of crazy question is that?" whereupon you can fall back to the more safe, "I mean, what thoughts or feelings might pass through your mind in that situation?"

Ask About the Customer's Customer. In BTB markets, most of your customers will have their own customers to satisfy, even if this is simply another group within their own organization. A good way to expand the focus of the visit outward from narrow product details is to ask your customer, "Who is *your* customer, and what do they require of you?" This is yet another way of focusing the visit on the broader business purpose that your product serves. As a general rule, if you can more effectively help your customers to satisfy their customers, you will satisfy and retain your customers.[3] This question makes the value chain, in which both you and your customer participate, salient and accessible to discussion.

EFFECTIVE AND INEFFECTIVE QUESTIONS

If the first requirement for success in asking questions is recognition of the need to balance consistency and spontaneity, the second requirement is understanding that you can usually obtain valuable information merely by avoiding the worst flaws in question delivery. In other words, you don't have to be a terrifically smooth, articulate, and poised interviewer to succeed in customer visits. It is enough that you avoid the more egregious errors. Such mistakes can be grouped under two headings: (a) unclear and (b) inappropriate questions. A third requirement for success is accepting that whereas a minimum level of interviewing skill can take you quite far, the ceiling in terms of interview skill is very high. You can spend your entire working life getting better at asking *productive* questions.

Unclear Questions

Perhaps the most common cause of lack of clarity is a question that is too long, or whose syntax or clause structure is difficult to process. We tend to forget that what can be processed through the ear is far less than what can be processed through the eye. A question that might just be comprehensible if delivered in writing is likely to be beyond the pale if delivered orally. As a rule of thumb, you may assume that any question that, if written, would be punctuated with a semicolon is almost certainly going to be unclear.

Sometimes a question becomes unclear because it is forced to do too much. A typical response of someone new to interviewing, who is experiencing anxiety and fear of failure, is to attempt to ask "the perfect question." For example: "Assuming we make the changes you requested, and assuming that the national economy recovers in the third quarter, and given that our leading competitor does not change its price-performance ratio, what will the timing look like on your upgrade of this system?" This question may be "perfect" in the sense of covering all relevant contingencies, but it is unanswerable! You should apply the KISS principle here: keep it short and simple. When you must address a complex issue, build up to the crucial point using a series of relatively short and clear questions.

Yet another condition that tends to produce unclear questions is the failure to use visual aids where appropriate. It is far easier to clearly and efficiently probe responses to a new product concept or other initiative if you can point to a picture as you focus on the details. To think that you can deliver an oral description of something complex and novel, and then ask productive questions about the details of what you just described, is absurd—it ignores the very real limits of attention and information processing in human beings. A better idea is to bring diagrams, flowcharts, and other graphic representations whenever you are discussing a system or process. By the way, it is important that these graphics not appear overly slick. The more finished these graphic aids appear, the less inviting they are to comment on, critique, or edit. You want something that looks relatively preliminary and rudimentary. This sends a message to customers that their input is welcome, even necessary, and will have an impact. Too slick a graphic sends the opposite message—we have already decided, you have no role.

Do not limit yourself to graphic visual aids. It can be very helpful when discussing a product concept to slide across the table a page containing four or five key points that outline the essential features of the concept. Although it is still a good idea to describe the concept orally, the ensuing discussion will benefit in two ways. First, you can point to specific items and invite a detailed response focused on that item. Second, the written summary makes it easier for the customer to grasp the concept as a whole and makes it more likely that they will comment on interconnections between aspects of the concept.

Most interviewers, even veterans, ask unclear questions from time to time. Occasionally, it is simply a matter of not being able to accommodate a particular customer whose style of thinking happens to be quite distinct from your own. Good interviewers will quickly notice that they have asked an unclear question and do their best to correct the situation. Here, a little self-deprecating humor, or a graceful acknowledgment of having erred, will often allow you to recover.

Inappropriate Questions

Any question that obscures the truth, produces inaccurate responses, or leads to misunderstanding may be considered an inappropriate question. In my experience, such questions tend to come about as a result of (a) your emotions getting the better of you or (b) bad faith on the part of one or more team members. The most important categories within this classification are *leading* and *biased* questions.

A leading question is one that makes one response from the customer more likely than another. Such a question is fundamentally manipulative. As a general rule of thumb, any question that begins with a negative contraction is probably a leading question. For example, "Don't you think that Windows NT has gained the upper hand over Unix?" or "Isn't it the case that maintenance costs far outweigh the initial purchase price?" Such questions put words into the mouth of the customer. In all probability, your own need for reassurance or confirmation is the underlying cause. But it is important to recognize that such attempts to cue a particular answer undercut the whole rationale of customer visits, which is to create an arena in which discovery and new learning can occur.

A biased question is one that indicates that you already know the "right" answer, or that you are simply seeking confirmation for what you have already decided to be the case. Biased questions can be even more off-putting to the customer than leading questions. They suggest that the interview is not really an attempt to listen, but simply a pro forma exercise. If the customer perceives questions as being biased, he or she is likely to grow cynical and to withdraw from the interview. Some examples of biased questions would be: "Our lab is really excited about this idea. What do you see as its advantages?" or "We know that Acme's ads irritate people. What do you think is their most bothersome feature?" or "Our studies show that the whole industry is moving in this direction—what is your time frame for making the change?"

The underlying cause of biased questioning is typically a defensive attitude around some decision that the interviewer favors, some pet peeve of a team member, or a gambit within a larger political agenda (i.e., a team member may have lobbied for inclusion of some feature in the product and is seeking support for this preference from the customer). If you do find yourself or your team asking leading or biased questions, you may attempt to recover using the same grace and self-deprecating humor as suggested earlier in the discussion of unclear questions. However, I am less optimistic that you will succeed. Leading and biased questions really are poisonous to the sort of interview atmosphere that a good customer visit requires. They are strongly alienating to the customer, in part because they make a mockery of your promise that the purpose of the visit is to listen and learn.

There is also a more subtle kind of biased question that you should guard against. Suppose, for instance, that you ask a customer what they like about a new concept. You phrase it as an open-ended question, and you probe diligently after the initial query. Suppose also that you never turn around and ask what the customer *dislikes* about the new concept. Then, despite good intentions, you will have pursued a biased line of questioning. The bias lies not in the phrasing of the individual queries so much as in the selection of which questions to ask and which to avoid. The likely result is that you will return from the visits with an unduly positive model of customers' responses to the new concept.

In reflecting on the difficulty of avoiding these more subtle kinds of biases, you may come to understand why it is so important to conduct customer visits dedicated to research and free of any pressure to sell. If your visit had to serve a double agenda, both your choice of questions and the wording thereof would be constrained. It is, after all, common practice in selling to ask a series of questions, all of which must be answered "yes," in order to build commitment to a viewpoint. Similarly, many sales encounters are designed to create a positive, upbeat atmosphere. And, competent salespeople know how to anticipate and overcome objections. But in a research visit, you don't want to overcome objections; you want to identify and understand them.

Productive Questions

Although it is important to avoid fatal flaws in question delivery, you should also actively seek the most productive questions possible. You know you have asked a productive question when the customer has to stop and think, not because they are stymied but because the question both requires and deserves a thoughtful answer. A productive question is one that matches the customer's orientation (as opposed to questions that are opaque because they use language or rest on assumptions that are foreign to this customer). Productive questions typically open up new avenues of discussion. A productive question takes advantage of the unique motivational potential of an in-person interview as opposed to a phone or mail survey. An interview is motivating because questions are asked by a visitor who really seems to care about the answers and who is sufficiently knowledgeable to understand a complex answer. A customer is going to be willing to work much harder to answer questions from a key decision maker than questions from an anonymous individual with minimal involvement in the issues, who is largely following a script and is present only as a disembodied voice on the phone. Any question that effectively takes advantage of this motivational aspect of the interview may be deemed a productive question.

A productive question asks the customer to think, to draw connections, to explain, or to give the big picture. It is difficult to be more precise about productive questions; one of their key characteristics is that they are tightly tied to the context of a specific interview and as varied as the topics pursued. It is possible, however, to point to two common ways of failing to ask a productive question: the too-easy and too-hard questions. A question is too easy when it can be answered yes or no, answered from memory, or answered from conventional wisdom. Whereas you will certainly have to ask some easy questions during customer visits, these properly belong to survey research. If most of your questions can be answered yes or no, or with a phrase or two, you probably ought to use some other research technique such as a questionnaire. At the other extreme, questions that are too hard are also not productive. Examples would include questions that demand knowledge the customer does not possess, demand a level of analysis that is impossible without patient reflection over a sustained period, or demand that the customer use concepts that are unfamiliar. Questions are also too hard when they are not obviously relevant to the purpose of the interview. An example of a question that often fails to be productive is "Describe the ideal or dream instrument for this application." From the customer's standpoint, the "ideal instrument" doesn't exist, isn't likely to exist, and probably would cost too much anyway. Hence, what is the point of trying to answer this question? Besides, thinks this customer, isn't it the vendor's responsibility to come up with bright new ideas? A more productive question might be, "Are there any measurements that you would like to take, but which this instrument does not permit?" A focus on a specific gap is more likely to be productive than an invitation to dream.

Specific Questions to Avoid

Here are three questions that often come up for consideration when preparing for an interview:

1. What features would you like to see in this product?
2. How much would you be willing to pay for a product like this?
3. Where do you see this technology going over the next five years?

At first glance, Question 1 would appear to be a reasonable attempt at asking an open-ended question. The first problem is that *features* represents marketing jargon. Although people who plan products have to make lists of features, what customers care about is how the product can help them perform some task. A better approach is to focus directly on the task that the product performs, and to probe for aspects of that task that are not being handled effectively, or perhaps not addressed at all. The second difficulty with this question is that it tends to produce unrealistic wish lists. Ultimately, the question rests on the dangerous fallacy that the customer can tell you what to design. No. In most cases the customer can only tell you what task they are trying to accomplish and what obstacles they have encountered. The goal in visits is to make certain that the design engineers who are responsible for developing your technology are intimately familiar with the customer's task demands. You want to bring these people face to face with customers, so that when they return to the lab they can say, "Well, if that's the problem they have, then any solution must have the following characteristics . . . ." The responsibility for technological invention remains the vendor's; what the vendor hopes to get from the customer is a sense of the problems that most need to be solved.[4]

The problem with Question 2 is that it converts the interview into a negotiating session. If the customer wishes to behave in a rational and self-interested fashion, he or she has to either give a lowball estimate, or refuse to answer. Interviews may be the world's worst technique for doing pricing research! Good pricing research requires an experimental design in which choices are made among different product profiles priced at different points.[5] The best that one can do in an interview is identify substitutes for the product or service (the cost of these substitutes provides an indirect estimate of the value the product or service provides), or identify the benefits of the product in sufficient detail that you yourself can compute the value provided. Alternatively, you can name a specific price (only one; a second price moves you into haggling and away from research) and see how the customer responds. If you know that a tentative price has been set, mentioning it can be a useful disaster check (as when the customer replies, "I can buy two of the competitors' old model instruments for half that figure and get the job done more or less as well!").

The problem with Question 3 is that it assumes that the customer is as fascinated by, and familiar with, the technology that underlies your product as your design engineers are. Asked "where the technology is going," an ordinary user might well reply, "if I knew the answer to that question, I'd be working for you!" If you want to ask that question that way, then you can't visit ordinary users—you must seek out opinion leaders, industry experts, power users, and so forth. If you need to visit ordinary users, then you must rephrase the question. Try one of the following:

"What problems are you unable to solve with current technology?"
"Is there anything your customers have started to demand that you don't know how to supply using current technology?"

Each of these alternative phrasings returns the focus to matters on which the customer is an expert—the obstacles and difficulties of doing a job with what is currently available. It remains your job to reason how technology must evolve, given the pressing business problems faced by your customers. It is unrealistic to suppose that ordinary customers can draw that connection for you.

THE IMPORTANCE OF FOLLOW-UP

The gist of this chapter has been the importance of working out your questions in advance, getting the wording right, and avoiding common pitfalls. Preparation of this kind will make your visits more productive. I should acknowledge, however, that much of the real work in interviews happens after you have asked a carefully phrased, well-formed question. As often as not, the customer will give you a vague, general, or partial answer in reply. You must recognize that your question has not really been answered and follow up with additional questions to more fully unpack the customers' response. These questions must be developed on the fly; in many instances these follow-up questions will be some form of "Could you give me an example?" "What specifically was the problem?" "What caused that to happen?" "Then what happened next?" "What other reasons?" (See the next chapter for more on the topic of probing). It is the opportunity to clarify answers and pursue a lengthy line of questioning that underlies many of the distinctive advantages of *interactive* face-to-face communication. Do not fall into the trap of assuming that there exists some set of questions that, without further effort on your part, will unlock everything the customer has to offer on a topic. On the contrary, in most cases your performed questions only initiate a dialogue, which only later yields the richest material.

TIME FRAME

Setting objectives, selecting and recruiting a sample, organizing and briefing teams, and preparing a discussion guide are the necessary preludes to a productive customer visit. For planning purposes, you should allow for 4 to 8 weeks to elapse between the moment the idea of visiting customers dawns on you and the day the first visit of the program takes place. More specifically, 1 to 2 weeks will be required to get agreement on objectives, and 1 to 2 weeks to devise and finalize a sample frame. You will probably have to schedule interviews 3 to 4 weeks ahead. Team selection and preparation of the discussion guide can go on in parallel with recruiting.

NOTES

1. The books on focus groups by Goldman and McDonald (1987) and Greenbaum (1998) can be consulted for examples of discussion guides and additional advice on their preparation.

2. For a rather different approach to this problem, see Von Hippel (1987).

3. Lynn Phillips and his consulting firm have built an entire approach to visiting customers from this key question. Although to my knowledge no definitive published account of their approach exists, some idea of it can be gained from Guillart and Sturdivant (1994).

4. Note that this position is at variance with that of Von Hippel (1987), who argued that lead users are often the best source of innovative solutions. I believe Von Hippel is correct in the case of some industries, and I would urge you to be attentive to any user-designed solutions that you encounter during your customer visits. But as a general rule, I think the customer can only specify the need, whereas the vendor must develop the specifics of the solution.

5. See Simon (1989, 1992) for advice on pricing research.

CHAPTER SEVEN

Conducting the Visits

The face-to-face interview is the heart of the customer visit program. The preparation activities described in the preceding chapters, and the follow-up activities described in the next, are designed to maximize the value of the time you actually spend with customers. This chapter focuses on things you can do during the interview itself to increase your learning.

INTERVIEW FORMAT: TIME BOUNDARIES

Most interviews undertaken as part of a customer visit program will occupy between 1 and 2 hours. The limits of the human attention span, together with the difficulty of convincing someone to block out more than 2 hours on their calendar, suggest that 2 hours is the practical maximum. Shorter interviews of about 1 hour make sense when you are interviewing an individual customer, the customer's business is small and relatively straightforward, and/or your questions are relatively less complex. Longer interviews are required when several people from the customer participate, the application or product is more complex, or you want to explore more difficult issues. As a general rule, managers can be scheduled for longer interviews of close to 2 hours, whereas individual contributors will often require only a shorter interview of an hour or so. As suggested earlier, sometimes the only way to determine whether you are dealing with a 1- or 2-hour topic is to conduct several pilot interviews and see how long they take.

However many minutes the interview consumes, it can logically be divided into three parts: the opening, the middle, and the close. Each part of the interview presents specific opportunities and challenges, and each portion has to be approached in the correct frame of mind. The fundamental task during the opening portion is to build *rapport* with the customer. Rapport refers to a relationship of comfort, trust, and receptivity between interviewer and interviewee. When you first sit down together, you and the customer are strangers to one another—rapport does not yet exist. Building good rapport is the key to obtaining as much information as possible. Because the primary task in the opening is to build rapport, you should choose your first few questions carefully, both when constructing your discussion guide and in the interview itself. Good questions for the opening are those that are straightforward, clearly relevant, relatively easy to answer, and safe (meaning that the customer is unlikely to feel embarrassed or incompetent in attempting to answer them). These opening questions should also be designed to require more than a one-word answer. You want to get the customer into the mode of talking, and talking at length. In light of these criteria, a question about the customer's application for your product is usually a good opener. Queries about the customer's job responsibilities and how these intersect with your product are also generally appropriate.

Questions to be avoided during the opening include those that are irrelevant or nothing more than chit-chat (e.g., "How's your golf game?"). The opening questions should clearly correspond to the expectations that you set in your confirmation letter. You also want to avoid questions that are too microscopic in focus (e.g., precise measurement tolerance for one of several functions performed by an instrument) or too difficult and challenging (e.g., how this product technology stacks up against a competing technology).

It is in the middle of the interview that you do the bulk of the substantive work in gathering information and getting answers to your questions. This is where you ask the hard questions, probe for in-depth information, and follow up on surprising new information.

In terms of actual time elapsed, the middle portion accounts for the bulk of the interview.

The point of distinguishing the close of the interview as a distinct component can be made by reminding you that just as a good interview requires a steady ramping up of intensity, so also it benefits from a winding down. It is *not* a good idea to ask your last substantive question, stand up, shake hands, and leave. Instead, strive to finish 5 or 10 minutes before your allotted time is up. Psychotherapists sometimes joke that all the really good stuff comes out in the last 5 minutes of the therapy hour. A similar phenomenon holds true in market research interviews. Often the customer has held back some telling complaint, novel perspective, or crucial bit of information, unable to incorporate it into answers to your prepared questions. You want to allow time for, and be receptive to, this kind of unexpected input toward the end of the interview.

Once you have worked through your discussion guide, you might say something like: "Those are all the questions I have for you. Is there anything else you would like to say on this topic?" In metaphorical terms, you are handing the reins of this conversation over to the customer. You want to see where he or she will take it. As always in research, an item or perspective that is spontaneously volunteered by a customer will more powerfully reflect that customer's true concerns than any prompted answer. True, some customers will simply seize the opportunity to quiz you about new product schedules and the like. But other customers will surprise you with insights that you are grateful to obtain but would never have thought to inquire about.

INTERVIEW FORMAT:
SPATIAL CONSIDERATIONS

If possible, you want to hold the interview in a conference room in order to minimize distractions. A customer's office is often a less-than-ideal setting because it is vulnerable to interruptions from the phone, drop-ins, and the like. Nonetheless, if you do a lot of customer visits you will find yourself conducting many of them in an office setting. If you are meeting in the customer's office, choose a seat that puts you a comfortable distance from the customer— neither too close nor too far. If there is a separate conversation area (as will be true above a certain managerial level), it is more desirable to conduct the interview there than sitting across the desk from the customer. You want to take advantage of the more informal setting, and you want to avoid a seating position associated with subordinates and salespeople. Avoid conducting the interview over a meal whenever possible. Interviews are work, not play, and a great deal of labor is required to achieve a successful result. The social norms that surround eating together in a professional context are at best neutral, and at worst hostile, to the kind of probing that a good interview requires. Of course, if you are going to spend an entire day at a customer site, you might very well find yourself joining these people for lunch or dinner. But you should consider such meals, and whatever conversational openings they provide, as a kind of bonus. Although they provide an extra opportunity to learn more about the customer, make certain that they function as a supplement to, and not a substitute for, an actual interview.

Given a conference room setting, try to achieve the following seating arrangements. If there is one customer and two or three people on your team, place the customer at the head of the table or at one of the first seats on either side. Place your moderator (see next section for an explanation of the moderator role) at the first seat on the other side, so that he or she sits immediately across from the customer or diagonal to him or her. Have the other members of your team sit a few seats down the conference table. This arrangement accomplishes several goals. By placing one team member close to the customer, it encourages the customer to focus on that person. This improves the moderator's ability to exert leadership during the interview, and it also improves the moderator's ability to build rapport with the customer. For the customer, this arrangement increases the comfort of the situation because it indicates clearly who is leading the interview and who should be examined for cues as to how to proceed. Finally, placing the other members of the team at a slight remove makes them less conspicuous, so that if they yawn—or begin to scribble notes furiously—it is less distracting.

If there are multiple individuals from the customer and multiple people from your side, stay away from any seating arrangement that would array the customer's people on one side of the table and your people on the other. That is a seating arrangement associated with nuclear arms talks, union disputes, and other negotiations between adversaries. Beyond this caveat, try to seat the moderator close to, and preferably directly across from, whoever is the most important person on the customer side. In any case, the moderator should sit where he or she will have good eye contact with all members of the customer's group. It is difficult to exercise leadership in a group discussion unless you occupy this vantage point.

In conclusion, it is true that spatial considerations are, in the larger spectrum of things, a minor issue. You can have productive interactions with customers over a meal, across a desk, in an airport, and under any conceivable seating arrangement. However, these spatial factors can make a difference at the margin, at least as far as the comfort of the interview situation is concerned. And, as often as not, you can control these arrangements if you so choose. In that case, think of these suggestions as ways to optimize the encounter.

A point that is by no means minor and in fact goes to the heart of the contribution of customer visits is this: *Seldom should you confine your visit to the conference room.* Whereas the conference room provides a pleasant and functional environment in which to pursue a sustained conversation, it is also generally a sterile, homogenous environment that provides few clues to anything that may be distinctive about a particular customer's environment or product usage. Every visit should include some kind of tour of the customer's facilities in order to view product setup and usage.

The value of the tour can range from low to high. If you sell something that is essentially invisible (e.g., insurance), and your questions predominantly concern such intangibles as how this type of insurance fits into the customer's long-range business plans, then there are limits to what the tour can contribute. I think it is still a good idea, however, because you always want to have clear and vivid images of the customer in your mind, and in particular in the minds of your technical people. An encounter with the physical aspects of the customer's business is part of the process of building a mental model of who the customer is and what they need. As a researcher at an insurance firm remarked, "We did a program 2 years ago with plastics manufacturers. Although you can read all this technical information about how plastics manufacturers work, probably unless you are an engineer, you won't understand it until you are actually in the plastics plant and can see the process."

A tour will be of moderate to strong value whenever you sell instruments or mechanical equipment. Here you will often be concerned with such questions as: How is the product set up? Where is it, and what else surrounds it? How does it fit into the total process of which it is a part? How do people interact with it? Many factors that are important in product design may not be sufficiently "top-of-mind" for the customer to be able to retrieve and verbalize them during the interview. From another angle, your understanding of your product and what may be important aspects of its functionality extend far beyond your own ability to frame specific questions. The physical encounter with the work site helps to overcome these limits (recall the Skyhook example mentioned in Chapter 1).

In order to maximize the value of the tour, you may want to consider the use of a variety of recording devices such as still and video cameras. In such cases, it is essential to ask the customer's permission well in advance. (Don't try this in a defense industry factory!) In addition to cameras and the like, consider developing a kind of observation checklist that can be used to develop a profile of each customer site. Comparing interview responses across distinct profiles as determined by the observation checklist may be quite illuminating. Moreover, developing and applying the checklist may stimulate insights and a much more thorough understanding of the conditions of product use. This can be particularly important for individuals in the quality function who are seeking to identify and eliminate subtle impediments to total satisfaction. For example, perhaps a wire comes out of an instrument in such a way as to interfere with some normal or necessary interaction with the instrument, for instance, where one would otherwise like to hang a clipboard. While easily observed, such factors are unlikely to be verbalized spontaneously.

GROUP VERSUS INDIVIDUAL INTERVIEWS

As mentioned in the previous chapter, typically you will want to speak to more than one individual at the customer site. Let's assume for the moment that you could potentially spend a half day or a whole day with a customer organization. There are three possible arrangements: (a) your team interviews individuals one at a time, in series; (b) your team interviews all these individuals at once in a single interview; or (c) you take a mixed-mode approach, involving some combination of the first two. No hard and fast rules can be given as

to which approach is superior. Instead, you should understand some
of the factors involved in making one arrangement or the other more
attractive. Realistically, however, you will not always get to choose,
and you should be prepared to deal with any one of these arrangements. It is advantageous to interview customers one at a time, in series,
under any of the following circumstances:

1. The individuals you are interviewing have very different competencies,
   and/or your questions for each individual are quite distinct.
2. You have reason to believe that the various individuals have conflicting
   viewpoints or desires, and you want to isolate and examine the opinions
   uniquely held by each.
3. You are interviewing people at different status levels, as in the case of
   superiors and subordinates.
4. You are hesitant to attempt the greater difficulties associated with group
   interviews, due either to the challenging nature of your research topic
   or the inexperience of your team.

In each of these cases, a group interview is *not* the best choice. You
should avoid a group interview whenever you would have to continually put one individual "on hold" while you ask a series of questions
of another. For example, this is likely to occur if one individual is
very technical and the other is not. The second issue, concerning
conflicting viewpoints within the customer organization, can cut
either way. If you wanted to maximize the depth of your understanding of *each side* of the conflict, it would make sense to interview
the parties separately. On the other hand, if you wanted to maximize
your ability to *integrate* these conflicting views, you would interview the parties jointly. The issue behind the status rule is simple:
You won't hear very much from subordinates when superiors are
present. Finally, you need to recognize that group interviews are
inherently more difficult to manage than individual interviews. They
simply tend to be more chaotic, thus placing greater demands on the
moderator's leadership, ability to exercise just the right degree of
control, and skill at establishing rapport.

Despite the difficulties inherent in group interviews, it is advantageous to interview individuals as a group when you need to understand how individual customers interact around the topics under
discussion. As mentioned earlier, most organizational purchases are

discussed, debated, and ultimately agreed on by a group of people within the customer firm. If you don't understand the different ways in which, say, the MIS director and the telecommunications director view your technology, you may select a strategy that alienates one or the other. The great virtue of a group interview is that you can see conflicts play themselves out right in front of you. Moreover, you can ask one individual to respond to the views just expressed by another. Group interviews are also efficient. If various individuals each have something to say about a topic, and their starting points are not too dissimilar, then you might as well interview them together and enjoy whatever synergy results.

In certain situations involving very complex products or services (I have encountered this situation in the computer networking industry), a hybrid approach may make sense. Here you would begin the day with a group meeting that brings together your team and the various people from the customer. This provides an opportunity to articulate goals and set a direction for the day. Next, you would either have your team interview customers one at a time or split your team up so that your technical person talks to their technical person, and so forth. Finally, at the end of the day you would reconvene and discuss the results (especially any conflicting results) of the individual interviews.

INTERVIEW ROLES

It is a good idea to assign a specific role to each member of the visit team. The two most important roles are the *moderator* and the *listener;* if you have a third person on the team, this person can fill the role of the *observer.* Each of these roles corresponds to an important function that has to be performed if the interview is to be successful. One of the reasons for preferring team visits to individual visits is that it is very difficult for one person to effectively perform all three functions simultaneously.

Moderator Role

The moderator manages all aspects of the interview. The moderator asks most of the questions, introduces all topics, and handles transitions between topics. The moderator is also responsible for executing the discussion guide, keeping the interview on track, and watching the clock. Moreover, the moderator orchestrates the contributions by other members of the visit team. In all respects, the moderator acts as "captain of the ship." Other members of the team need to recognize the moderator's authority to cut topics short or redirect the conversation. (Sometimes controlling one's own teammates is the most challenging part of the interview.)

SIDEBAR 11

Problem: The Interview Resembles a Rugby Scrum *The assignment of moderator, listener, and observer roles is intended to prevent this problem. Of course, team members must accept the moderator's authority for this arrangement to work. The team has to recognize that in cases where there are three to four people facing a single customer, rapid-fire questions coming from all corners can be both overwhelming and intimidating. Similarly, when there are three to four customers and three to four of you, air time becomes limited and the need for firm leadership most pressing.*

The advantages of appointing one person to be moderator should be apparent. The alternative is often an ill-coordinated free-for-all in which each member of the visit team pursues his or her own agenda. As a point of comparison, we have all sat in committees and other meetings that floundered because the chairperson abdicated his or her leadership responsibilities. Similarly, interviews benefit when one person is designated the leader. With a moderator, the visit team's efforts are more likely to be focused and implemented consistently across interviews. You may also find that customers are more comfortable when one individual is clearly in charge. An acceptable way to signal to the customer that one individual is going to lead the discussion (without having to be painfully explicit) is for the moderator to be the first to greet the customer. Moreover, the moderator should speak first once everyone is seated. As part of the introduction, the moderator might say something like the following: "I'll be leading the discussion today. My companions will also have questions for you when we discuss matters on which they are particularly expert." Such an introduction allays any concerns the customer might have about the role of the quiet team members, even as it avoids going into unnecessary detail about interview roles, none of which really matters to the customer.

Which team member should be designated as moderator? The person with the best communication skills should assume this role. Often, this will be someone from the marketing function, if only because communication skills are not a featured part of most engineering curricula. However, there is no necessary relation between business function and fitness for the moderator role. All that matters is that the moderator have the necessary people skills. Communication and interpersonal skills are crucial because the most important functions of the moderator are to build rapport and to probe for clarification. Because these two activities lie at the heart of any good interview, detailed discussion of them is postponed until the next section. Can team members take turns playing the moderator role across interviews? Certainly. Can two team members take turns within an interview? Probably. Taking turns across interviews makes sense if several people on the team have the necessary skills to be a moderator. Taking turns within the interview may make sense if very different topics, each demanding a different kind of expertise, will be covered. What doesn't make sense is to take turns at the moderator role simply for the sake of sharing or team building. There is work to be done, and you want the person most capable of performing the work of moderating to take that role.

Listener Role

The fundamental responsibility of the listener is to take good notes on the content of the interview. You might ask why such notes are necessary, as in many cases you will also tape-record the interviews. The explanation is that audiotape suffers from a key limitation: It is not a random-access storage device. This means that if you want to compare and contrast customer responses, across 12 interviews, to a question asked during the middle of each interview, you have a very laborious task ahead of you if you must rely on tape recordings alone.

Moreover, tape recordings quickly become voluminous, with most of the content being of little interest. Besides, who in your organization really has time to review 20 tapes, each 2 hours in length? And who will authorize the thousands of dollars required for a complete set of transcripts? Rather, the key advantage of tape recordings, and the justification for them, concerns those few rich interchanges within every program of visits that demand to be listened to several times, in their entirety. Hence, whether or not a tape recorder is used, in most cases the analysis of customer visit data must be carried out using the detailed notes taken by listeners.

A set of notes can be spread out over a conference table, copied, cut up, sorted by topic, and so forth, thus facilitating analysis. An approach used by some people to facilitate the note-taking process is to expand the discussion guide to fill 10 or 20 pages, leaving lots of white space between each topic. In this way, notes can be taken in a semiorganized fashion, thus making subsequent comparisons and contrasts between interviews that much easier. The combination of tape recordings (so that you can review certain passages and, if appropriate, share them in all their complexity with other decision makers) with detailed content notes is an important part of the discipline underlying a programmatic approach to customer visits.

In addition to taking notes, the listener should also strive to listen "between the lines" of what is being said. (If there is a three-person team, this responsibility can be assigned to the observer.) As mentioned earlier, face-to-face communication is an extremely rich communication channel, and the kinds of information being offered by the customer go far beyond the content of the words spoken. The listener should attempt to construct a global impression of the customer, including their level of sophistication, their emotional hot buttons, and their underlying priorities. The moderator is far too busy managing the flow of conversation and framing future questions to adequately handle these tasks.

Part of the justification for distinguishing the moderator and listener roles is to reinforce the point that effective moderating is a demanding task that leaves neither time nor energy for note taking (and also that note taking is a demanding task that gets in the way of good moderating). In general, moderators should refrain from taking any content notes whatsoever during the course of the interview. Jotting down reminders to oneself about questions to ask or topics to return to at some later point in the interview is, of course, both acceptable and necessary. Nonetheless, if the moderator is doing his or her job, he or she will be fully occupied managing the interview and framing questions, and literally cannot take notes. The importance of freeing moderators from note taking was brought home to me several years ago when I worked with a visit team from a computer company. They had invited me to accompany them on their initial pilot visits to serve as an interview coach who would observe their conduct of the interview and offer feedback on the strengths and weaknesses of their interview style. For this project, the computer firm wanted to visit value added resellers (VARs)—small, independently owned firms that bought the company's computer hardware, packaged it with their own software, and sold the result as a total solution aimed at a particular market niche. At one point during an interview, the president of the VAR began to express what it felt like to own a small business dependent for its success on the whims of this multibillion-dollar computer firm. It was clearly an emotionally rich moment and a topic of discussion that held considerable implications for the strategic choices that had motivated this computer firm to conduct the visits with VARs in the first place. The moderator also grasped the significance of the moment and began to scribble furiously to get this valuable material down on paper. As a consequence, he broke eye contact, bent his head down, and lost the opportunity to nod sympathetically and draw the customer into an extended reflection on these matters. In sum, he abandoned his primary task as a moderator by usurping part of the listener's role. He should instead have placed his confidence in the listener's ability to take notes, and devoted himself to drawing the customer out further.

Observer Role

If the team has three members, then you can assign one of them to the observer role. This person's task is to absorb the total communication presented by the customer. The observer does not have to manage the conversation, and the observer is also freed from the responsibility to take detailed notes. These two tasks will often demand the full attention of moderator and listener. Because the observer is freed from these tasks, he or she has the opportunity to think creatively about what is being said. Among other things, the observer should spend time thinking about specific questions, not anticipated in the discussion guide, that ought to be put to this customer based on their initial responses. The observer should also be comparing this customer to those previously visited, building all the while a model of the factors that determine the responses of different customers. In all respects, the observer should use his or her relative freedom from task demands to think about and process the content of the interview as it unfolds, and to consider how the later portions of the interview might be customized to capture uniquely relevant information from this particular customer.

If the team includes a very technical individual, or someone of high managerial rank, it is generally best to assign this person to the observer role, for both negative and positive reasons. On the negative side, very technical people are sometimes too easily distracted by topics of great interest to them but peripheral to the discussion guide, making them less-than-ideal candidates to play the moderator and listener roles. Similarly, high-level managers tend to be too quick to go into reassurance mode, promising "we'll take care of you," when it is really more important to probe for the root source of the complaint. Such managers may also be too readily distracted by big-picture issues to serve as diligent note takers. On the positive side, the very technical person and the high-level manager are exactly the people who can benefit most from the observer role. You want these individuals to be freed from the mundane tasks of managing and recording the interview so that they can really think about what is being said, and soak up the full richness of this face-to-face encounter with customers.

The advantages of the observer role for executives were brought home to me when I moderated some visits for the president and vice president of a small publishing business. The president, who, like most individuals in his position, had many hours of customer meetings under his belt, was struck by both the comfort and the opportunity to reflect that the observer role afforded him. He contrasted it favorably with those situations where he had to run the customer meeting himself. He felt more relaxed and more able to articulate the essential questions that had to be asked of each customer.

On a final note, it is important not to be overly rigid in carrying out these roles. Although the moderator will ask the majority of questions, any member of the team should feel empowered to ask a question from time to time. In fact, both the listener and the observer should function as a backstop for the moderator. Inevitably, over the course of the visits, a moderator will miss the significance of some remark, fail to probe for clarification, or simply lack the necessary background or perspective to ask the appropriate follow-up question. It is at this point that some other member of the team should clear his or her throat and interrupt with a comment such as: "Excuse me, if I could just ask one more question along these lines . . . " Obviously, such transitions can be handled well or poorly. An advantage of having one visit team stay together for 6 to 12 visits is that team members learn how to support one another smoothly (one never wants to look like the Keystone Kops). In any case, part of a team's preparation prior to its first visit in the program should be a discussion of how best to handle such transitions. The visit is truly a team effort and enhanced teamwork will improve the overall yield from the visits. One piece of advice for managing team involvement is to have the moderator look to his or her teammates at the conclusion of each major topic, and invite them, silently or out loud, to jump in if appropriate.

INTERVIEW SKILLS

The Proper Attitude

The most important thing to remember is that you are not there to interrogate your customers. Your model is *not* Mike Wallace of *60 Minutes,* and it is not Ted Koppel of *Nightline.* You are not an investigative reporter, you are not a credit analyst, you are not a police sergeant, and you are certainly not a prosecuting attorney.

Instead, imagine that you are taking a long flight and discover that the person next to you has just returned from Costa Rica—one of several destinations you are considering to celebrate your tenth wedding anniversary. In this situation you would pursue a directed conversation with this person. You would want to learn anything and everything they could tell you that would help you decide whether or not to go to Costa Rica, and what to do if you went. In a word, you would treat your seatmate as an expert informant. That is exactly the attitude you want to bring to the customer visit: This person across from you is an expert on what it takes to do their job using your products, and you want to tap into that expertise. In turn, you are a curious listener eager to understand and assimilate the perspective of this knowledgeable person to whom you have just been introduced. If you can maintain this attitude, you will avoid most of the worst sins in a customer interview.[1]

SIDEBAR 12

Problem: You Start to Sell During the Interview *This is most likely to occur when you are exploring reactions to a product concept or program initiative, rather than approaching the customer with a blank slate (realistically, blank slate visits are not all that common, because in most technology markets technical advances are occurring all the time, and product policy is always evolving). In trying to avoid the trap of selling, it helps to remember that during a research visit customer objections are to be explored, not overcome, acknowledged, rather than denied. Or, as Peter Drucker once remarked, "The aim of marketing is to make selling superfluous." You don't want to sell the customer; you want to learn what kind of product this customer would clamor to buy. Experience suggests that the selling trap is very common, extremely seductive, and quite hard to avoid.*

In view of the audience for this book, many of whom are people whose training lies outside of the social sciences, I would also like to offer you this reassurance: Most professional interviewers got that way without receiving very much formal training. Interviewing has always been a skill learned on the job. In fact, if your training were to consist of nothing but a 1- or 2-day course on conducting customer visits, this would probably place you at the median among practicing professionals in terms of amount of training for interviewing. People mostly learn how to interview by doing interviews and learning from their mistakes. You can develop your skills further through reading books such as this one, observing role models, being self-critical, and simply growing older and wiser.

It is best to approach interviewing as more art than science. Think of it as a craft or skill; do not approach it as a process that can be precision engineered. Think of the interview as a messy, human event, full of surprises, and ultimately uncontrollable. There *are* rules of thumb; practice *does* lead to improvement; and procedures *can* be developed to improve your conduct of interviews on average and over time. But a good qualitative interview is always going to remain an improvisational, extemporaneous event.

SIDEBAR 13

Problem: You End Up Talking More Than the Customer
It is important to avoid long-winded introductions because you want to set the expectation right away that the customer will do much of the talking. In general, you would like the customer to speak 75% of the time, with your participation mostly taking the form of questions. One cause of excessive talking by the interviewer happens when the customer starts to interview you. It is often tempting to answer customer questions in order to show off your expertise (more validly, you don't want to seem overly withholding or controlling). But as often as not, when the customer asks you a question of the type, "How fast is the transfer rate?" your best response would be along the lines of, "How fast should it be/do you expect/would you need?" This reply provides an opportunity to discover the task that drives demand for this aspect of product functionality, and it may also serve to reveal the customer's own metric. The customer's metric may have nothing to do with bits per second, and everything to do with some much more concrete and holistic test that the customer will actually apply during a purchase decision. For example, "Fast enough that I won't have to interrupt this other task to wait for it." A metric cast in terms of "no waiting" differs fundamentally from a bits-per-second metric, and may suggest rather different avenues for product development.

Finally, let me warn you away from a tempting but ultimately bankrupt solution to the anxiety you may feel concerning interviews. In most bookstores you can find a scattering of paperbacks with titles such as *Master the Secrets of Body Language,* and *How to Discover What She's Really Saying.* The premise underlying all such works is that you can manipulate the outcomes of an interpersonal encounter if only you grasp certain techniques that the author promises to reveal. An example of the kind of dictum found in such books might be, "Always assume the same body posture as the interviewee. If they cross their legs, you cross your legs. If they stroke their chin, you stroke your chin. This will create a bond of sympathy between the two of you that will allow you to steer the encounter as you wish."

In the context of customer visits, I strongly discourage you from seeking or following such advice on how to successfully manipulate people. The argument against attempting any such maneuver is twofold. First, you want to avoid any mannerism that smacks of sales behavior. Sad to say (as a marketing professor, it particularly hurts to admit this), salespeople in this culture have acquired a reputation for relating to people by means of a bag of interpersonal tricks designed to unduly influence others. One of the most disruptive things that can happen in a research visit is for the customer to conclude that the real purpose of the interview is to push something. Second, you probably think of yourself as a sophisticated and savvy individual who is not easily manipulated. And, when you realize that a sales maneuver is being applied to you, your immediate response is probably to become guarded and self-protective. You should give your customers the benefit of the doubt and assume that they too are savvy people who are likely to react in the same way. If so, then attempting such manipulation is probably the single most damaging thing you could do during an interview. Of course, if you find yourself spontaneously mirroring the customer during an interview, don't be horrified—it's a natural human response. And, of course, that's the real key to successful interviewing: be yourself. True, a cleaned-up and edited version of yourself, with certain unproductive habits removed; but authentically yourself, rather than a puppet moving according to some manipulative design. An engineer who is genuinely trying to understand what a customer needs is going to have a positive impact, even if he or she is something less than poised, articulate, and charming.

Moderator Skills

The most common mistake made by beginning moderators is a failure to probe. The ability to ask probing questions is something every moderator should strive to develop. To probe means asking for clarification when an answer is opaque, difficult to follow, or uncertain in its implications. It means recognizing when your initial question hasn't really been answered and finding a way to ask that question again in a more effective way. It means pursuing a topic in depth rather than settling for a superficial overview.

SIDEBAR 14

Problem: The Information Uncovered in the Interview Is Shallow, Vague, or Not Particularly Helpful *This is most often due to a failure to probe. It might also come about when your questions focus on features rather than the underlying conditions that create a demand for those features. Remember that form follows function: The most important thing is to understand the task the customer is trying to accomplish, and the context for this task—how it fits into the customer's larger business objectives. It is task demands that ultimately drive demand for product features, and a focus on task demands will be much more productive than collecting a wish list of desired features.*

To illustrate the importance of probing, suppose you work for a manufacturer of instruments or computers. During the interview, you inquire about what the customer is looking for when they buy this product. He or she replies, "Well, it has to be easy to use." If you simply make a note of that and proceed to your next question, you have missed the whole point of in-person, in-depth interviews with customers. Incorporating *easy to use* into the emerging specification for the new instrument won't do you a bit of good. Let's face it, *ease of use* is probably the single most unilluminating term in all of engineering today!

To probe means that you bring further definition to the customer's request. Do they mean easy to learn? Or do they want the operation to be intuitive with respect to their current ways of working? Or, do they mean the instrument has to be equally accessible to experts and novices alike? Is their comment a function of problems using the manuals that accompany the existing model, or a deeper concern with the basic design of the user interface? Only when customer visits yield information at this level of specificity do they begin to contribute to improved product design.

To probe also means that you expect, and are prepared to elicit, second, third, and fourth responses to an open-ended question such as "Please describe some of the problems you have been unable to solve using this product." Thus, the interviewer's favorite expressions include "Anything else?" "Can you give me an example?" "Why do you say that?" and "Are there any other reasons?" The experienced interviewer expects to have to dig for information, even with very cooperative customers. Probing is required because customers do not naturally or habitually express themselves in an analytic, self-aware, or detailed way. By contrast, the novice interviewer, anxious that the interview should proceed smoothly, applies a model in which each question is supposed to be followed by a single complete answer, which is supposed to be followed by the next question, without delay or diversion.

Skillful probing clearly requires a light touch. Although you must be persistent if you are to learn everything you need to know, you must never browbeat the customer. You must be alert to indications of customer impatience or exhaustion with a topic. Tone of voice and manner are crucial in communicating a sincere desire to learn (as opposed to a brusque demand). Case in point: There are two entirely different tones of voice you can use in asking *why*. The first tone sounds like this: "Why (would you do a stupid thing like that)?" This is not the tone you want. The second sounds like this: "Why (help me out here, I'm missing something)?" This tone suggests an attitude of incomplete understanding, very helpful in drawing out the customer.

Probing is the first of two important skills demanded of moderators. The second skill is the ability to quickly establish rapport with a wide range of different types of customers. As mentioned earlier, rapport is a relationship of trust and empathy in which the customer feels free to express his or her perceptions and emotions, without fear of ridicule or rejection. The greater the rapport, the harder the customer will work for you, and the greater the depth and richness of the information you will obtain.

To some degree, the ability to establish rapport with a stranger is probably based on personality, character, and temperament—things that you cannot change about yourself. This is why you need to pick the person on the team with the best interpersonal and communication skills to be the moderator.

Nonetheless, whatever the natural limits imposed by your character and temperament, there are specific things you can do to improve your ability to establish rapport. Most of these fall under the heading of removing obstacles to rapport. To cover this topic in seminars, I invite two people, one after the other, to come to the front of the room, where I ask each of them the same question. However, I pursue this question using two very different styles. In one case, my tone of voice is peremptory and my manner brusque. I do not look the person in the eye. I interrupt their answers with tangential questions. I am somewhat cold and curt; I look often at my watch. I take out my wallet and examine papers in it. I fidget constantly. As you might expect, the person I am interviewing soon becomes discombobulated; in some cases, he or she is simply struck dumb. With the next person, I proceed differently. My tone of voice is warmer and my questions less abrupt. I look at the person as he or she speaks, and I nod in response. My later questions follow logically from the answers to earlier questions. My body is turned toward the person, I sit in a relaxed fashion, and my manner is calm. This interview, as you can imagine, is much more comfortable for the respondent and yields far more information.

The point of this exercise is that small things you do with your body, your face, and your tone of voice can have a big impact on whether the customer wants to invest time and energy in the interview. We have all had the experience of talking to someone who seemed receptive and interested in what we had to say. Such a response stimulates us to speak at length, to speak with more feeling, and to go to a greater depth. Most of us have also had the experience of being questioned pro forma, without any sign that the questioner really cared about our responses. In customer visits you want to be perceived as an attentive listener, one who communicates in many small ways that he or she regards the interview as a valuable experience and a good use of his or her time.

Most of us know and unconsciously practice at least some effective bits of body language: the nod, the responsive smile, the receptive manner, and so forth. You want to build on this foundation, without going off the deep end and engaging in the sort of manipulation decried earlier. Similarly, most of us are saddled with one or two ineffective mannerisms, of which we are quite unconscious, but which interfere with the effort to establish rapport. Case in point: Some of us, when we listen hard, wrinkle our forehead into two vertical lines. You know you are concentrating—but what does your customer see? Someone frowning at them, for no discernable reason! Part of conducting visits as teams is giving constructive feedback to one another concerning ways to improve rapport.

Having raised the issue of rapport, it is important to emphasize what is *not* required of you as a questioner. You do not need to be enthusiastic, excited, or emotionally moved by the customer's statements. In fact, you should at all costs *avoid* trying to reward or stroke the customer with replies such as "Terrific!" "Great idea!" "Neat!" and "How interesting!" There are three problems with such attempts. First, such attempts tend to remind customers of unfortunate experiences where they were bamboozled. Second, the customer is unlikely to believe you in any case. This is deadly, because you must not give the impression of insincerity. Third, if you say "terrific" on several occasions, sooner or later you are going to omit this response (maybe you were distracted, or didn't understand a remark). Immediately the customer is going to wonder what was wrong with this most recent remark—why was it *not* a terrific thing to say? Overall, the customer will perceive that his or her responses are being evaluated rather than registered. If some remarks are terrific, then it follows that others are probably terrible. "I'd better watch what I say" is the likely response, and this is not the mode that you want the customer to adopt.

A useful concept for understanding the proper attitude to strike in developing rapport is the notion of *unconditional positive regard,* which is taken from client-centered psychotherapy. This is best explained by contrasting it with *conditional* positive regard. You show conditional positive regard when you act positively toward someone only so long as they behave themselves. In other words, as long as the customer speaks positively about your product, you are all smiles and warmth; but when they begin to speak positively about a competitor, your manner grows cold and distant. Conditional positive regard has been shown to have a variety of negative effects on an interview. Such a manner (which we would colloquially refer to as "critical and judgmental") causes the interviewee to speak less, to invest less of himself or herself, and to give more shallow and superficial responses. The essence of unconditional positive regard is that the content of what the customer says has no effect on the tenor of your response. The customer may be pleasant and engaging, or difficult and gruff. They may like your product or criticize it severely. They may be a smart and sophisticated user, or a slow and thick-headed one. You treat them all with the same respect, curiosity, and interest. Each one is a customer, and each one is important to understand.

Probably the most difficult test for technical people doing customer visits is the encounter with the unsophisticated or less capable user. This is where rapport is most likely to slip or fail. As one manager (jokingly) remarked, "The problem with our division is we only want to sell to people who are as smart as we are—and that's a very small market." No, no, no—you want to sell to people who have money, period! You have to ask yourself and your engineers: Are there really any stupid customers? Or are there just customers who you haven't yet figured out how to satisfy? Sometimes one of the most beneficial impacts of the customer visit on engineers is that it brings them face to face with the real world of nontechnical users. If rapport can be maintained during the visits, a real change of heart on the part of engineers may result. Absent such encounters, engineers often focus on the needs of technical users like themselves or hobbyists who are highly involved with the product.

Implicit in these remarks about rapport and unconditional positive regard is the requirement that as an interviewer you maintain some degree of control over your face. You have to be able to restrain, or refrain from showing, your instinctive reactions of dismay, disdain, or disappointment. This can be difficult! Such discipline is essential, however, if you are to avoid chilling the atmosphere or biasing the results of the interview. Of course, it is precisely the difficulty of masking one's reactions when passionately involved with the issues under investigation that originally led to the use of neutral outside professionals in standard textbook approaches to market research.

In summary, the idea of unconditional positive regard helps to delineate an effective middle ground in terms of the moderator's self-presentation within the interview. That is, you don't want to project an unsustainable enthusiasm, or seem insincere. At the other extreme, you should not try to maintain some kind of poker face from which all human reaction has been purged. It's quite all right to appear startled, confused, or struck by some remark the customer has made. You certainly don't want to come across as an impassive psychoanalyst or as some kind of blank slate that offers no reinforcement. Rather, you are a professional with a job to do. Your job is to understand everything you can about this customer.

Although probing and the ability to establish rapport are the major skills required of the moderator, there are several other skills that are desirable to have or develop. Perhaps the most important of these is *tenacity*. Effective probing requires you to be tenacious: to keep digging. The importance of tenacity was brought home to me during some of the initial Hewlett-Packard customer visits in which I participated. My initial bias was that as a professional interviewer, I would be much better at asking good, unbiased questions than these HP managers. I quickly discovered that I was mistaken on this point; it turned out that they were just as capable as I was of framing a useful and productive question. But what I observed time and again was that a manager would ask a good question, and the customer would bobble the answer—just not understand the question at all. Whereupon the manager would nod, smile, and go on to the next question. That is not tenacity! It is imperative that you continue to pursue your questions until you have an answer. Remember that although customers will almost always *reply* to your questions, that reply is often not really an *answer*. You have to listen, note that the question was not answered, and find a way to pursue the matter further.

If you are going to be tenacious, then you had better be fluent! It is important to be fluent because otherwise your tenacity may come across as a kind of interrogation: "You didn't answer my question. Now I am going to ask it again . . . " Good moderators are able to ask the same basic question in half a dozen different ways. Fluency is also important because every customer has a different cognitive style. A phrase or choice of words that is transparent to one customer may be opaque to another, so that it helps to be able to frame questions in a variety of ways.

Other skills that are useful to acquire include the ability to think on your feet (so that you can capitalize on unexpected developments), a good memory (so that you can summarize customer comments), and the ability to paraphrase a customer's comments in order to check your understanding. Here is a counterintuitive point about paraphrases: You should be content if the customer rejects about 50% of your paraphrases. To see why, suppose that the customer were to accept 100% of the paraphrases you offer. If so, then you are probably paraphrasing too often or at points where it is unnecessary, as in the following example:

Customer: Your spooler really stinks.

You: You seem to be having difficulty with our spooler.

Rather, you should attempt a paraphrase whenever you find yourself thinking, "Did he understand my question?" or "I'm a little confused here," or "Did he mean X or Y?" Assuming you can trust your instincts, quite often these are points where you have not correctly understood the customer, hence he rejects your paraphrase. Provided your ego is not hung up on being correct all the time, his rejection should please you because you will certainly learn something from it. Of course, if the customer can accept none of your paraphrases, it will be difficult for him to believe that you are really listening.

Please do not mistake my meaning here. I am not saying that you have a quota to fill when you paraphrase. I am saying that you should only (and always) paraphrase when you feel a real need to check on your understanding. As that instinct develops, you will naturally find that a good portion of your paraphrases are rejected. This is a sign of success. In other words, in those instances you did need to check on your understanding. Every one of your paraphrases should be made in good faith, with each representing your best attempt to say what you thought you heard. But necessarily, many will not be quite accurate, thus allowing the customer to correct your misunderstanding.

Listener Skills

Listening is the responsibility of everyone on the visit team. Indeed, perhaps the ultimate challenge in customer visits is learning how to really listen. I like to joke that, "In America nobody listens— your spouse doesn't listen to you, your boss doesn't listen, your kids don't listen, your employees don't listen. Nobody listens!" Alas, the joke is all too true. Listening is not a widely practiced skill. One of the reasons that customer visit research, when done well, is rewarding for customers is that to be listened to, intently, for 2 hours, is such a rare and delightful experience.

Effective listening in the context of customer visits has a number of components. The most important task of the designated listener is to grasp and retain the *specificity* of what the customer said.[2] What often happens instead is that an almost instantaneous process of translation and assimilation intervenes, with the effect of masking and distancing the impact of the customer's words. The danger is particularly acute when the subject matter is highly technical and the temptation to apply one's own in-house jargon almost irresistible. For example, suppose the customer says, "I never could make head nor tail of your manuals." If the listener only makes a note to the effect that "Ease of use is a concern," much is lost. The customer did not say the instrument was hard to use; he or she said the manuals were difficult to understand. There is little point in putting your decision makers into direct contact with customers if they are automatically and immediately going to impose their own frame of reference! Similarly, if the customer says, "Our maintenance funds were slashed this year," it does little good to note down, "Cost of ownership is important to this customer." The customer was much more specific than that. Certainly, it is true that once the interviews are completed, you may conclude that cost of ownership is the underlying theme that unites a variety of comments. However, it is premature during the interviews themselves to substitute this abstract term at the expense of the concrete, specific remarks made by the customer. Instead, the most effective analyses will be firmly based on a record of what the customer concretely said, with abstraction naturally progressing over time rather than usurping the initial fact gathering.

Part of listening for specificity is staying alert to *context*. The great advantage of in-person interviews conducted by managers themselves is the opportunity to explore the total gestalt of the customer's buying and using experiences. Specific remarks, even when transcribed verbatim, are of limited usefulness apart from the context in which they were spoken. Key to the discipline of listening is integrating separate remarks made at different points of the interview into a global perspective. This is a matter of realizing, for instance, that the customer at hand is not very technically sophisticated, and understanding how their lack of technological expertise has shaped a variety of specific reactions to both your own product and the alternatives offered by your competitors.

A third aspect of good listening is the ability to recognize and retain the *range* of customer responses discovered over the course of the interviews. A great danger in doing one's own market research is truncating this range. Suppose that you have explored reactions to a product concept in six interviews. Three customers liked the concept, one didn't understand it, one disliked it, and one gave a response difficult to characterize. Too often, the conclusion drawn from such a set of interviews is, "most customers responded favorably." In other words, the inconvenient responses, that were not positive, have disappeared from view by the time the analysis is completed.

In one example from my own experience, we were asking a customer how they felt about putting the operating manuals for a computer system onto videotape. In the first week's visits in Los Angeles, response appeared quite favorable: "Sure, everyone has a VCR in the office," "Yeah, nobody reads anything anymore," or "That way you could demonstrate with live action how to handle such and such a problem." Next week in Denver, reaction was quite different: "That would never work, the VCR will always be in some other room," "You really need a combination of personal tutoring plus manuals," and so forth. The proper conclusion, then, was that some people liked the idea (with specific reasons indicated) and some disliked it (again, with specifics noted). You should expect that many conclusions from customer visits will take exactly this form of "some customers felt X, other customers felt Y." This kind of qualitative research conducted with small samples often does not allow for anything stronger or more definitive. Hence, it is crucial that you not truncate the range of responses uncovered through the visits. Given the high degree of variability inherent in small, nonrandom samples, for all you know the response heard only *once* in six interviews may actually be the single most common response in the population at large. Remember that customer visits can discover that certain responses exist and define their character, but can seldom estimate their frequency in the population at large (see Chapter 9).

The fourth component of good listening is the ability to understand responses in *depth*. Good listeners look beneath the surface of what is being said. The richness of face-to-face communication makes it possible to assess the emotions underlying specific responses. Listeners should come away from an interview with a firm grasp of the most emotionally powerful moments for the customer. Similarly, listeners should note the nature of the emotions that color specific comments. Listeners should always be asking themselves, "What is this customer really saying?"

One final tip is useful in communicating to the customer that the visit team truly is listening. Where possible, you should draw connections to previously made remarks. A natural point at which to do this is when you experience a sudden connection between what is being said now and something said earlier. Go ahead and share such realizations with the customer. In a way, this proves that you are listening. Whereas, if you review the earlier discussion about building rapport, you might recognize that many used car salesmen have mastered all the positive mannerisms that were described—and we know they don't listen! Drawing a connection to something said 20 minutes earlier is strong evidence that you are paying attention.

Observer Skills

It is more difficult to be specific about what the observer should do. Ideally, the observer is intelligent, capable of imaginative understanding, and a big-picture thinker. Ultimately, a good observer is simply a quick learner and an analytic thinker. A more concrete suggestion is that the observer should play with the development of frameworks or models within which responses by various customers can be compared. The observer should be intimately familiar with key business or technical issues and should constantly ponder the implications of specific customer statements with respect to these central issues. The observer should be integrating information from different parts of the interview, and comparing this interview to others in the program. The observer should always strive toward a conceptual level of understanding.

FIVE DIFFICULT
INTERVIEW SITUATIONS

Many of your customer visits will be relatively pleasant and uneventful; at worst, a little dull. However, if you make it a practice to visit customers, then over the years you will inevitably encounter some of the situations described next. These represent some of the difficult situations that I have been quizzed about repeatedly in the course of teaching workshops on customer visits. Each is followed by some suggestions on how to cope.

The Customer Repeatedly Goes Off on Tangents

The important thing to realize here is that the "office" you hold—your role as an interviewer—allows you a latitude of behavior that is not granted to you when your mother-in-law comes to visit. Specifically, you have the privilege and responsibility of making strategic interruptions. When you encounter this situation, you might let the first tangent or two go on without interruption. It is probably early in the interview, you are still building rapport, and you want to allow for the fact that this customer may have a roundabout way of expressing him or herself. If the tangents continue, you can begin to cut them short by carefully interrupting the customer. *Carefully* means that you always attempt to project a humble and apologetic manner when you interrupt. You want to *nonverbally* express the following: "I wish we could pursue this topic at more length, but I know your time is limited and we must move on." (You shouldn't say this out loud because it would sound disingenuous.) Your ability to interrupt without giving offense rests on the fact that at some level the customer understands that you are here to do a job and that you will naturally be more interested in some topics than in others.

In terms of how to interrupt, you wait for a pause, even a micropause in the customer's delivery, and then you telegraph your desire to enter the conversation. This is a matter of opening your mouth, beginning to lift your hand in a gesture, and starting to speak: "Bob, I . . . " If the customer has worked up a good head of steam, it may take more than one attempt to actually break in. Make sure that your telegraphing becomes a little more vigorous each time. I can assure you that it takes a real bulldog to survive more than four or five progressively stronger and more obvious attempts to enter the conversation! Turn taking is the norm in human conversation, and if you signal that you want to speak, sooner or later you will get a chance. Then, you should ask a timely and relevant question to bring the conversation back on track.

However, there is one situation where you should *not* attempt to interrupt and redirect a customer. This is covered later under the heading of the hostile or upset customer.

The Customer Appears to Contradict Himself or Herself

You must not let perceived contradictions pass without investigation. Any time you perceive a contradiction there is an opportunity to learn something. Perhaps you heard early in the interview that the customer had four installations. Later, they mention six. In answer to your query, they might explain that they have four installations here and two more at another site—something of which you were unaware until this point and which may be important to understand.

Of course, you must be very careful when you follow up on a contradiction. You don't ever want to give the impression of asking, "John, are you lying to me?" Again, you want to adopt a humble tone and manner, and communicate nonverbally that "I must have missed something," so that you must seek clarification.

Sometimes what you will learn, as you attempt to resolve an apparent contradiction, is that this customer may indeed be lying, or at least, withholding information. Perhaps this customer has already made some commitment to a competitor's offering, and they don't wish to reveal that fact. Because it is difficult to successfully maintain a fiction for 2 hours, you have started to notice inconsistencies. If you believe that a customer is in fact lying or withholding information, it is best to back off and let the matter drop—there is no point in pushing your luck by playing detective or cross-examiner. Rather, this may be an interview that you have to bracket, because you can't trust the information received.

The Customer Is Argumentative

Within a research context, you cannot win an argument with a customer. If you prove you are right, you humiliate them and they don't want to talk. If you are proven wrong, you humiliate yourself and they don't want to talk to you. The solution is not to get drawn into arguments in the first place. This can be very difficult advice to follow for some technical people. A customer's negative statement about a certain technology often functions like a red flag waved in front of a bull. If the technical person's ego is hooked or if the customer appears to be mistaken, the urge to jump in and lecture, instruct, or educate can be irresistible. But resist you must; few things are more injurious to the proper atmosphere for a research interview than a team member who tries to score points in a contest with the customer.

Although arguments are to be avoided, a challenge directed back at the customer may sometimes be appropriate. It was pointed out to me that some highly technical customers would occasionally make an argumentative or inflammatory comment about a technology as a means of testing the technical competence of the interviewer. The purpose of such comments was to see whether the interviewer was sufficiently knowledgeable to be taken seriously. Hence, the invitation to argue functioned as a kind of test. If you are a technical expert and you find yourself in a situation where the customer has stated something like, "Everyone knows Unix is a dead end as far as desktop computing is concerned," it may be appropriate to respond to the challenge, in a very polite and mild-mannered way, as follows: "I'm struck by your comment. From our perspective, Unix has the advantage of X." Then pause and wait for the customer's rebuttal. Through skillful questioning from that point, you should be able to identify the perceived strengths and weaknesses of the technology in question from the point of view of this customer (and, at the same time, establish that you are sufficiently knowledgeable to be worth the time and attention of this expert).

Note that if you were not being challenged and tested, a better reply (because it is more open ended) to the customer's statement about Unix would be, "What are Unix's most important limitations, as you see them, in the case of desktop computing?" It is only when you believe that you are being tested that it is appropriate to go one step further and name an advantage in order to establish your credibility. Again, the difference between challenging and arguing is that in an argument, someone must win or lose, with all the ego impact that those words suggest. In a challenge, you identify and explore areas of disagreement, without a need to prove anything. Finally, this discussion of challenges and arguments shows once again why it is not advisable to send marketing people out alone on customer visits while leaving engineers at home. Many technical people in customer organizations are simply not interested in talking to a marketing person and will not agree to be interviewed on that basis. You will not gain access to these people unless the visit team includes someone whom they regard as a technical peer. And, sometimes that status has to be earned.

The Customer Makes Negative Remarks
About Your Product, Plans, or Capabilities

Sooner or later, a customer will criticize your product. More specifically, they will criticize something that you personally have slaved over for months or years. This is the acid test of your ability to successfully carry out a program of customer visits. You have two choices: get defensive or seize this opportunity to learn. The instinctive response, of course, is to respond in an overtly or subtly defensive way: "You don't understand—that's not a problem, it's a product feature!" Or, "If your people were better trained, this wouldn't be an issue!" More subtle forms of defensiveness are also possible, as when your probing becomes more aggressive and more insistent in locating the root cause of the complaint in some incapacity of that customer. But, as soon as you become defensive, the research portion of the interview is over.

As Harry Truman used to say: "If you can't stand the heat, get out of the kitchen." There are great advantages in having product designers meet customers face to face. But a prerequisite for success in this endeavor is a willingness to listen to bad news as well as good, and sufficient professionalism to remain unruffled while the customer tears into your pet project. In all honesty, I expect many of the people who attempt customer visits will fall short on this count, at least initially. It is not in most people's nature to take kindly to criticism. There are good reasons why the textbook model of market research emphasizes the use of objective, unbiased outsiders to conduct interviews: It is easier for outsiders to remain unfazed by criticism. It's not their project, it's not their promotion, and it's not their career on the line. An outsider can easily smile and then follow up on a comment such as, "Your user interface comes right out of the Stone Age!"

With practice, self-criticism, and a commitment to excellence, you can learn to take criticism gracefully. What helps is the realization that negative comments from customers may be among the most valuable moments in the entire project. Critical comments, particularly if they uncover what could potentially be a "lock-out" failing (i.e., a deficiency that automatically excludes you from bidding for the business), may in themselves pay for the entire program of visits. After all, when would you prefer to hear bad news—during product development, when there is still time to do something about it, or after the product has been introduced, as an explanation for its failure?

Of course, if you are conducting these visits for inappropriate reasons, as when you go out in search of confirmation for design decisions you've already made, then it is not going to be possible to comfortably receive criticism. Similarly, if you have attempted to mix selling and research objectives into a single visit, you will find it difficult to respond appropriately to negative comments. An important part of selling is responding to and overcoming customer objections. A good salesperson knows that turning around an objection is often the key to closing a sale. A good researcher knows that it is important to identify, explore, and fully understand the roots of an objection, and that granting it legitimacy is the key to obtaining this understanding. Alas, the two responses are not compatible. Furthermore, mixing troubleshooting and research objectives also makes it difficult to respond appropriately. If you are there to solve problems, then either the customer will expect, or you will be inclined, to make commitments or promises in response to complaints. A researcher does not make promises; he or she attempts to understand.

Your ultimate test in responding to negative comments will come in those cases where the comment is wrong—that is, when the customer is mistaken as to the facts or is ignorant of the larger context. You are likely to experience a powerful temptation to correct them, to explain the situation. Nonetheless, you should resist the temptation, partly because the temptation stems from ego (a desire to show that you are right) and partly because it has deleterious effects on your research agenda. It's fun to be the expert and to display your superior knowledge to the customer, but that's not why you embarked on these visits. Worse, the customer is all too happy to have you play expert; that yields more immediate rewards than assisting you in your research. As a consequence, once you begin correcting and educating the customer, it may be difficult to resume the role of researcher. Besides, your attempts to correct their misunderstanding are all too likely to sound defensive.

In certain cases, the customer's negative remarks will stem from a problem that you *do* know how to solve. You've encountered the problem before, and a workaround has been devised or a more recent release has fixed the bug. Again, my advice is to wait. Do not offer this solution immediately. Instead, mention it at the end of the interview. After all, you do want to solve customer problems, but not at the expense of your research. Even better: Call the local field or support office after the interview and let them be the hero. If you're the hero, then you're the one who will be called the next time this customer has a problem—and it is probably not in your personal best interest, or in the interests of your organization, to add customer support to your other responsibilities.

The Customer Is Hostile Toward You or Your Firm

Negative remarks about a product are one thing; hostility presents a more daunting challenge. This hostility may be relatively cold or relatively hot; in the latter case, the customer is going to be upset, angry, or emotional. The crucial thing you must do in response is to let the customer vent steam. You must let the customer rant and rave for as long as it takes, without getting involved in a wrangle.

This is one circumstance where you must not attempt the kind of strategic interruption described earlier. I emphasize this point because you will often be tempted to cut these hostile interchanges short and move on to more productive areas. This is particularly true when the customer is upset about a decision in which you personally played no part (or which may involve a product sold by a different division entirely!). As the ranting and raving goes on for 20, 30, or 40 minutes, and you see the opportunity for executing your research agenda slipping away, you may feel compelled to break in and take back control of the agenda. Restrain yourself—that's like trying to put out a fire with gasoline. What the customer hears when you do this is, "I didn't get through to him. I better turn up the volume and let the tape play longer."

What you must do instead is patiently wait for the customer to run out of steam, even if this consumes an enormous amount of the time available. In most cases, you can expect this point to arrive after 30 to 50 minutes. In the meantime, you should strive to be receptive, concerned, and empathetic. You too are disturbed by the events the customer recounts. You ask clarifying questions as you normally would. Fundamentally you communicate that you accept the *legiti-*

macy of the customer's reaction. Eventually, the customer will run out of steam. They may even turn a little sheepish—here they have been ragging mercilessly on you for 40 minutes, and you weren't even personally involved. It is at this point that you look directly at the customer and, mustering all the sincerity and concern at your command, say something like, "Problems such as you have just described are one of the reasons we embarked on these visits. If I can ask you a few questions, this may help us to avoid future problems." Then, launch into whichever of your priority topics is most relevant and learn what you can in the time remaining.

If you can muster the discipline to listen patiently with genuine concern as just described, you will be able to turn around most initially hostile encounters. If your firm has been relatively successful at satisfying customer needs, and you have had good cooperation from the field in selecting the sample of customers to visit, then you may only encounter a hostile customer a few times in a hundred visits, and you will be able to turn most of these around. Even in those rare cases where the entire interview has to be sacrificed to the venting of steam (perhaps because you have been set up), all is not lost. It won't be the most enjoyable day of your working life, but it may be productive nonetheless. It is probably useful to be reminded from time to time that your firm is not perfect. And, many people have told me that when the customer is allowed to vent, even at the cost of the entire interview, that customer tends to be in a much better frame of mind at the next contact. Thus, you will have served the long-term interest of your firm in building customer relationships even if the session was most unpleasant for you personally in the short term.

There is one other response to the hostile customer that is best avoided. You might reason that because it is obviously inappropriate to brush off this customer, a helpful solution might be to actively agree with their criticism: "Yes, we certainly did screw up there." This is not wise. First of all, you don't know the full story, and there may be a tangled history to this dispute. Second, you may find your agreement used as ammunition by this customer in future disputes on this matter. Third, the local field and support offices, who ultimately bear responsibility for resolving this dispute, will not thank you for undercutting their position. The point here is that granting legitimacy to the customer's complaint is not the same as ratifying that complaint. The customer needs to feel that their upset has registered and been acknowledged, but that is all that is required from you within the context of a research interview.

You should also realize that the defusing tactics just described are not going to work very well if your firm has made a practice of ignoring customer complaints. If top management only cares about financial numbers and subscribes to the belief that your competitive strengths make it impossible for customers to defect, then your interviews are going to be stormier than otherwise. If this customer has told the last three visitors this same tale of woe, without visible result, then the patient listening proposed earlier is not going to be enough. Similarly, if you have been set up by the sales force, you are going to have to take the fall. If your sample selection did not exclude *hot sites* (i.e., customers known to be acutely unhappy), no amount of interview skill is going to rescue you. Recall that the customer visit is only one tool within TQM, and interview skills are only one competence among the many required for effective visits. Much else has to go right before the coping mechanisms described in this section can work for you.

NOTES

1. Although quite old, two of the best books to read to maintain this attitude are Merton, Fiske, and Kendall (1956) and Payne (1951). There are quite a number of more recently published books on interviewing, but these tend to have a narrower focus, with the bulk falling into four groups: (1) advice to managers on how to conduct personnel interviews (i.e., hiring, firing, promoting), (2) advice to psychologists, (3) advice to survey researchers who will use in-person interviews to collect quantitative data, and (4) advice to journalists. I suspect the typical reader of this book will find these to be too far afield. A better supplement would be the books on focus groups by Goldman and McDonald (1987), Greenbaum (1998), and Stewart and Shamdasani (1990), and the article by Wells (1974), which all have useful and pertinent things to say about how to interview customers.

2. This section draws heavily on Merton, Fiske, and Kendall (1956), who develop the ideas of specificity, context, depth, and range in considerable detail.

CHAPTER EIGHT

Completing the Visit Program

Just as preparation is crucial to the success of the actual interviews, so also follow-up activities are crucial to getting the most value from whatever has transpired during the interviews. Skill in interviewing is only a means to an end. What really matters is getting valuable information and performing the appropriate operations on that information so as to maximize its impact. If I were a hiring manager in a business where customer visit programs were growing more important and I had to choose between an individual who was a poised and articulate interviewer but could do little more than transmit the responses of customers, and another interviewer who was halting and somewhat clumsy in the interview but who had excellent analytic abilities in terms of processing what customers said, I would choose this latter person every time. You do not have to be poised and articulate to get value from customer visit programs (although it certainly helps), but you *must* be able to understand and interpret what customers have said.

171

DEBRIEFING

One thing you can do to improve the analysis of visit data is conduct a debriefing session *immediately* following each visit in the program. I do mean immediately: When you start the car to drive away from the customer site, start the debriefing session right then and there. The intent of the debriefing session is to begin the process of fixing in memory the key outcomes of each interview. Waiting until dinner that evening defeats the purpose. An interview is a complex and chaotic event that yields intangible as well as tangible impressions. These begin to fade as soon as the interview ends, hence the importance of holding a debriefing session right away.

More generally, the debriefing session serves three functions: facilitating midcourse corrections, jump-starting the analysis, and maintaining organizational harmony. The opportunity to make midcourse corrections is part of the flexibility of customer visits. As a team works through the 6 to 12 customers it will visit, it generally becomes apparent that some lines of questioning are working better than others. Similarly, new questions will occur, and new approaches to central topics will develop as the interviews proceed. In this regard, the debriefing session serves as an opportunity to edit and revise how the team approaches subsequent interviews. Although the core of the discussion guide must be preserved, lest the visit program fragment into a welter of idiosyncratic efforts, it is both necessary and desirable for the team to further elaborate the basic guide and make additions as the interviews proceed. The debriefing session provides a forum in which a team member can say, "This is not working—we have to try another approach here," or "Tom, that question you asked opened up a whole new domain. Let's be sure to ask it in the remaining interviews."

A second function of the debriefing session is to begin the process of analysis. As the interviews proceed, it becomes possible to compare and contrast each additional interview with those that came earlier. When a pattern is discovered or a unifying theme found, these can be shared with the team for immediate feedback, debate, and enhancement. There is often a fair amount of creative energy available during debriefing. The team has had to sit still and receive for 2 hours, and now has a chance to let loose with observation and speculation.

Because of its complexity, an interview often leaves rather different impressions on the members of the visit team. Also, because each team member brings his or her own filters and biases to the interview, which bits of information are retained and which forgotten may vary a good deal. Without a debriefing session, you run the risk that the engineer on the team will return and report one finding or interpretation, whereas the marketer returns and reports something quite different to his or her peers. These separate reports then propagate through the engineering and marketing functions. As a consequence, the findings of the visit program become one more thing about which the two functions can disagree. With effective debriefing, however, team members can correct each other's memories while the total gestalt remains fresh. This increases the likelihood that cross-functional customer visits will have a unifying rather than a divisive effect on the organization.

As a practical matter, you might organize your debriefing sessions around the following five questions:

1. What were this customer's most important points? (Use your discussion guide to give structure to this inquiry.)
2. Did the customer seem to have any unexpressed reservations?
3. How does this customer compare to those we interviewed earlier?
4. Is there any aspect of our interview procedure that we should change?
5. What new ideas did this visit stimulate?

You may also find it useful to tape-record your debriefing sessions. In a large visit program, these debriefing tapes can give a quick overview of those visits that were not personally conducted by the individual writing the report. The debriefing tapes may also capture some of the spirit of the creative interchanges between the team members.

ANALYSIS AND REPORTING

It is much easier to describe the nature, scope, and schedule for reports than it is to describe the process for analyzing data from visit programs. In fact, procedures for the analysis (as opposed to the collection) of qualitative data are probably among the least developed and most opaque aspects of qualitative research. Because the analysis of visit data also raises knotty issues of generalizability and the appropriate and inappropriate use of customer visits, discussion of the substance of these analysis procedures will be postponed until the next chapter. Suffice to say that 3 to 4 weeks should be allowed for the analysis of a standard-sized visit program.

In terms of written reports, two levels are almost always necessary in any substantial program of several dozen visits conducted by multiple teams. First, each team needs to write a *trip report* that captures the results from the customers they visited. And, the program coordinator needs to write a *summary report* that integrates the various trip reports.

Perhaps it is your feeling that many business reports are really no more than time-wasting exercises in bureaucratic obfuscation. Hence, it is worthwhile to ask, "Why bother? Why not just discuss the visit program findings among participants until an action plan evolves?" Three rebuttals come to mind. First, in many businesses, individuals change jobs frequently. Without a written record, it may be impossible to determine, after a year or two, what was learned during these customer visits and how a certain course of action evolved. Second, the written report brings together in one place all that was learned by the various participants and makes this learning accessible to a wider audience dispersed in space and time. Third and most important, to write is to think. The task of reporting serves as a spur to better analysis. The level of understanding required to execute a written report is more demanding than the level of knowledge that allows a team to comfortably conclude a meeting.

The trip report should be prepared according to a format that is standard for all teams in the project (ideally, this will reflect a consistent standard used by all visit projects conducted within the business unit). In this regard, several types of report organization are possible. However, in my experience a thematic organization generally is most effective.

A thematic organization presupposes a successfully concluded analysis of the visit data in which you have identified major insights, unifying principles, key contrasts, and the like. The best way to apprise a wider audience of these findings is to lead with the big news. That is, today everyone is busy and every one's inbox is stuffed. Hence, as early as possible in the trip report you must lay out the major finding, the big idea, the exciting insight. This is followed by the other themes that have emerged, each with its own subheading. Within each theme, you may want to present one or two verbatim quotes from customers to vividly illustrate the point being made. A summary section will often focus on similarities and differences between groups of customers.

The most common alternative to the thematic organization is the customer-by-customer account. This is generally less successful because it becomes repetitious at the level of themes, even as it makes it difficult for these themes to emerge clearly. This organization quickly degenerates into mere reporting devoid of analytic insight. Or, valuable insights get lost in a tide of verbiage necessary to recount the details pertaining to each customer. The only situation where this organization might make sense is when you have a small number of very large customers who account for the bulk of your revenue, so that your thought world really is organized customer by customer.

The summary report should be written at a higher level of abstraction than the trip report. It should integrate points made in the individual trip reports and resolve any discrepancies. Most important, the summary report should contain background and methodological material. (In a small study consisting of a dozen visits there may be only one level of report, in which case that report must discuss methodology.) Why was this program of visits initiated? What were the objectives? How was the sample selected? Who participated on the visit teams? What discussion guide was used? The point of all this material is to allow an individual who is distant from the project, in either time or space, to assess the relevance and the merits of this visit program vis-à-vis his or her knowledge needs.

When this is not done, institutional memory suffers. A manager once told me, "When I took over my new position I found a file drawer full of old customer visit reports. I was delighted because I thought these reports would provide me with an invaluable briefing. Instead, the reports were so lacking in contextual data, and so heterogeneous in structure, as to be essentially useless for the purpose of providing me an understanding of the division's customers and markets." It doesn't have to be this way. Well-written summary reports have an important role to play in building institutional memory.

There are a few other report components worth mentioning. First, if the visit teams have included decision makers, per the advice given earlier, then each level of report should list recommended courses of action, as judged by the visit team. Second, as discussed in more detail in the next chapter, visual representations provide a powerful means of conveying patterns in the data and should be featured in most reports. Third, an appendix may be included that contains a one-paragraph thumbnail sketch recounting some specifics for each customer visited. This appendix helps bring the sample alive. In addition to written reports, you might consider scheduling an oral presentation of the findings to an appropriate forum. Written and oral reports have offsetting strengths and weaknesses. Written reports are permanent, but every manager's inbox is overflowing with written material. Oral presentations are evanescent, but have the power to break through the clutter and get the attention of those present. The best approach is to ask the highest level manager you can approach to serve as host and be the source of invitations to the presentation. This works particularly well when the visits are conducted in the context of a business unit that is trying to improve its customer focus. At the presentation itself, have each team leader do a brief presentation on key findings. You can reasonably hope that a presentation of this kind will galvanize attendees to act on some of what has been learned from customers.

DISSEMINATION OF RESULTS

Although the key decision makers for the project in question should be personally involved in the visits, there will always be other people in the organization who should receive a copy of the report. It is the responsibility of the program coordinator to identify these people. One sign of an organization that is customer focused is that people in all parts of the organization spend a portion of their time thinking about customers and perusing information on customers. This is an argument for wide rather than narrow dissemination of the results of visit programs.

In larger business units where there is a considerable amount of customer visit activity, the challenge of disseminating results takes on a new aspect. Although each of the visit programs undertaken by various teams will be focused on highly specific issues of paramount concern to that team at the time the visits were conducted, each visit team will nonetheless also uncover findings of wider import. It is in the nature of qualitative research to be diffuse and wide ranging.

SIDEBAR 15

Problem: Analyses Are Too Solution Oriented *Because customer visits are seldom confirmatory or definitive, they mostly serve to set the stage for either follow-up research or a judgment call. With respect to the latter, many times in business it simply is not possible to do the kind of conclusive research that one ideally should. The important thing, when a judgment call must be made, is not to hide behind the customer visits and not to pretend that the visits provided the data that justified the decision. A sentence beginning, "I think that . . . " is a supportable statement based on 15 customer visits (or one visit, or no visits), whereas a statement beginning, "The data show that . . . " is unlikely to be true when 15 visits are all the data you have with which to evaluate two products, or infer how common some event is. Fifteen visits cannot show that one concept is better; but you may think that one is preferable, based on the visits in combination with all the rest of your experience. As a manager, I would always want to know what you think; but I would not want to be confused about which statements represent data and which represent your reflections on data. The conclusions that can safely be drawn from a small sample of unknown bias are quite limited, and as a matter of intellectual honesty it is important that analyses of visit programs respect these limits.*

Similarly, the essence of TQM is that many things besides defect rate or speed of performance may influence customer satisfaction. This poses the issue of what to do with visit findings that, however valuable and thought provoking, go beyond the intended scope of a specific project. Absent a plan for capturing them, such findings are likely to fall through the cracks and be ignored or slighted.

Here is one practical suggestion. In the case of a business that manufactured a variety of medical equipment, all of which was sold to hospitals, but each piece of which was the responsibility of an individual project or product manager, my recommendation was to hold quarterly meetings. At each meeting, the agenda would be straightforward: to summarize all customer visit activity undertaken by each product manager during the past quarter. More specifically, the meeting was to serve as an opportunity to compare notes, to cross-check perceived trends or emerging problems, and more generally to see whether each person might have a piece that, although trivial in itself, could be combined to form a larger picture. Such meetings can serve to diffuse best practices and to function as an early warning system for emerging trends in the marketplace.

As further discussed in the next section, the growth of intranets provides new opportunities for wider diffusion of and easier access to customer visit findings. The unique benefits of intranets—worldwide access 24 hours a day, automated indexing, cross-linking, and so forth—are perfectly matched to the needs of a large organization generating a fair number of customer visit trip reports that may possibly be relevant to a difficult-to-specify audience beyond the visit team. Blanket mailing of hard copy would be a terrible waste of paper; instead, posting to an intranet allows for serendipitous discovery on the part of others, especially if there is a culture of curiosity and learning.

STORAGE OF RESULTS

Most customer visit programs produce information that continues to be relevant for a long time after the visits have concluded and that deserves careful storage. Yet I can say with confidence, based on my experience of visit efforts at numerous firms, that most businesses have only begun to address issues of information storage. This is unfortunate. Advances in computerized text retrieval have vastly improved the ability to conduct searches of reports and other written information.[1] Moreover, most visit reports will be prepared on a word processor. It would be a relatively simple matter for a business unit to compile all the customer visit reports conducted by that unit into a free form text database and to analyze that database systematically both each quarter and opportunistically as the need arises. For example, one might search for every mention of a key competitor in visits conducted over the past year. What is the image of that competitor? How is it evolving? Such a database might also be useful for orienting new employees so as to help them get close to customers from the day they join your organization. From another angle, before undertaking a visit to a customer, wouldn't it be nice to pull up the reports from the last few visits your unit made to that customer? Might that not help you avoid reinventing the wheel, or going back to the same small circle of customers too many times?

It's easy to wax enthusiastic about the benefits of such a database and hard to understand why so few firms have done anything like this. Realistically, however, I recognize the obstacles to implementing such a database. First of all, it requires long-term planning (always rare). Such a database will not begin to achieve its potential until it has been in existence for some time. Second, the database needs to be implemented at the business-unit level or above. That means that visits sponsored by a variety of functions and under diverse auspices need to be brought together. Such organization-wide coordination is typically difficult. Third, the database is unlikely to yield immediate, substantial benefits to any single party. Hence, even given good intentions, the task of its development will always tend to slip to the bottom of the to-do list. That is a shame; the long-term value of such a customer visit database could be very high.

To conclude this discussion of storage, let me venture this observation: In the 1980s, some firms began to gain an advantage simply because they took the concrete step of personally visiting customers. As the 1990s proceed, however, simply visiting customers will no longer be enough. The advantage will move to those firms that conduct visits systematically, and who can extract the maximum value from those visits. By the year 2000, even that will not be enough. The ability to effectively store and search the constantly accumulating database of customer information will become a new source of competitive advantage.

CLOSURE FOR
CUSTOMERS AND THE FIELD

Your visit program is still not quite complete once the report is written and stored. You need to provide some kind of closure for customers. You want to lay the foundation for future visit efforts, you want to nourish any good will that the visits may have created, and you want to extract the maximum in public relations value. As a first step, the team leader might send out a brief thank-you note in the

---

SIDEBAR 16

Problem: Bad News Is Buried *Sometimes customers are quite harsh in their judgments. For all kinds of understandable reasons, you may be reluctant to fully report the bad news heard from customers. However, this reluctance can produce a situation where research is done but not heeded, with the result that the firm fails to become market driven despite good intentions. If research can only bring home good news, then it is not really research at all; it is politics. For your own protection, I would certainly encourage you to let the customer be the bearer of bad news, whether through direct quotes or the personal presence of your management during visits; but the bad news has to be communicated in some way while there is still time for the organization to respond.*

---

week following the visit. Second, some kind of letter or memo should go to customers once the analysis of the visit program is complete. You have to walk a fine line here. Because there can be no guarantee that such a letter will remain confidential, you cannot go into too much detail about what was learned or how you intend to respond. Once in a while, such letters will fall into the hands of your competition, and you do not want to give away your market research for free. But, neither can you afford a letter full of empty generalities. That will frustrate the customer, and provoke the thought that it was all a waste of time. Your goal is simply to communicate, in a convincing way, that you did listen and that customers' input is going to have an impact. If you are successful—if a customer comes away from the entire visit experience with a sense that it was a worthwhile use of time—then it is going to be much, much easier to recruit that customer to participate in future visit programs.

The field sales and support organizations need closure just as much as the customer. From their standpoint, arranging for you to conduct visits in their region has few immediate or tangible rewards. Yet, their cooperation is crucial to the program's success as developed earlier. You will find them more supportive of future efforts if you can establish that you learned something important as a result of these visits. You also should take this opportunity to share any information you gained from customers that may be directly and immediately relevant to the field. Again, the basic motivation is simply to show that something happened or will happen as a result of the visits, so that the field accepts that their time and effort was well spent.

NOTE

1. A text-retrieval program called ZyIndex is available for the PC (there are other low-cost programs available as well). Much more elaborate search capabilities are available in a program called Topic from Verity Corporation in Mountain View, California, and in the personal version of Digital Equipment Corporation's Altavista search engine. Text retrieval is an active focus of software innovation and you can expect to see a steady increase in program sophistication throughout this decade. Check a website such as www.yahoo.com for the latest software tools.

CHAPTER NINE

The Analysis of Visit
Data and the Question
of Generalizability

OVERVIEW

The analysis of survey data, by comparison with the analysis of interview data, is quite straightforward. Moreover, contemporary business education, together with the familiarity of questionnaires and survey research in American culture, combine to give most managers an intuitive understanding of how to analyze the results of a survey. The most important thing to recognize about the analysis of customer visit programs is that you must bracket and put aside any habits you have acquired in the course of analyzing answers to questionnaires. This is more difficult that it at first appears. Based on the seminars I have taught, most people who are new to customer visits are "closet" survey researchers. Their native and intuitive approach to analyzing visit data is to seek opportunities to express the results in terms of percentages; for example, "A total of 75% of the customers we visited preferred to pay for support services separately, rather than have them bundled into the product purchase price." Such a conclusion from visit data will almost *never* be appropriate or helpful. In fact, a rule of thumb is to avoid reporting percentage breakdowns or mean values as part of the analysis of visit data.

Those of you with more experience in conducting interviews will often have come to distrust percentages in the context of visits, out of an instinctive uneasiness with drawing anything so exact out of something so approximate as a set of exploratory interviews. But, as often as not, the fallback position is to use fuzzier language to state a similar sort of conclusion; for instance, "most customers preferred" as opposed to "75% of customers preferred." It is important to realize that "most" is every bit as suspect as "75%," and has neither more nor less validity. "Most," in this context, is nothing more than a fudge.

Whenever we use language such as "75%" or "most," we are drawing a conclusion about the incidence or frequency of some customer response. You will avoid some of the worst pitfalls in the analysis of visit data if you can discipline yourself to avoid drawing conclusions about how common or rare any customer response is in the population at large. By extension, you should also avoid conclusions about whether more customers prefer Option A relative to Option B, since such judgments ultimately rest on an inference that one response (i.e., a preference for A) is more common than another in the population.

This injunction is often difficult for seminar participants to accept. Typically, they feel under pressure to produce research findings that can be plugged directly into a spreadsheet or forecast. They may also sense that there will never be any research performed subsequent to the visit program. They indicate that their management demands precisely this sort of exact, definitive result from visit programs. However, once you understand how thoroughly sampling characteristics condition the kind of generalization that can be made, you too will be most reluctant to base conclusions as to the incidence of some phenomenon on visit data.

Here it helps to distinguish between two types of generalization that one might wish to make based on contact with a sample of customers (Table 9.1). The first type of generalization concerns the *incidence* of one or more phenomena in the population at large, whereas the second type of generalization concerns the *existence* of some subset of phenomena in the population. Note that incidence generalizations correspond to the ordinary use of the word *generalization* in social science research. An example would be a Gallup Poll finding that only 720 out of 1,500 voters surveyed intend to vote for the incumbent, leading to the generalization that the incumbent will

TABLE 9.1 Two Types of Generalization

Type 2: Existence (What Kind?)		Type 1: Incidence (How Many?)								
	10%	20%	30%	40%	50%	60%	70%	80%	90%	100%
A										
B										
C										
D										
•										
•										
•										
K										

NOTE: Let the set of elements **A** through **K** represent consumer responses or actions (e.g., various applications for an instrument). To make an incidence generalization one would attempt to determine how common any given application is in the population of consumers based on its frequency in the sample. To make an existence generalization, one would attempt to identify all elements of the set of k applications found in the sample.

lose the election by a 48% to 52% margin. The category of existence generalizations is a new one and represents an attempt to contribute to the discussion of the kind of information that qualitative market research can and cannot yield.

Here is an example of the existence type of generalization. Suppose that you sell an instrument that can be used in a variety of different ways in the manufacturing environment. Your research objective is to understand the sorts of applications that now exist and also those that are just now emerging. This corresponds to the "What Kind?" question that is characteristic of qualitative research (see Chapter 10). With respect to Table 9.1, your goal is to identify the set of K applications that are characteristic of the instrument usage of your customers. In judging the fitness of customer visits to this task, the question reduces to this: How likely is it that you will encounter, in your sample of 12 to 30 visits, at least one of each of these K applications? More generally, what is the probability that the *k* different applications enumerated in your sample reflect the K applications that exist in the total population of customers? Continuing with this example, suppose instead that your research objective were to determine the two most common applications for this instrument (perhaps you plan to segment the market based on application and wish to identify the two largest segments). Here, you would have to make a generalization of the first type, as to incidence. The question now is this: What are the odds that the frequency with which you found each application in your sample reflects the true incidence of each application in the total population?

As a general rule, the sampling requirements for an incidence generalization are much stricter than the sampling requirements for an existence generalization. Specifically, a larger sample, and a greater degree of representativeness, will be necessary if the percentage breakdown on applications found in the sample is to serve as a good indication of the incidence of each application in the population. A smaller sample, and a greater degree of bias, can be tolerated when we only wish to make an existence generalization. This involves a weaker kind of inference that places less stringent requirements on the sample.

The ability to make valid existence generalizations from customer visits is not absolute; it is limited by such factors as (a) how fragmented and various the applications for this instrument are and (b) how "bad" the sample of customers selected for visiting is. If there are 50 different applications, each present in between 0.5% and 2% of the customer base, then a customer visit program involving 30 customers is unlikely to be effective at exhaustively identifying the applications for this instrument. If, on the other hand, there are seven distinct applications, each of which is present in at least 10% of the customer base, the odds are good that a program of 30 visits will identify all seven applications. As to the badness of the sample, if you have drawn a tiny sample of seven customers, each of whom is a favorite customer of the only two sales representatives who would return your phone calls, then you may not be able to support even an existence generalization. But if you have drawn a judgment sample of reasonable size, as described in Chapter 5, then I think you will usually be able to support statements of the form, "There are seven distinct applications for this instrument" (recognizing, of course, that there may be N additional applications that are quite idiosyncratic or unusual).

One more illustration (this in the language of probability theory) may help to clarify the distinction between the two types of generalization. Imagine an urn filled with beads of different colors. You will be allowed to draw 30 beads from the urn. If, after you obtain your sample of beads, you must estimate what proportion of the beads remaining in the urn are black, what proportion are white, and so forth, then you have to make a generalization of the first type, as to incidence. If, on the other hand, your task, based on the sample of 30 beads, is to identify all the different colors of beads that may be found in the urn, then you have to make a generalization of the second type, as to existence. If there are five different colors, each of which accounts for 20% of the beads in the urn, then you almost certainly will be able to identify all the colors (i.e., successfully perform a generalization of the second type). However, the odds that your draw of 30 beads will allow you to correctly estimate that each color accounts for 20% of the beads are rather lower. Of course, if you had an opportunity to draw 200 beads from the urn, then the odds of making a successful generalization about the incidence of each color would go up considerably.

Continuing this example, suppose that the black beads in the urn lie mostly near the bottom. If you reach into the urn and grab the first 30 beads you find (a "bad" sample), you may miss the black beads altogether. Even if you take care to draw beads from several different parts of the urn (a metaphor for the advice given in Chapter 5), you might still come up with only one or two black beads. Hence, the danger of drawing conclusions from a small sample of customer visits of the form, *"few* customers are interested in X" or *"most* customers prefer product concept A." Hence, also, the relative safety of concluding "there are some black beads in the urn" or "customers gave three different reasons for their lack of interest."

The point of distinguishing between the two types of generalization is to explain why visit programs involving 12 to 30 customers cannot yield useful point estimates of the incidence of some customer response, with the basic problem being that the sample of customers visited is too small and rarely, if ever, a probability sample. I sometimes present this under the heading of "The Brutal Truth About Confidence Intervals." Suppose that you visit 16 customers during your program. Twelve respond negatively to some proposal that you broach, and four respond positively. This is where people are tempted to conclude that "75% of customers disliked the idea." Now, whether or not you have formal training in statistics, you probably recognize that 75% is only an estimate of the proportion of all customers who would dislike the idea if it was presented to them. The true proportion of dislike in the total population may be higher or lower than 75%. A confidence interval is the formal term for the band around the percentage obtained in the sample, within which the true population value is expected to be found were the research to be repeated an infinite number of times. Here is the punch line: Given an estimate of 75% dislike based on a sample of 16 interviews, we can expect, 95 times out of 100, that the population value will fall somewhere between 53% and 97%![1] Is that the degree of precision that you need in order to make sound business decisions? Note furthermore that this confidence interval, wide though it is, assumes that the 16 customers were randomly selected. If instead this sample was filtered through the sales force, then the confidence interval can only be wider.

In summary, it is foolish to state percentages in drawing conclusions from a typical customer visit program. The seeming exactitude of these figures is a sham. You are on much firmer ground when you indicate that customers who liked the idea gave the following reasons in explanation, whereas those who disliked it mentioned these other reasons. In naming and describing these reasons you are making a generalization of the second type, as to existence, which is more likely to be valid despite the small sample size and uncertain representativeness of the sample of customers visited.

ANALYSIS STRATEGIES

The baseline approach for the analysis of qualitative market research was developed decades ago. Although advances have been made in recent years, it is useful to begin with this baseline approach, inasmuch as it requires no special tools or procedures. The basic technique has been named "scissors and paste."[2] You begin by assembling the notes from all the interviews (or, if available, transcripts made from tapes of these interviews). You then cut up the notes and transcripts into smaller pieces, with each piece containing a single viewpoint, perspective, need, or fact. As you cut, you perform a sort. For example, verbatim quotes from customers that share a common theme would be put into a pile together. As you work through the entire set of notes or transcripts, the number of piles of clippings grows to reflect themes and clusters of responses. After everything has been cut up, you examine each pile resulting from the initial sort. You will often decide at this point to subdivide some piles, or group other piles together, and you may also find it necessary to reassign certain clippings to different piles.

Once you have finished this sort, the process of writing the report is straightforward. Each pile of clippings corresponds to a section or subsection of the report. The individual quotes or remarks can be juxtaposed, sequenced, situated, and elaborated in order to produce the content of the report. The sorting process stimulates the discovery of underlying themes and motifs. Seeing in one place the various comments on a topic made across all the interviews produces additional insight. Moreover, reviewing the verbatim quotes and the notes made by listeners helps to highlight what is missing from them: The more intangible and global impressions or intuitions that are an integral part of your learning, but that cannot be located in any single remark made by a customer.

In sum, the sorting technique works because the human brain is a pattern-finding organ. Confronted with all the material gained from the interviews, inevitably you will be able to weave a story that illuminates what has been learned. The greater your native intelligence, the more in-depth your knowledge of the product and market, and the more intense your engagement with the business problem that stimulated the visits, the more valuable this report will be.

A variation of the scissors-and-paste technique, evolved to meet the needs of engineering teams, takes a slightly different approach to stimulating the pattern-finding abilities of the human brain. To begin, the interview notes or transcripts are again separated into individual facts, reactions, and so forth. After an initial culling, these are reproduced on Post-it notes. The team adjourns to a room with a large expanse of bare wall. The task is to arrange the Post-it notes—individual bits representing the voice of the customer—into clusters that reflect themes and connections. Given enough time and commitment on the part of team members, the patterns identified (and augmented) through this exercise can be extremely valuable. A not unimportant side benefit is that the whole team will feel ownership of the resulting analysis.

VISUAL REPRESENTATION
OF VISIT DATA

In recent years, more elaborate techniques for the analysis of qualitative data have been developed. These go under a variety of esoteric names, and many reflect the actual or supposed practice of Japanese firms.[3] Perhaps the best known is the House of Quality, or quality function deployment (QFD).[4] The House of Quality describes a set of matrices for capturing and processing the voice of the customer. The core matrix has customer requirements as the rows and product design elements as the columns. (Note that customer visit programs are an excellent means of discovering these customer requirements.) A set of symbols is entered into the cells of the matrix to indicate how strong or weak the connection is between specific design elements and customer requirements. Other matrices incorporate other aspects of the design.

In its original form as a specific technique requiring a complex series of prescribed steps, QFD has not aged well in the 1990s—at least, that is what I gather from discussions with clients.[5] Unfortunately, the complete House of Quality is a bewildering mass of half a dozen or more intricate matrices requiring the mind of a Talmudic scholar to decipher. In practice, QFD too often led to analysis paralysis, in which accurate completion of the matrices, rather than timely delivery of a profitable new product, became the primary goal. However, the spirit of QFD, which I will define as "the impulse to graphically depict the voice of the customer in an analytically useful way," remains alive and well, and firms that have learned how to keep the process simple continue to benefit from the procedure. Hence, rather than asking, "Is QFD the best way to analyze customer visit data?" a better question is, "What kinds of visual representations can be used to gain insight into customer visit data?" Anyone making a serious study of this question will want to read *Qualitative Data Analysis* by Miles and Huberman, a work without parallel in this area.[6] What follows is a brief sketch of several possibilities for visual representation, intended mostly as thought starters.

Matrices

A matrix can be used to array items of information from two different domains against one another. One of the most useful matrices from the standpoint of customer visits is the core matrix or main room within the House of Quality, in which customer requirements function as the rows and key product features or design specifications function as the columns. Any such matrix facilitates two valuable kinds of analyses. First, note whether there are any empty rows. These indicate customer requirements that are not addressed by any design element and that may lead to customer rejection due to product insufficiency. Next, note whether there are any empty columns. These indicate design elements that do not relate to customer needs and that may lead to customer rejection due to product prolixity, or lack of cost effectiveness (the "Cadillac fallacy").

Some other examples of matrices that might be useful in the analysis of visit data include a matrix that arrays customer requirements as the rows against market segments as the columns. Here, the goal would be to capture and make readily apparent the key differences between market segments. Another possibility is a matrix arraying requirements as the rows against job roles as the columns. This kind of matrix may be helpful when purchase of your product requires a complex group decision on the part of the customer.

Although all the matrices mentioned so far make use of requirements, other matrices can be envisioned (for instance, a matrix that lists specific product applications as the rows and then lists problems, complaints, or bugs as the columns). The identification of requirements is a good example of the existence type of generalization described earlier. The goal of the customer visits would be to identify requirements that exist and understand each one well enough to complete the kinds of matrices under discussion. The visits will probably not be adequate to accurately rank order the relative importance of each requirement in the marketplace, but will lay a solid foundation for the kind of quantitative research that can accomplish that ranking.

In summary, any matrix will map one dimension or domain onto another and will allow you to code the intersection using a variety of symbols. One can note the presence or absence of a connection, its strength or weakness, and so forth, using an appropriate symbol. Hence, matrices help you to perceive relations across information domains.

Process Maps

The process map is another technique pioneered in the quality literature. It is basically a kind of flowchart that traces a complex process, especially one with multiple inputs or outputs, or one that may branch in different directions. One possible target would be the buying decision. A process map would allow you to see who enters the decision process, when, how they enter, what criteria are applied, what activities are undertaken by the various parties, and the like. All of this is captured in a single compact representation.

To appreciate the value of a process map, a comparison to the earlier matrix example may be useful. The matrix of requirements by job roles is useful in mapping the one dimension onto the other, but is static and limited in the amount of information conveyed. By contrast, the process map will be more useful for capturing events that develop over time and on balance can convey a larger amount and more diverse types of information. Some of the possible targets for a process map might include the installation of new equipment, the customer's troubleshooting process, or the transmission of information through the customer organization.

It is routine today to hear talk of "business processes." To the extent that this is more than a cliche, a mapping of these processes must be possible. If it is true that your product is designed to facilitate some business process, then it behooves you to construct good maps of that process.

Conceptual Tables

A conceptual table may be thought of as a set of vectors—the columns—each listing some category of information, which when combined serve to characterize some set of entities—the row elements. An example would be a table listing market segments as the row elements, the key themes that emerged from the visits with respect to each segment as the first column, some key pieces of evidence relevant to each theme as the second column, and action implications pertinent to each theme as the third column. A conceptual table is a device to jointly map more than two domains or types of information (conceptual tables are better recast as matrices if there are only two domains). Because each column can be structured differently in terms of number of items, and so forth, the conceptual table is an enormously flexible format for pulling together a diverse assembly of evidence. Thus, in the example, you may list three themes with respect to one segment, and five themes with respect to another; two pieces of evidence with respect to one theme, and four pieces with respect to another; and so forth. Tables can have four, five, six, or more columns, as needed. Thus, another example of a conceptual table might use columns to depict, for each application of your product, the specific competitors active in that arena, competitor advantages with respect to that application, competitor disadvantages, and action implications.

As shown by Miles and Huberman,[7] the whole technique of arraying qualitative data using matrices and other graphical aids holds great promise. I encourage you, after familiarizing yourself with existing work, to experiment with different types of graphical displays tailored to your specific situation. You need not assume that someone else, whether a Japanese firm, quality guru, or academic author, has already invented the best way to display and process the voice of the customer. In fact, the best ways to represent the voice of the customer have probably not yet emerged—the field is too young. You could be the pioneer.

SPECIFIC ADVICE FOR IMPROVING THE ANALYSIS OF VISIT DATA

Match Deliverables to Objectives

One of the most important benefits of having clearly stated and specific objectives is that these help to guide the process of analysis. For example, if you set out to identify new opportunities for distributing your product, then a list of the opportunities identified through the visits should be a centerpiece of your report. As your experience with programmatic visits grows, you will probably find that you are able to set more precise and achievable objectives up front. It is a grim task to attempt to make sense of a mass of interview notes generated as a result of a fuzzy and ill-defined search for customer input. Moreover, asking yourself, at the beginning of a project, whether you would be satisfied to come away at the end with a list of things identified is a good means of checking whether an objective of the type "Identify . . . " really captures your goal for these visits.

Always Include Verbatim Quotes From Customers

Please recognize that as a professional or manager, your write-ups of visit programs will tend to devolve toward that stuffy and vague style known as bureaucratese. This tendency can and should be fought, but it will continually reassert itself for reasons that are beyond your control. You are perforce aware of the political sensitivities of your audience, which causes you to hedge; your work will be reviewed by your superiors, which breeds caution; and at a fundamental level, you are interpreting the experience of other people, which produces a certain distance that robs your writing of the vivid and immediate qualities so characteristic of the interviews themselves. A partial solution is to always feature verbatim quotes from customers in any report. These can be used to headline a section, to make a point, to set up a contrast, to serve as flesh on the bones of a schematic analysis, or to provide an epigram at the conclusion of a section.

Customers sound like customers, not bureaucrats. Verbatim quotes serve as a reminder to readers that your information comes from the source—the people who buy your product. The rhetorical impact of "the customer says" is always going to be greater than "marketing thinks" or "engineering believes." Verbatims also reinforce the message that you conducted a kind of research that is distinctively capable of uncovering rich, detailed information. Each quote will generally do more than reinforce the point that it serves, conveying as well an impression of the world of the customer, the gestalt from which the specific findings spring. Of course, an organization or a management that does not wish to grow, or is not capable of changing, can find ways to reject even direct input from customers. But the virtue of direct quotes is that they make such rejection more difficult.

Include Both Conclusions and Recommendations, but Keep Them Distinct

A conclusion arises from the data. If valid, it should in principle be possible for another person, exposed to the same data, to draw the same conclusion. A recommendation comes from a person, and may draw on the data at hand, all the other data available to that person, and the unique skills and experiences of that person. Recommendations typically go beyond the data. Teams at any level of reporting should be encouraged to offer both conclusions and recommendations, and to keep them distinct. You don't ever want to be confused about which statements arise from the data and which arise from the author. You want both, but you don't want one to substitute for the other.

SIDEBAR 17

Problem: Lack of Management Support *One pitfall looms over all the rest: lack of support and understanding from management. The most difficult problems in executing visit programs are organizational and cultural. Does your management even believe in research? Is your management committed to investing in research? Are individuals at the project-manager level empowered to get and heed customer input? Negative answers indicate that even a visit program conducted according to all the precepts in this book may not succeed. After all, the customer visit is just one piece of the puzzle, and many other factors have to be in place before visits can truly benefit a firm that seeks to be market focused.*

Highlight Discoveries

Among the most appropriate uses of customer visits is to reveal to you what you didn't know you didn't know. You only have to hear of a new application or a new competitor once to learn of their existence. Hence, the analysis should always identify, discuss, and highlight those findings that are novel or unexpected.

Draw Contrasts

Encountering flesh-and-blood customers in all their immediacy and complexity often stimulates comparisons and contrasts. These may clarify differences between segments, between the demands of certain applications, or between usage environments. Such contrasts are a basic expression of the pattern finding that underlies all analysis of visit data and are to be encouraged. Due to sample limitations, most contrasts between groups should be thought of as tentative and awaiting further confirmation. However, such confirmation is unlikely to be found unless you go to the trouble of putting these contrasts on paper so that readers can relate them to other data they may have.

Provide Thick Descriptions

A thick description is one that provides both detail and context. A great advantage of any form of field research (thick description is an anthropological term) is the wealth of information gained simply through being there. It is often useful to provide a thick description of the customer's task environment: what they are trying to accomplish through purchase of this product, what other tasks interface with the primary task your product accomplishes for them, and how the primary task advances their overall business strategy. The observational component of a customer visit program—the tour of the plant—is often very helpful in working up such a thick description.

Generate Hypotheses

A small and biased sample is no bar to generating possible connections or causal linkages. In fact, this sort of learning is characteristic of good exploratory research. If customer visits are part of a research program committed to the use of multiple and overlapping research techniques, then one can legitimately assign to the visits the task of uncovering potential causal links to be confirmed or disproved through subsequent research. Asking the visits to be the source of hypotheses, rather than to provide a conclusive answer, is one means of avoiding pitfalls and getting the most value from your research effort.

Stay Alert to Parables and Epiphanies

The point of customer visits is not to pin down specific facts but to gain new insight. Because customer visit data will always be quite limited as to generalizability, the important thing is to focus on what you learned as a result of exposure to these customers. For instance, a parable is a teaching story that instructs how to act properly. Perhaps you heard a story that made vividly clear why a particular competitor is so successful in taking away a certain kind of customer—and what you would have to change in order to successfully respond to this challenge. Reproduce that story so that it can have a wider impact within the organization. An epiphany is a moment of realization where everything comes together into a gestalt. Customer visits lend themselves to epiphanies, and you should build on any that occur when you conduct the analysis and write the report.

NOTES

1. To compute a confidence interval around a proportion, first find the standard error, which is equal to the square root of $P \times Q/(N-1)$, where P and Q are the two proportions (e.g., 0.75 and 0.25) and N is the sample size. Then multiply the standard error by 1.96 and add and subtract the result to the proportion of interest. This gives the 95% confidence interval.

2. See Wells (1974) for a discussion. Like so many other aspects of customer visits, the literature on focus groups is helpful in suggesting analytic techniques that might be applied.

3. The Center for Quality Management has sponsored a number of studies of QFD-like techniques, including work by Gary Burchill at MIT's Sloan School.

4. See Hauser and Clausing (1988) and American Supplier Institute (1987) for an introduction to QFD, and Griffin (1991) for some empirical evidence.

5. See Griffin (1991) for an account of how QFD has fared in specific applications.

6. For a recent example of how matrices can be used, see Brynjolfsson, Renshaw, and van Alstyne (1997).

7. The most sophisticated account of how to analyze qualitative data is Miles and Huberman (1994). Although the context of their work—evaluation of educational programs—will be remote for most readers of this book, the serious student of

qualitative data analysis needs to grapple with their work. An encounter with Miles and Huberman is also useful for escaping the faint air of mystical reverence that sometimes surrounds the adoption of Japanese analysis techniques by American managers. The basic idea of arraying qualitative data in some kind of matrix is far more general and flexible than its implementation in the House of Quality.

CHAPTER TEN

The Customer Visit
in Perspective

Customer visits constitute an important part of the total market research effort because they offer a distinct mix of advantages and disadvantages not duplicated by any other market research tool. You must remember, however, that no customer visit effort, no matter how well designed, can replace a comprehensive market research effort. Good research planning means finding the proper place for customer visits, neither neglecting visits nor giving them undue prominence. Hence, the goal of this chapter is to position customer visits within the context of the larger market research toolbox.[1] It is intended in part to serve as a check on any excess enthusiasm that may have been generated in the reader.

I sometimes begin a seminar by telling participants that one of the most valuable outcomes of the course might be that they will decide *not* to do a program of customer visits, because they have learned that other, better techniques exist to address their particular information needs. In this connection, I suggest that they think of the market research discipline as a toolbox containing a variety of techniques, each one of which is optimized for certain information-gathering purposes, but no one of which is an all-purpose tool. Given this metaphor, it would be foolish to talk about a hammer being a better tool than a screwdriver, and similarly it is not helpful to think of customer visits as a better tool than market experiments or a worse tool than survey research. A screwdriver is a fine tool, unless you need something with which to drive a nail. A hammer is a very useful thing to have, excepting those situations where you must set a screw. Continuing the metaphor, your task under a market orientation is to build an understanding of customer needs. It would be freakish indeed to try to build a house using only a wrench and no other tool. Similarly, building your understanding of customers requires that you flexibly combine different market research tools and that you use the right tool for each task. There are many ways to learn about customers, and it is just as important to recognize when customer visits are inappropriate and the wrong solution as it is to appreciate the unique value of customer visits.

SOME HELPFUL DISTINCTIONS

The market research toolbox contains a couple of compartments that are useful for grouping together similar research techniques. Among the most important of these distinctions are qualitative versus quantitative research, exploratory versus confirmatory research, and market intelligence gathering versus market research projects. A brief review of these key distinctions will facilitate a discussion of the research planning process and the place of customer visits.

Qualitative Versus Quantitative Market Research

A contrast that organizes and illuminates many controversies about the capabilities of specific research techniques is that between qualitative and quantitative research.[2] The major qualitative techniques include focus groups, customer visits, and in-depth interviews, whereas the major quantitative techniques include survey research (whether in person, or by phone, mail, e-mail, or Web) and experiments of all kinds, including choice modeling techniques such as conjoint analysis. Contemporary MBA education, along with the technical backgrounds of many managers in technology firms, tends to bias business people in favor of quantitative research techniques. In fact, surveys based on large probability samples, and experiments designed for causal inference, are precise techniques that are ideal for giving accurate answers to questions such as: "How many?" "How much?" "How often?" and "Which one?" The results of these procedures can be projected to the larger population of customers, and bias is minimized. It is important to recognize that many of the decisions faced by business people require a survey or experiment for optimal results. As discussed later, one of the classic errors in research planning is expecting customer visits to take the place of a survey or experiment.

What is less often realized is that there is a very different type of question, no less important in business, that requires another style of research. This question takes the form of "What kind?" rather than "How many?" or "Why?" rather than "Which one?" It concerns the essential quality of some response, rather than its quantity or frequency. In other words, it seeks to identify members of a set and grasp these essential qualities, rather than determine whether one member of the set is more common than another (see Chapter 9). Typically, the best way to answer such questions is a loosely structured interview. When the decision maker conducts the interview (i.e., a customer visit), there are enhanced opportunities to make discoveries and achieve in-depth understanding. Discovery and understanding are just as important to business success as precision and accuracy. Sometimes what you need is not a number, but a picture; not a count, but a contrast; not a significance test, but an illuminating anecdote. Under those circumstances qualitative research is the way to go.

Exploratory Versus Confirmatory Research

You perform exploratory research to widen your horizons, expand the number of decision options, and in general to make room for discoveries, new insights, and alternative perspectives. You perform confirmatory research to separate truth from supposition, to discard ineffective decision options, and in general to focus on the one or two best alternatives, explanations, or frameworks available. Exploratory research generates questions; confirmatory research selects answers. You can readily see that exploratory research typically will be performed prior to confirmatory research, so that in many cases *early stage* can serve as a synonym for exploratory and *late stage* can serve as a synonym for confirmatory. However, exploratory research can also be done to better understand specific troublesome results achieved in the course of confirmatory research, thus reversing the standard sequence.

As a general rule, customer visits are incapable of achieving the goals of confirmatory research. The only exception is when you have a very small number of large customers and you essentially visit all of them. In the more typical case, all of the problems discussed in Chapter 9 render customer visits unsuitable for confirmatory purposes—namely, the use of small, nonrandom samples, variance across visits in interview procedures, problems with interviewer bias, and so forth. In a word, it is difficult to prove anything with customer visits.

Market Intelligence Gathering
Versus Market Research Projects

A market research project is a specific data collection effort generally designed to assist in making an upcoming decision. Market intelligence gathering is an ongoing effort, proceeding on diverse fronts, designed to identify trends, stay on top of changes in the marketplace, and stay close to customers. Market intelligence provides the foundation for specific research projects. When intelligence gathering is absent or rudimentary, specific research projects tend to grow unwieldy, as they are asked to do too much or too many different things. Much market intelligence makes use of data gathered by other people or for other purposes (industry reports, sales history, etc.). By contrast, market research projects are conducted by the firm or its agents for the explicit purpose of answering a current question.

Ad hoc customer visits represent market intelligence gathering, whereas customer visit programs are an instance of a market research project. Thus, the number of customer visit programs a business unit conducts will typically be limited in number, in contrast to the number of ad hoc visits. Similarly, specific customer visit programs are facilitated when there is effective harvesting of ongoing ad hoc visits along with other market intelligence.

RESEARCH PLANNING

To select a research tool intelligently requires an understanding of how research fits into the overall process of business decision making. Table 10.1 gives a simple four-step model of decision making.[3] For example, suppose that your overall strategy dictates development of a new generation of some instrument. At the earliest stage of your decision cycle, your research question will be some version of "What's going on?" You want to understand how the present generation is being used, what customers like and dislike about the existing product, and so forth. As you gather information, your decision making evolves to the next stage: "What are the possibilities?" Here you will try to identify capabilities that might or might not be built into the new instrument. More generally, you will try to formulate specific alternative directions that your development work might take.

The third step is quite different. Resources are always limited and time is short, and you must begin to discard the least attractive options generated earlier and focus in on a subset of the data gathered. Hence, you must select the best option from among those available. In the fourth and final step, you evaluate the success of the decisions you made (i.e., the option-selection process). Did the ad campaign raise awareness? Did customer satisfaction improve? This evaluation of outcomes lays the foundation for the next decision cycle as new questions are raised.

More elaborate models of business planning are possible, and most firms have developed their own frameworks for this purpose. However, the basic distinctions between early and late, exploratory and confirmatory, finding possibilities and then evaluating them, generating ideas and then narrowing the set, are universal features of such models. The four-step model makes the point that customer visit programs will be most useful in Steps 1 and 2 in the decision cycle. Taking stock, looking around, getting a feel, stumbling on the unexpected, gleaning an idea, defining the opportunity, generating a hypothesis, exploring the possibilities—these are the applications where customer visits pay off. For BTB and technology firms, this can be put more strongly: When basic exploration is the goal, there are few good alternatives to customer visits.

From the beginning of my seminar teaching, I have found this point—that customer visits are of limited but crucial value—to be

TABLE 10.1 Decision Stages, Research Objectives, and Research Tools

		Tools	
Stage	*Objectives*	*Primary*	*Supporting*
Scan environment • What's out there? • What's going on?	Identify, Describe, Monitor	Secondary research, Customer visits	Focus groups, Surveys
Generate options • What are the possibilities?	Generate, Define, Explore	Customer visits, Focus groups	Secondary research
Select option • How much will we achieve • Which one is best?	Evaluate, Test, Select, Prioritize	Experiments, Surveys, Choice models, Usability tests	Secondary research
Evaluate outcomes • How well did we do?	Measure, Track	Surveys, Secondary research	Customer visits

among the most important messages to be gotten across. Participants tend to come to the seminars holding a position to either side of this happy medium. Either they do not recognize how important it is to get out and visit customers early in the decision cycle, or they have a naive faith that customer visits can function as an all-purpose research tool. At some firms, use of the customer visit has reminded me of the little boy with a hammer—to whom the whole world looked like a nail! At other firms, the obsession with hard, quantitative research, performed without any preparation in terms of customer visits or other exploratory research, highlighted the risk of getting wonderfully precise answers—to the wrong questions.

The gist of the research planning process is that there is a time and place for customer visits. Do visit customers early in the decision cycle. Do visit customers when your goal is to perform exploratory research. Don't visit customers when the goal is to narrow your focus and select the one best option.

THE MARKET RESEARCH TOOLBOX

Table 10.1 also arrays research tools against the four decision-making steps.[4] Secondary research is performed using such things as sales reports and accounting breakdowns, reports of previous primary research, government data, commercial databases, syndicated reports by outside research groups, and the like.[5] Secondary research will almost always be the quickest and cheapest kind of market research available to you. However, sooner or later you will face questions that have never been addressed before. This is where the three basic techniques of primary research become useful:

1. The survey
2. The interview, which can take the form of a focus group, individual interview at a central site, or a customer visit
3. The experiment, which might take a variety of forms, including

   a. Various kinds of choice modeling, such as conjoint analysis— analysis of customer preference for different bundles of product features, so that you can mathematically determine the utility of each feature.

   b. Comparisons of stimuli administered to two or more randomly selected groups of customers—as in research on product demand at different pricing levels.

   c. Usability tests—where customers encounter products or documentation under controlled conditions and their responses are observed and measured.

Secondary research is a staple of market intelligence gathering, whereas primary research generally takes the form of a market research project.

Many research tools can provide useful descriptive information to facilitate the first step in decision making. In particular, this is one of the strong suits of secondary data and of survey research. If you want answers such as "Our largest customers have slowed their rate of purchase whereas smaller customers have maintained their pace," then secondary data is often the place to look. Similarly, if you want to come away with an answer of the form, "This application characterizes 42% of the installed base, whereas this other application is present in only 10%," then you should probably conduct a survey.[6]

Interviews are also useful here, as long as description is understood to mean getting the lay of the land, or providing an in-depth profile of how the product is used. It is more difficult to find or generate *new* ideas and options through surveys and other conventional forms of market research. Although secondary data and surveys may occasionally be a source of suggestions or insights, the very best tools at this stage of the decision cycle are loosely structured interviews, especially when they include opportunities for observational learning. Hence, this is where customer visits are not only valuable but often essential.

Note that there is generally only one effective tool when the goal is to perform a conclusive test of options, and that is to conduct some kind of experiment. It is surprising how frequently I encounter businesspeople who nonetheless expect a dozen customer visits to reliably and validly evaluate consumer preferences with respect to a set of options. Stories are told of entire R&D efforts being steered down one path instead of another, based on a few interviews. I want to state in the strongest terms that customer visits are not the best tool when the goal is to evaluate two or more alternatives and select the best. The small sample size, the highly variable circumstances of interviewing, the possible bias due to the vendor name tag worn by visitors, the lack of random assignment of customers to test groups, and many other factors combine to make customer visits unreliable as a test of preference (see Chapter 9 for more on this point).

Lastly, customer visits are of limited use in evaluating decision outcomes. Secondary research and surveys will generally be the best choice here.

CUSTOMER VISITS COMPARED TO KINDRED TECHNIQUES

In my experience working with managers attempting to decide whether to do customer visits, I have encountered three areas of confusion with particular frequency. Many of the questions that could be addressed through customer visits seem as if they might also be pursued via survey research. From another angle, many of the virtues of customer visits, as developed earlier, are similar to the kinds of things one hears in discussions of the focus group technique.[7] Lastly, accounts of the benefits of usability testing suggest an overlap with customer visits. Hence, a more in-depth comparison with these three related research techniques may be helpful.

Customer Visits Versus Survey Research

Early in new product research, or when undertaking a fundamental examination of customer satisfaction, survey research is generally not suitable. The reason is that so much is unknown at this point. Customer visits tend to be more useful than surveys when you don't know precisely what questions to ask, you don't have a clear vision of the person who will have to answer those questions, you can't be sure that their answers will make sense, and you can't even state in writing your really interesting questions because they are too complex and depend too much on answers to previous questions. *That* describes a situation where you need to do in-person visits. An interview that you personally conduct with a customer allows you to explore, make discoveries, refine understanding, and pursue complex inquiries at length and in depth. The rigidity of the question formats in a survey and the narrow scope of freedom allowed to the respondent make the survey technique unsuitable when discovery and exploration are the goals.

By the same token, customer visits make a poor substitute for surveys when your purpose requires exact numerical results. Surveys, when properly conducted on a large probability sample, are very effective at identifying the frequency, incidence, or average value of a wide range of phenomena, including specific applications, typical level of expenditure, most common equipment configuration, evaluation of competitors, and so forth. If your purposes require a reasonably precise comparison of subgroups, a large sample survey is ideal. More generally, if your primary questions about customers are fundamentally in the form of yes-no, choose-from-a-list, or rate-on-a-scale questions, then you probably want to do a survey. Put another way, if the answers to your most important questions could best be represented in a tabular display of numbers, or in a chart or graph, then you probably shouldn't rely on customer visits—a survey is more likely to produce the data needed for that table or graph.

Customer Visits Versus Focus Groups

A focus group, like the customer visit, represents a kind of qualitative interview technique. The first thing to remember, faced with a choice between the two, is that most of what customer visits cannot do, focus groups cannot do either; each is a kind of interview and each is limited by this fact. However, there are shades of difference that can occasionally make the focus group the more advantageous choice. For instance, focus group research allows the sponsor to remain anonymous through the use of one-way glass and a professional moderator. This anonymity can be a crucial advantage when investigating brand perceptions, service quality, and the like. A videotaped record can also be made, so that a wide variety of people in the organization can encounter the same customer input. Moreover, the use of an outside professional to moderate the groups may increase the objectivity and credibility of the analysis.

On a more subtle level, conducting several focus groups may be one of the best ways to get your bearings in a totally unfamiliar situation. A fundamental process that occurs in a group discussion held among strangers is the search for common ground. Watching, say, nurses search for this common ground in front of your eyes, when your entire business effort has heretofore been directed at medical technologists, may reveal basic assumptions that characterize the nurse perspective. A second process that occurs in groups is polarization. As the discussion proceeds, the group tends to split into factions (a good moderator can help orchestrate this). Customers are free to challenge one another and argue points in a way that the moderator or interviewer is not. These arguments can help you understand the diversity of viewpoints that may exist among customers with respect to some issue.[8] For that reason, focus groups are an excellent tool for identifying points of difference between market segments. Although a program of customer visits can also reveal commonalities and key dividing points among customers, on the whole, the focus group is probably a more efficient tool—or at least, a better place to begin—if this kind of understanding is of primary interest.

A final advantage of any group discussion is that participants can help one another. That is, there are many issues important to vendors that are simply not top of mind for many customers. In a one-on-one interview or customer visit, a customer may draw a blank when queried on these matters. Faced with that nonresponse, there are strict limits on how much coaxing or prodding an interviewer can do, without violating the canons of unbiased, open-ended interviewing. By contrast, in a group discussion, there are 8 to 10 opportunities, corresponding to the number of participants, for that query to click with a customer. Moreover, the response given by the first group member to answer can serve as a retrieval cue for the other participants; similarly with second and third responses. Hence, focus groups become advantageous when you anticipate that the central topics of your inquiry are not top of mind for many customers, so that it may be difficult for them to respond individually at any length. Similarly, if you expect that you only have 15- to 20-minutes worth of interviewing with each individual customer, it is far more efficient to schedule a group than to arrange interviews with these same 8 to 10 individuals.

Despite these specific merits of the focus group, I tend to think that overall the customer visit will be more advantageous and have wider applicability in the case of BTB and technology markets.[9] A key advantage of customer visits is the ability to pursue highly technical issues at length. The professionals who moderate focus groups, by contrast, typically are not physicists, software engineers, chemists, and the like, and often cannot probe deeply enough or grasp the opportunity to ask crucial follow-up questions. As you can imagine, it is quite frustrating to sit behind a one-way mirror, helpless to intervene as a crucial issue is dropped. Similarly, in a focus group, an individual customer has at most 15 to 20 minutes of air time available. Is that enough for one of your customers to fully acquaint you with their circumstances, business strategy, and product needs? If not, then you have to consider whether a series of customer visits might be more productive. Another difficulty with focus groups is that they are essentially a laboratory procedure. Customers are interviewed outside their workplace and apart from their fellow workers. Hence, none of the advantages of observation and field research accrue to focus groups. Moreover, all of the advantages of a group discussion are balanced by cognate disadvantages: conformity pressures, bandwagon effects, biasing influence of unduly vocal participants and so forth.

Lastly, you may be under the impression that focus groups are superior to customer visits when the purpose is brainstorming or idea generation. In fact, research in both psychology and marketing has demonstrated that when the goal is the maximum number and quality of ideas generated, then, say, four groups of eight people will be *inferior* to 32 individual interviews. The problem can be traced back to the air-time limitations and conformity pressures inherent in groups (the cuing effect of responses made by other participants also functions as a constraint on innovation).[10]

Hence, if you want to generate the greatest number of ideas, you will prefer customer visits to focus groups; whereas, if you want to focus on segment differences, particularly for topics not top of mind, you will prefer focus groups. There is, of course, no bar to conducting both customer visits and focus groups as part of a larger research project, and I have encountered situations where that dual effort constituted a good use of resources. In that scenario, I tend to think that the focus groups should be done first, as the more high-level and cursory technique, followed by customer visits, which can go into much more gory detail.

Customer Visits Versus Usability Studies

In usability research (actively pursued by many software firms), the goal is to examine the interaction between user and product. Almost all other kinds of market research focus on customer actions or reactions with respect to products or issues, and not on interaction. In usability testing proper, a laboratory setup is used. Customers interact with the product under controlled conditions and all interactions may be recorded. As an experimental procedure, usability testing can function as quantitative and confirmatory research—for instance, to select the best of two competing interface designs based on a statistically significant improvement in speed of task accomplishment or number of errors.

It is in usability studies more broadly conceived that one encounters some overlap with customer visits. In fact, at one level, "usability" is not a research technique but a research topic, analogous to market segmentation, advertising strategy, market expansion, new product definition, and so forth. Hence, the customer visit technique can be pressed into the service of usability studies just as customer visits can serve the purposes of market segmentation studies. This point is important because, in circles where the customer visit has never been separately conceptualized as a market research technique, one might react to this book along the lines of "Why, this is really about usability studies"; but that would be equivalent to saying, in another context, "Why, the customer visit is really just a form of segmentation research."

The confusion is compounded by the fact that marketing is often a weak function in software and other technology firms. Hence, usability professionals have sometimes stepped up to the plate and broadened their charge to include much of what would be classified as "strategic market planning" or "market research" in more mature firms. I think it is more effective to think of usability as a *topic,* one that may be relevant to strategic planning and also an appropriate focus for market research (of many kinds), while distinguishing usability testing—in the laboratory context—as a specific (and new) kind of market research *technique,* quite distinct from customer visits.

Whatever stance one takes on terminology, one important distinction between customer visits and the whole area of usability studies rests on the following: *Customer* has a much broader and more inclusive reference than *user. Customer* includes nonusers of the product category, decision makers who manage users, opinion leaders who influence purchasers, and channel partners, as well as product users. Hence, on the whole, the customer visit will be a research technique with broader applicability than any specific usability technique, especially those that take place in a usability lab.

TWO MISTAKES TO AVOID

To be very concrete, here are two danger signs that suggest that a customer visit program has been misused. The presence of either one of these telltale signs in a report alerts me that the visit program sponsors may not understand the limits of the tool.

Percentage Breakdowns

A percentage, by intention, is a context-free number. In a customer visit report, a percentage invites your readers to project the results of the visit program to the population at large, without even thinking twice. These percentage figures become particularly risible when worked out to the decimal point. I guess "67.5% agreed that" sounds quite a bit more impressive than "five of the eight customers we visited agreed that." The reality remains that you visited a small, nonrandom sample of customers using a highly variable set of questions and probes. Percentage figures give the lie to these limitations, and are to be avoided for that reason. In short, if you are going to do qualitative research, do it well and let it be itself—don't try to dress it up as something it is not by using the vernacular of survey research.

Go–No Go Tests

The other danger sign is a report that picks a winner or derives a go forward or kill the project decision based on the visit data alone. Any such judgment fundamentally rests on a comparison of two magnitudes. Product Concept A is judged the winner over Concept B because customer preference for A—a quantity—exceeded the positive reaction to B—another quantity. Selecting a winner or making a go-no go decision presumes that one has conducted appropriate quantitative research capable of precisely estimating quantities based on a large sample representative of the population of interest.

You may be dismayed by these strong statements, in part because of a sinking feeling that upper management is never going to authorize the budget needed for effective quantitative research. You may be cheered if I remind you of the distinction between a conclusion or recommendation, corresponding roughly to "The data show that" versus "I think that." Customer visit data can rarely if ever show that one product concept wins over another or that negative reactions exceed positive reactions. But you, as an intelligent manager who must act based on whatever information of whatever quality happens to be available right now, are always free to decide and recommend, based on your gut feeling and the gestalt of data available to you (e.g., customer visits, industry experience, strategic insight, etc.), that Product Concept A is in fact a better bet or that the project has to be a go. In other words, much of the time, managers do not have enough information to claim that "The data show" anything. Decisions must still be made, raising the question of when some data (i.e., customer visits) is better than no data. Generally speaking, doing some customer visits, rather than not doing any at all, will usefully educate a manager so that a marginally better decision can be made.

What you must avoid is claiming that you are acting on data, when in fact you have based your decision on personal judgment. Such dissembling undermines both managerial credibility and organizational accountability. Managers do not get promoted for mumbling that they need more data before they can act. The proper response to this fact is not to claim to have data that you do not, but to have the courage to stand up and say, "I think that." Take the credit, or the blame, for exercising judgment.

COMBINATION STRATEGIES
FOR CUSTOMER VISIT RESEARCH

The obvious solution to the limitations and restrictions highlighted in this chapter is to combine customer visits with other research techniques so as to capitalize on strengths and compensate for weaknesses. The following two combinations have widespread relevance:

Customers Visits Followed by a Survey. Here, the purpose of the customer visits would be to discover the key questions to be answered definitively by the survey research. Visits would reveal the issues that matter to customers, and the survey would determine what proportion of customers had positive or negative reactions to each issue, or the rank order of importance of each issue. In other circumstances, visits might identify the answer categories (e.g., what kind of applications for the product exist), and surveys would estimate the frequency of each answer category. In yet other conditions, visits might suggest key contrasts among customer groups or a possible segment structure, whereupon surveys can confirm that the differences do characterize the population, while estimating the size of each segment. The point of these examples is that a good survey requires that you already know a great deal about your customers and markets. Of course, any manager can construct a survey of some sort in an hour or two. But for that survey to be of much use, you must know which few questions out of the vast set of possible questions are worth pursuing and what answer categories are meaningful. In BTB and technology markets, customer visits may be the best means of obtaining that knowledge.

Customer Visits Followed by Conjoint Analysis. In conjoint analysis, and in choice modeling procedures generally, customers give their reaction to various configurations of product attributes. Given a large representative sample, mathematical analysis can compute the optimum price-feature bundle based on these judgments. As with surveys, any manager can generate a few dozen feature combinations with little effort, whereupon a good statistician can reduce these to the most efficient set for statistical estimation. But which features, from among the many possible features engineering could provide, really matter to customers? Which words for describing features would be most meaningful to customers? Which new features unanticipated by engineering ought to be examined?

Each of these questions can be addressed in an initial stage of customer visit research. The resulting conjoint analysis will be grounded in real customer concerns. Here again, identification of product attributes is logically prior to their prioritization, and identification is a discovery task that requires qualitative research. In other words, conjoint analysis is only as accurate as the information used to construct the product configurations. If important features are left out or misrepresented, then the mathematical analysis merely selects the most optimal configuration from a suboptimal set. Customer visits make this unfortunate result less likely.

SUMMARY

The advice in this chapter can be summarized as follows:

1. The less you know and the greater your uncertainty, the greater the value of customer visit programs.
2. The greater the intangibility and complexity of the issues under study, and the more the need for perspective as opposed to facts, the greater the value of visit programs.

These criteria help to illuminate what is unique about the knowledge contribution that customer visits can make to the organization. In terms of overall context, note that these conditions will almost inevitably arise in the course of efforts to develop new products or markets and efforts to improve customer satisfaction. There are other reasons for undertaking customer visit programs, but developing new products, entering new markets, and initiatives to improve satisfaction are prime opportunities for engaging in visits.

NOTES

1. See McQuarrie (1996) for an expanded treatment.

2. For contemporary thinking on qualitative and quantitative research, see McCracken (1988) and Patton (1990) and the references therein.

3. My rendition of the four-step decision model was influenced by materials developed in the mid-1980s by Professor David Stewart at the University of Southern California and Bill BonDurant, Director of the Market Research and Information Center at Hewlett-Packard.

4. For a more extensive discussion of the advantages and disadvantages of each tool, see Barabba and Zaltman (1991) and Churchill (1991).

5. See Stewart and Kamins (1993) for more information.

6. A good source of advice on survey design and execution is Dillman (1978).

7. Contemporary wisdom on the merits and demerits of qualitative market research largely developed in the context of discussions of focus groups. In a focus group, 8 to 10 consumers meet in a special facility for a 2-hour discussion led by a professional moderator. Vendor personnel set the topics for the discussion and have an opportunity to observe from behind one-way glass. If you are going to become heavily involved in customer visits, you might benefit from consulting works on focus groups, including Goldman and McDonald (1987) and Wells (1974)—the best book and compact reference, respectively. See also Greenbaum (1998)—best from the vendor or client perspective—and Stewart and Shamdasani (1990)—the best guide to the academic literature.

8. This comparison is developed in greater detail in McQuarrie and McIntyre (1990a).

9. Several of the managers I interviewed during the MSI study emphasized this point.

10. Despite the popular literature on brainstorming, experiments in both market research and psychology have shown that 32 people interviewed individually will produce a larger number of ideas, of higher quality, than four groups of 8 people. For more information, see Fern (1982), Griffin and Hauser (1992), and McQuarrie and McIntyre (1990a).

CHAPTER ELEVEN

History and Future
Prospects of Customer Visits

How did the idea of programmatic customer visits first evolve? I believe the practice was originally invented by West Coast electronics firms. I have heard of programs dating back to the 1970s at Tektronix in Oregon and Xerox in California, and I have heard tales that the procedure originated decades earlier at Hewlett-Packard. Along these lines, a Massachusetts-based director of engineering confirms that it was his impression as well that the impulse for this kind of work originated out West. What may have happened is that the freedom from convention characteristic of the western United States, combined with the rapid cycle of technical invention in the electronics industry, together with the fact that electronics engineers were accustomed to making products for other engineers, led naturally to the idea of conversations with customers as part of product development. This laid a cultural foundation that supported and encouraged direct customer contact between technical personnel and customers.

In more recent years, the advent of the computer—a product requiring a high degree of engineering expertise, but sold to and used by nonengineers—in turn may have forced the development of a more systematic approach to customer visits. In the case of computer products, a few conversations with the engineer who sat at "the next bench" were no longer enough; something more deliberate and sustained was required. Still more recently, the increase in competitive pressure worldwide, together with the quality revolution and the adoption of the marketing concept in BTB markets, has impelled an even wider diffusion of the customer visit program beyond its base in the electronics industry. The following quote summarizes the evolution of systematic customer visits at one firm. The development it describes has probably occurred at many firms over the past 10 to 15 years:

> Years and years ago, we did customer visits but nobody did it in any regular sort of fashion; it wasn't true research. Then we went through a research phase where you have to do focus groups and telephone surveys; and then we said well, wait a minute, that's not getting us enough information. So now we are back doing customer visits but in a much more structured mode. *(market researcher, financial service firm)*

CURRENT STATUS

If an omniscient observer were to assess current practice in the area of customer visits, that observer would probably note characteristics of the following sort. He or she would find first of all that marketing managers have been visiting customers for many decades. The idea of consultative selling has similarly existed for many years. Hence, almost any firm in BTB and technology markets could rightfully claim, "Yes, we visit our customers regularly." In the case of key national accounts, many firms could also claim that the engineering function plays a role in these visits.

Our observer would soon realize, however, that a far smaller number of firms make it a routine practice to form joint marketing and engineering teams that then visit customers together. If the observer looked further in an attempt to find businesses that also encourage personal contact between production and the customer, few firms indeed would qualify.

Looking only at those firms that send cross-functional teams out to visit customers, our observer would soon come to realize that this activity often occurs by happenstance, on impulse, in fits and starts, and sometimes as an afterthought. Our observer would further note the very small number of customers visited (on the order of four or five), the often chaotic interview process, and the breathtaking generalizations made on the basis of these interviews. Although our observer would also find numerous examples of carefully planned customer visit programs, he or she would soon note that they are the exception, rather than the rule.

I believe the preceding paragraphs accurately describe normal customer visit practice in the United States during much of the 1990s. This book was written, and now revised, with the hope of raising the sophistication of customer visit practice. The ever-increasing cost of travel and lodging, together with the expense of managerial and professional talent, make it imperative to get the maximum value from the visits that are done. The growing futility of attempting to compete on the basis of technological advantage alone, together with the intensity of global competition, similarly drive firms toward ever-closer relations with their customers, with customer visits being an attractive means to this end.

EXHIBIT 11.1

Training Can Help

A study by Corporate Marketing Education at Hewlett-Packard (see Appendix A for details) examined the impact on customer visit practices of taking a 2-day course designed to encourage the programmatic approach described in this book. Course participants were compared with a group of nonparticipants matched on job title, functional area, and business unit. The study showed that course participants were more likely:

- To have explicit objectives and to set fewer and more appropriate objectives
- To give the users of information from the visit program an opportunity to influence its design
- To experience more effective teamwork among the various functional areas involved in the visits

- To visit a larger number of customers and to proceed programmatically
- To use a written discussion guide
- To assign specific roles to members of the visit team

This study also examined the association between specific planning procedures and the perceived value of the visit program. A statistically significant correlation was found between valuable outcomes and the following procedures:

- Involvement of information users in the design of the visit program
- Effective teamwork among functional areas
- A clear plan for using the information gained from visits
- Perceptions that customers felt free to respond candidly

With the exception of the latter point, which is a function of interview skills, note how important good planning and organizational coordination are to achieving positive results from visit programs.

FUTURE PROSPECTS

Beyond a movement toward cross-functional team visits, organized as a program and conducted at the appropriate point in the decision cycle, I can see two directions for future progress. First, I expect the customer visit program will take its place as one of several nontraditional market research tools for obtaining customer input. Second, I see increasing sophistication in the analysis, storage, and dissemination of customer information, whether gained through visits or other means. Again, leading firms will be those that develop tools for harvesting an increasing fraction of the unceasing flow of customer information.

Most nontraditional market research approaches, whether these be programmatic customer visits or the hybrid forms mentioned in Chapter 3, share a common trait: They rest on direct interaction between customer and nonsales personnel of the vendor. By contrast, traditional market research techniques are indirect and mediated.

Either some individual, such as a professional interviewer, or some instrument or procedure, as in survey or experimental research, comes between the decision maker and the customer. (As an aside, I suspect that one reason that the focus group technique has always held a special fascination for business people new to market research is precisely because, of all the traditional tools, it makes the customer most visible as a person.) Conventional market research will continue to be important, and BTB and technology firms will continue to play catch-up in making good use of traditional techniques. However, I expect the future will see an even more dramatic increase in the direct involvement of all kinds of people, at all levels and across all functions, in learning about customers and markets.

Beyond more diverse and participatory approaches to collecting data, I also expect to see more attention paid to retaining and processing customer information, whatever its source. Here is an example. At one firm I visited, there was a group of application specialists—a fairly common job function in technology firms. Their function was to help customers get more value out of the firm's photographic products. The application specialist teaches seminars, visits customers, and responds to information requests. Recently their director imposed a new responsibility: Each specialist owes him 12 customer profiles per month (see Chapter 3). The profile is a simple one-page document that describes the customer and their application. The specialist is encouraged to note problems in using the product and new applications for it. Once collated, these profiles are used to identify unsuspected problems or unexpected applications, to diagnose common user mistakes that can be addressed in product literature, and to suggest to the sales force the types of businesses most likely to be in the market for specific types of products.

This example illustrates several points. First, it functions as a means of getting down on paper the sort of knowledge that typically remains locked in the heads of individual vendor employees. Second, the requirement to submit a profile stimulates and directs curiosity. The director makes it clear that the profile can be based on any kind of customer contact: a conversation in the hallway, a phone call, a full-dress visit. The profile form is short, but provides a common format facilitating the integration of data. The basic idea behind this arrangement has probably been reinvented many times. A manager in the pension-management division of an insurance company told me of a similar procedure. The practice there was that someone from client relations would visit each customer of any size at least once a year. This manager had devised a form indicating three to four basic questions that were to be asked of every customer.

What is being described here is a culture of learning and curiosity. I believe it is those firms that succeed in becoming learning organizations that will be most successful at instituting customer visits. I invite the reader to imagine how his or her business might be transformed if key producers—the scientists and engineers who really understand and own the firm's technology—were to steadily receive, often firsthand, a stream of customer information that is vivid, specific, and focused on key concerns. That is the near future. Now imagine if anyone in the firm were able to log on to the corporate intranet and access past profiles and trip reports pertaining to a specific customer firm of interest, or search by keyword for topics such as a specific application, complaint, or competitor. That is the more distant future of customer visits.

Appendix A

Methodology for Research Conducted at Hewlett-Packard (HP)

THE 1990 HP CORPORATE MARKETING EDUCATION STUDY

The primary purpose of this study was to evaluate the success of the customer visits course sponsored by Corporate Marketing Education in changing the behavior of participants in the direction of more effective practices. We gathered the names of everyone who attended the course during the first 2 years it was offered ($N = 193$, after eliminating people who had left the company or could not be reached). To create a comparison group, we selected people who had taken other corporate marketing courses but had not taken the customer visit course. These people were randomly selected from within strata created by differentiating job title (e.g., project manager vs. engineer), functional department (e.g., marketing vs. R&D), and business group (e.g., computers vs. instruments). The selection percentages were set so that the comparison sample approximately matched the control sample in its distribution across titles, function, and business group ($N = 192$, after eliminating those who could not be reached). Note that because other corporate marketing courses discuss the proper use of customer visits, and because some members of the comparison sample probably work in the same unit as course graduates and thus had an opportunity to learn the material vicariously, it was unlikely that there would be large differences between course graduates and the comparison group. A cover letter and questionnaire and two follow-up notices were sent to course graduates and the comparison group. A total of 232 questionnaires were returned (60% response rate). We concluded from the study that the course was successful in promoting improved visit practices. The advice in the course and this book appears to be self-validating; people are willing to put these recommendations into practice once they have become acquainted with them, and to perceive the advice as valuable. Of course, these findings by no means prove that the advice is correct in any absolute sense, and the study does not even begin to broach the question of whether other, better advice might exist.

Moreover, several limitations should be kept in mind. First, self-report data of this type have an obvious positive bias. Second, the response rate to the survey (60%) indicates an unknown degree of nonresponse bias. Third, individuals who sought out corporate training offerings in marketing may not be representative of HP as a whole.

THE 1991 CORPORATE
ENGINEERING (CE) STUDY

This study was intended to provide a snapshot of actual practice in customer visits at HP, with a focus on the involvement of R&D project managers. These are first-level managers within the engineering function who have primary responsibility for managing the process of product design. Because HP is a highly decentralized organization, with at that time some 83 distinct business units, prior to this study no one was in a position to assess with any confidence what the corporation's practice really was.

A letter from CE was sent to the R&D manager at each of these business units explaining the study and asking for a referral to a project manager at that unit who was known to have conducted customer visits in the 12 to 18 months prior to June 1991. A total of 54 project managers were identified and agreed to participate. The time period was chosen so that questions could be asked about the outcome of the visits. However, in almost all cases, the product itself had not been introduced at the time this study was conducted.

Using a discussion guide, a manager from CE completed brief telephone interviews with each of these project managers. The topics and questions used in the discussion guide were developed through exploratory interviews with project managers. On the plus side, the interviews obtained are worldwide in scope and include all of HP's major lines of business. On the minus side, we may suppose that the request from CE led R&D managers to refer "showcase" projects. Hence, the results probably reflect an unrealistically positive view of actual practice. Moreover, the substantial degree of nonresponse (29 of 83 contacts), the qualitative nature of the interviews themselves (no attempt was made to ask the same questions the same way every time), and possible biases of the interviewer all suggest caution in interpreting the results.

A finding of note is simply the ease with which we could identify, within an 18-month time period, 54 customer visit programs involving R&D project managers. The worldwide extent of these programs across multiple product lines appeared to confirm the ubiquity of this practice at Hewlett-Packard.

Appendix B

Checklist for Conducting
a Program of Customer Visits

PREPARING FOR THE VISIT

1. Send a confirmation letter to customers who have agreed to participate and attach an agenda (the agenda should contain only the major topics from your discussion guide).

   - This helps the customer understand that the visit is for research purposes and allows him or her to prepare for the interview.

2. Send cross-functional teams.

   - A two-person team representing two different departments or areas will bring "stereo vision" to bear on the customer's response.

3. Select customers according to a plan and visit at least a dozen.

   - This is a matter of "garbage in, garbage out"—you have to visit the right number of the right kinds of customers to have any confidence in what you hear.

4. Don't visit the same small group of favored customers over and over. Visit competitors' customers, lost leads, lost customers, and any other group that might provide a valuable perspective.

   - Customer visits work best as a discovery tool.

5. Try to interview several different people at each customer representing the different influences on the purchase decision.

   - In technology markets, it is particularly important to interview both technical and managerial individuals.

6. Enlist the support of local account management. Make sure that they understand the research purpose of the visit. Seek their perspective

on the customer's situation and their interpretation of customer response.

- Otherwise, you may find yourself a victim of the "setup," wherein an account representative steers you toward a particularly irate customer, on the theory that corporate never listens anyway and needs to be hit over the head when they do deign to visit.

CONDUCTING THE VISITS

7. Use a discussion guide.

- Just as agendas make for better meetings, a 2- to 3-page, organized list of key topics and important questions will help keep interviews on track and consistent across the program.

8. Assign roles to team members.

- In any interview, or at least in each part of it, one person should lead the discussion while the other concentrates on listening and taking notes.

9. Emphasize open-ended questions.

- Open-ended questions maximize discovery and best take advantage of the possibilities inherent in interactive, face-to-face communication.

10. Don't ask customers to give solutions—get them to identify problems. Emphasize task requirements and business goals, not product features.

- Implementing profitable solutions is fundamentally a vendor responsibility. Whereas, the customer is the authority on what the real problems are.

11. Don't talk too much. Make any presentations after the research interview, not before.

- Dialogue, dominated by the customer, is the goal. Beginning with a presentation "poisons the well," diminishing the odds of discovery and surprise.

12. Probe customer answers. Elicit second, third, and fourth answers to your open-ended questions. Seek clarifying examples and additional elaboration.

- The number-one failing of beginning interviewers is a failure to probe. It's like leaving money on the table.

13. Use visual aids—sketches of equipment, network configurations, or bullet points describing key aspects of a concept.

   - These help the customer address all the issues that concern you.

14. Don't confine yourself to a conference room. Walk around. Watch the product in use. See how it's set up.

   - Observation can reveal needs and opportunities that the customer is unable to vocalize.

15. Accept criticism gratefully. Demonstrate unconditional positive regard—that you acknowledge the legitimacy of what the customer says, whether painful or pleasant to hear.

   - There's no reason for the customer to believe your claim that you are there to listen and learn—normal vendor behavior is by turns aggressive and defensive, not receptive. You have to earn the customer's trust.

FOLLOWING THE INTERVIEW

16. Debrief immediately after each visit.

   - Interviews yield a large number of tacit and subtle impressions that quickly fade. Plus, you'd be surprised how often team members come away with different impressions. These need to be integrated lest they become divisive.

17. Highlight verbatim quotes from customers in reports.

   - Customers tend to speak vividly with no holds barred. Use of verbatims can be particularly helpful when the visits have yielded bad news (they can't fire the customer!).

18. Every visit team should produce a trip report. Organize these reports by theme, not by customer, and lead with the big news.

   - Research leaves a record. On the other hand, fat reports won't be read. A thematic organization that highlights the most newsworthy discoveries addresses this problem.

19. Use matrices to analyze and interpret the results of visits.

- A basic matrix, where customer requirements identified through visits are the rows and product features are the columns, is often illuminating. Such matrices can reveal features that don't correspond to any customer need, and conversely, requirements not addressed by any feature.

20. Archive trip reports on-line with other marketing intelligence.

- Regular review of accumulated reports can identify trends, suggest opportunities, orient new employees, and in general keep the customer visible.

References

American Supplier Institute. (1987). *Quality function deployment: A collection of presentations and QFD case studies.* Dearborn, MI: Author.

Bailetti, A. J., & Guild, P. D. (1991). Designers' impressions of direct contact between product designers and champions of innovation. *Journal of Product Innovation Management, 8,* 91-103.

Barabba, V., & Zaltman, G. (1991). *Hearing the voice of the market: Competitive advantage through creative use of market information.* Boston: Harvard Business School Press.

Bonnet, D. C. L. (1986). Nature of the R&D/marketing cooperation in the design of technologically advanced new industrial products. *R&D Management, 16,* 117-126.

Bonoma, T., & Shapiro, B. (1983). *Segmenting the industrial market.* Lexington, MA: Lexington Books.

Brynjolfsson, E., Renshaw, A. A., & van Alstyne, M. (1997, Winter). The matrix of change. *Sloan Management Review,* pp. 37-54.

Chan-Herur, K. C. (1994). *Communicating with customers around the world: A practical guide to effective cross-cultural business communication.* San Francisco: AuMonde International Publishing.

Churchill, G. A. (1991). *Marketing research: Methodological foundations.* Chicago: Dryden.

Cleland, A. S., & Bruno, A. V. (1996). *The market value process: Bridging customer and shareholder value.* San Francisco: Jossey-Bass.

Cooper, R. G. (1986). *Winning at new products.* Reading, MA: Addison-Wesley.

228

Daft, R. L., & Lengel, R. H. (1986, May). Organizational information require-ments, media richness, and structural design. *Management Science, 32,* 554-569.

Daft, R. L., Lengel, R. H., & Trevino, L. K. (1987, September). Message equivocality, media selection, and manager performance: Implications for information systems. *MIS Quarterly,* pp. 355-364.

Day, G. S. (1991). *Learning about markets* (Report No. 91-117). Cambridge, MA: Marketing Science Institute.

Deshpande, R., Farley, J., & Webster, F. (1993, January). Corporate culture, customer orientation, and innovativeness in Japanese firms: A quadrad analysis. *Journal of Marketing, 57,* 22-27.

Deshpande, R., & Webster, F. E. (1989, January). Organizational culture and marketing: Defining the research agenda. *Journal of Marketing, 53,* 3-15.

Deshpande, R., & Zaltman, G. (1982, February). Factors affecting the use of market research information: A path analysis. *Journal of Marketing, 14,* 14-31.

Deshpande, R., & Zaltman, G. (1984, February). A comparison of factors affecting reseacher and manager perceptions of market research use. *Journal of Marketing Research, 22,* 32-38.

Deshpande, R., & Zaltman, G. (1987, February). A comparison of factors affecting use of marketing information in consumer and industrial firms. *Journal of Marketing Research, 24,* 114-118.

Dillman, D. A. (1978). *Mail and telephone surveys: The total design method.* New York: Wiley.

Dougherty, D. J. (1988). Interpretive barriers to successful product innovation in large firms. *Organization Science, 3*(2), 179-202.

Douglas, M. (1986). *How institutions think.* Syracuse, NY: Syracuse Univer-sity Press.

Drucker, P. F. (1954). *The practice of management.* New York: Harper & Row.

Feldman, L. P., & Page, A. L. (1984). Principles vs. practice in new product planning. *Journal of Product Innovation Management, 1,* 33-44.

Fern, E. (1982). The use of focus groups for idea generation: The effects of group size, acquaintanceship, and moderator on response quantity and quality. *Journal of Marketing Research, 19,* 1-13.

Goldman, A. E., & McDonald, S. S. (1987). *The group depth interview.* Englewood Cliffs, NJ: Prentice Hall.

Greenbaum, T. (1998). *The handbook for focus group research* (2nd ed.). Thousand Oaks, CA: Sage.

Griffin, A. (1991). Evaluating development processes: QFD as an example (Report No. 91-121). Cambridge, MA: Marketing Science Institute.

Griffin, A., & Hauser, J. (1992, Winter). The voice of the customer. *Marketing Science, 12,* 1-27.

Griffin, A., & Hauser, J. (1996). Integrating R&D and marketing: A review and analysis of the literature. *Journal of Product Innovation Management, 13,* 191-215.

Guillart, F. J., & Sturdivant, F. D. (1994, January/February). Spend a day in the life of your customer. *Harvard Business Review,* pp. 116-125.

Gupta, A. K., Raj, S. P., & Wilemon, D. (1986, April). A model for studying R&D-marketing interface in the product innovation process. *Journal of Marketing, 50,* 7-17.

Hauser, J. R., & Clausing, D. P. (1988). The house of quality. *Harvard Business Review, 66,* 63-73.

Holtzblatt, K., & Beyer, H. (1993, October). Making customer-centered design work for teams. *Communications of the ACM, 36,* 93-103.

Jaworski, B. J., & Kohli, A. (1993, July). Market orientation: Antecedents and consequences. *Journal of Marketing, 57* 53-70.

Jaworski, B. J., & Kohli, A. (1996). Market orientation: Review, refinement, and roadmap. *Journal of Market Focused Management, 1,* 119-135.

Kelly, P. J., & Hise, R. T. (1979). Industrial and consumer goods product managers are different. *Industrial Marketing Management, 8,* 325-332.

Kohli, A. K., & Jaworski, B. J. (1990, April). Market orientation: The construct, research propositions, and managerial implications. *Journal of Marketing, 54,* 1-18.

Kotler, P. (1994). *Marketing management: Analysis, planning, implementation, and control.* Englewood Cliffs, NJ: Prentice Hall.

Kotter, J. P., & Heskett, J. L. (1992). *Corporate culture and performance.* New York: Free Press

Levitt, T. (1960, July/August). Marketing myopia. *Harvard Business Review,* pp. 45-56.

Maltz, E., & Kohli, A. (1996). Market intelligence dissemination across functional boundaries. *Journal of Marketing Research, 32,* 318-335.

McCracken, G. (1988). *The long interview.* Newbury Park, CA: Sage.

McQuarrie, E. F. (1995). Taking a road trip: Customer visits help companies recharge relationships and pass competitors. *Marketing Management, 3,*(4), 8-21.

McQuarrie, E. F. (1996). *The market research toolbox: A concise guide for beginners.* Thousand Oaks, CA: Sage.

McQuarrie, E. F., & McIntyre, S. H. (1990a). Contribution of the group interview to research on consumer phenomenology. In E. C. Hirschman (Ed.), *Advances in consumer behavior* (Vol. 4, pp. 165-194). Greenwich, CT: JAI Press.

McQuarrie, E. F., & McIntyre, S. H. (1990b). *Implementing the marketing concept through a program of customer visits* (Rep. No. 90-107). Cambridge, MA: Marketing Science Institute.

McQuarrie, E. F., & McIntyre, S. H. (1992). *The customer visit: An emerging practice in business-to-business marketing* (Report No. 92-114). Cambridge, MA: Marketing Science Institute.

Merton, R. K., Fiske, M., & Kendall, P. L. (1956). *The focused interview.* New York: Free Press.

Miles, M. B., & Huberman, A. M. (1994). *Qualitative data analysis* (2nd ed.). Thousand Oaks, CA: Sage.

Moorman, C. (1995). Organizational market information processes: Cultural antecedents and new product outcomes. *Journal of Marketing Research, 32,* 318-335.

Narver, J. C., & Slater, S. F. (1990, October). The effect of a market orientation on business profitability. *Journal of Marketing, 54,* 20-35.

Narver, J. C., & Slater, S. F. (1991). *Becoming more market-oriented: An exploratory study of the programmatic and market-back approaches* (Rep. No. 92-128). Cambridge, MA: Marketing Science Institute.

Patton, M. Q. (1990). *Qualitative evaluation and research methods.* Newbury Park, CA: Sage.

Payne, S. (1951). *The art of asking questions.* Princeton, NJ: Princeton University Press.

Peters, T. J., & Waterman, R. H. (1982). *In search of excellence: Lessons from America's best-run companies.* New York: Harper & Row.

Ruekert, R. W., & Walker, O. C., Jr. (1987, January). Marketing's interaction with other functional units: A conceptual framework and empirical evidence. *Journal of Marketing, 51,* 1-19.

Shapiro, B. (1988). What the hell is "market-oriented"? *Harvard Business Review, 66,* 119-125.

Simon, H. (1989). *Price management.* Amsterdam: North-Holland.

Simon, H. (1992, Winter). Pricing opportunities—And how to exploit them. *Sloan Management Review, 34,* 55-65.

Slater, S. F., & Narver, J. C. (1995). Market-oriented isn't enough: Build a learning organization (Rep. No. 94-101). Cambridge, MA: Marketing Science Institute.

Souder, W. E. (1987). *Managing new product innovations.* Lexington, MA: Lexington Books.

Stewart, D. W., & Kamins, M. A. (1993). *Secondary research: Information sources and methods* (2nd. ed.). Newbury Park, CA: Sage.

Stewart, D. W., & Shamdasani, P. (1990). *Focus groups: Theory and practice.* Newbury Park, CA: Sage.

Tushman, M. L. (1979, Winter). Managing communication networks in R&D laboratories. *Sloan Management Review,* pp. 37-49.

Tushman, M. L., & Nadler, D. (1986, Spring). Organizing for innovation. *California Management Review, 28,* 74-92.

Utterback, J. M. (1974, February 15). Innovation and the diffusion of technology. *Science, 183,* 620-626.

Von Hippel, E. (1986, July). Lead users: A source of novel product concepts. *Management Science, 32,* 791-805.

Von Hippel, E. (1987). *The sources of innovation.* New York: Oxford University Press.

Webster, F. E. (1978). Is industrial marketing coming of age? In T. V. Bonoma & G. Zaltman (Eds.), *Review of marketing* (pp. 138-159). Chicago: American Marketing Association.

Webster, F. E. (1988). *Rediscovering the marketing concept* (Rep. No. 88-102). Cambridge, MA: Marketing Science Institute.

Webster, F. E. (1992, October). The changing role of marketing in the corporation. *Journal of Marketing, 56,* 1-17.

Wells, W. D. (1974). Group interviews. In R. Ferber (Ed.), *Handbook of marketing research* (pp. 2-12). New York: McGraw-Hill.

Index